CAPITALISM, SOCIAL PRIVILEGE AND MANAGERIAL IDEOLOGIES

T0382904

Capitalism, Social Privilege and Managerial Ideologies

ERNESTO R. GANTMAN
Universidad de Buenos Aires, Argentina
and
Universidad de Belgrano, Argentina

 Routledge
Taylor & Francis Group

LONDON AND NEW YORK

First published 2005 by Ashgate Publishing

Reissued 2019 by Routledge
2 Park Square, Milton Park, Abingdon, Oxon, OX14 4RN
52 Vanderbilt Avenue, New York, NY 10017

Routledge is an imprint of the Taylor & Francis Group, an informa business

A Library of Congress record exists under LC control number:

ISBN 13: 978-0-8153-8791-6 (hbk)
ISBN 13: 978-1-138-35664-1 (pbk)
ISBN 13: 978-1-351-16208-1 (ebk)

Contents

Contents

Preface

In our contemporary society, management is a discipline that enjoys much prestige. However, beyond its appeal and image of authoritative and 'serious' knowledge, many of its basic premises are beliefs that can be interpreted as ideological. The role of the discipline is not merely to provide normative models to govern organizations, but to sanction certain ways of organizing as good, efficient, valid, and/or desirable, thus legitimating these arrangements and the relation of domination that they entail. Many social scientists have observed the centrality of management discourse in contemporary capitalism, and this is an incentive to explore its evolution and function. The analysis of administrative thought as ideology began in the late 1950s, but still remains today, in my opinion, as one of the most promising research topics in the social sciences. That is the reason why I chose it as the subject of my doctoral dissertation at the University of Buenos Aires, which, after a process of revision and updating, gave way to the present work.

This book is a historical reconstruction of the evolution of administrative thought from the nineteenth century to the present. I wrote it with two objectives in mind: (1) to contribute to the existing debate about how managerial ideologies evolved, and (2) to present a critique of the discipline of management, calling into question its status as an authoritative source of knowledge by highlighting its ideological character. My hope is that this book will be useful to readers with diverse backgrounds in the social sciences. I consider it a starting point, an invitation to readers, to dig deeper into the primary sources themselves and to see how the historical narrative that I have developed can be complemented and extended. If the book serves to further the interest in the study of managerial ideologies and to stimulate the debate about how management ideas were instrumental for advancing the privilege of particular social actors, I will be more than satisfied. In case the reader is not yet skeptical about management thought, I think that the best service this book can render is to provoke suspicion in his or her mind about the usefulness and intentions of much popular management discourse. If this occurs, the book's mission, to use managerial lexicon, will be successfully accomplished.

My coverage of management thinkers has been deliberately partial. The history of administrative thought is older than most people believe – as are the supposedly innovative management ideas that are constantly appearing. Interesting insights can be found in the writings of ancient non-Western thinkers like the Chinese philosopher Han Fei Tzu, an authentic 'guru' of statecraft, whose fate however was much different than that of today's management pundits: he committed suicide after the monarch to whom he was advisor sent him to prison. The list of precursors is certainly long, but the focus of my work is on the relationship between management thinking and the social order that emerged with industrialism in the West. However, even within this historical period, there are several omissions; I made cursory or no mention to authors who could have developed relevant contributions to management but whose work, for diverse reasons, was not sufficiently diffused at their time.

I am indebted to a number of individuals and institutions that have contributed to the research leading to this book. In the first place, I want to express my gratitude to the three mentors of my academic career: Ricardo Gómez, who supervised my dissertation, Oscar Oszlak, and Francisco Suárez. I would also like to extend my appreciation to Mauricio Contreras, Norberto Góngora, Conrado Estol, and Roberto Martínez Nogueira, all of whom encouraged me in my academic endeavors. The Universidad de Buenos Aires and the Universidad de Belgrano provided excellent institutional support for this research. In addition, I am especially grateful to Martin Parker, Anshuman Prasad, and an anonymous Ashgate reviewer for their valuable comments and suggestions. Thanks also to Andrew Miller for helping me to improve my English prose. Finally, my thanks to Brendan George, commissioning editor at Ashgate, whose support made possible the publication of this book.

Chapter 1

Introduction: Ideology and Administrative Thought

Ideology and the legitimation of social privilege

The issue of ideology has been the object of diverse approaches in the social sciences. The term was first used in relation to an antireligious tradition associated to the Enlightenment movement. Ideology was born as the science of ideas that, guided by the force of reason, would unveil the fallacies of the dominant thought of the period by showing its roots in the mundane interests of the ruling class. This science disappeared along with its creator, Destutt de Tracy, but the term continued to be utilized with a variety of meanings by intellectuals from different disciplines and political persuasions. At present, there are two basic perspectives on the subject. The first is a neutral position that assimilates the concept of ideology to that of a belief system. The second perceives ideas and systems of symbolic action as resulting from a manipulation carried out by the dominant strata of society with the intention of making their own interests prevail. This latter view shares the same theoretical — and political — intentions of the first French *idéologues*: to expose the mystifying character of particular discourses by revealing how and why they present a distorted image of the social world, thus questioning the claims based on such discourses.

Ideologies play a constitutive or integrative role by supplying people with cognitive maps that serve to locate them in the social world. However, these representational maps are not a faithful mirror of reality but rather a distorted one (Ricouer, 1986). This deformation is not innocent, nor does it derive from cultural, methodological, or perceptual artifacts or from an epistemological impossibility to gauge the true essence of things. Although these causes may also be at work, there remains an underlying factor. Certain discourses may present the existing social inequalities in a particular society as being fair, legitimate, or even impossible to modify (Therborn, 1980). In such cases, their function is to legitimate the relations of domination characterizing such social structure, giving reasons to justify their existence by appealing to the natural, divine, or moral order in which those relations are based.

If ideology has a role to fulfill in the maintenance of relations of domination, then it also serves to legitimize the social privilege of the members of the society's ruling class. Social privilege can be defined as the existence of a differential access to goods, services, and personal relations on the part of certain individuals, which is the main outcome of social stratification.[1] The composition of the upper or privileged strata evolves with time. In the same way, the diverse ideologies that aim at legitimating the social privilege of the ruling class and their associated strata also change.

The functionality of ideology in the reproduction of social privilege is a central element in any social formation. Nevertheless, not all ideologies legitimate an existing social order; they may also endorse the subversion of that order, but this does not invalidate their function of serving particular social interests. An ideology may perfectly respond to the interests of a counterelite and may even turn into a legitimating ideology, as soon as this counterelite becomes an emergent ruling class. Therefore, it can be affirmed in a wider sense that an ideology is a system of beliefs functional to the legitimation of the interests of a social group. However, regarding the type of interests behind any ideology, a scope condition must be added to this definition, because otherwise, ideology becomes an all-encompassing notion that covers almost any human desire under any situation (as in Vilfredo Pareto's concept of derivations).[2] To be more precise, the interests that I deem relevant to the study of ideology are those associated to a claim about, or a dispute against, the maintenance of social privilege.

At this point, I have arrived at a definition of ideology that emphasizes its legitimating role, but it is also pertinent to ask how effective are ideologies in fulfilling that role. In my opinion, an ideology may produce the wished effect of legitimation, fulfill it only partially, or have no effect at all.[3] Moreover, the need to legitimize an existing social order does not aim solely at inculcating among the members of the nonprivileged sectors the conception that they inhabit a world subject to a just or natural order. The beneficiaries of social privilege must also perceive their situation of superiority as legitimate and deserving. Actually, in the case of managerial ideologies, which constitute the object of this book, the greater ideological permeability (understood as the degree of acceptance of premises or internalization of values from an ideological system) is found among the members of the privileged strata of society. It is clear that working in an organization implies an exposure to socialization in practices whose ideological foundations are communicated to all organization members in order to guarantee their adherence; yet those who are most exposed to these ideological discourses are precisely the members of the upper organizational strata.[4]

Ideologies exhibit diverse mechanisms to achieve their aims of legitimation. In my description of managerial ideologies, I will present discursive operations of construction of identities (e.g., the 'rational manager' in the ideology of systemic rationalism); of silencing or exclusion of certain issues (i.e., when a troublesome matter that appeared prominently in previous ideologies disappears as problem); and so on. Alvin Gouldner (1976) argued that contemporary ideological discourses are not founded upon tradition, divine inspiration, or intellectual authority. Instead, they typically base their claims on rational grounds. For him, their argumentative rhetoric emphasizes empirical tests and logical reasoning, thus obscuring any relationship with particular social interests that may be deemed as being served by them. If ideologies can be assimilated, as Gouldner believes, to relatively rational forms of discourse, then a scientific discourse can be considered as ideological. Economic theories are frequently analyzed from that point of view. J.J. Klant

(1988), for example, claimed that in the work of the classic economists there is a clear reference to a natural order that gives sense to political and social laws.[5] In a similar vein, Stephen Marglin (1984: 481) explained the preeminence of neoclassical theory, not by 'its superior explanatory or predictive capacity', but on the basis of ideological reasons.[6] Following this line of thought, I will consider in the next section the study of management theory as ideological discourse.

Management and ideology

The epistemological status of the discipline of management is an issue that is not quite settled. Some like the philosopher of science Mario Bunge (1980) consider it a technology. For others, it is an art.[7] But most management scholars assert it is a science, a label that they use to endow the discipline with a more respectable aura of 'authoritative knowledge' (Alvesson and Willmott, 1996). Whatever its real status, I believe there is a strong case for analyzing management as an ideology. Management is about how organizations should be directed or governed. It is therefore 'a political discourse *par excellence*' (Clegg and Palmer 1996: 3). Administrative or management knowledge is basically prescriptive in nature. However, most management books and articles also offer descriptive views not only of organizations, which are the basic object of the discipline, but also of human work and society at large. Not surprisingly, some management theorists, such as Taylor, Simon and Drucker, have been recently acclaimed as 'capitalist philosophers' (Gabor, 2000). There is an implicit, and in some cases even explicit, weltanschauung in the most important works of these authors. Management discourse, as presented in the writings of the most influential management thinkers, informs an orderly account of the nature of man and the functioning of society. The issues discussed in these works go beyond mere 'recipe-knowledge' to further construct notions about who is virtuous and deserves power in organizations, who should be punished or rewarded and according to what criteria, and under which principles should organizations and ultimately society be structured. In sum, a systematic set of beliefs that can be deemed as an ideology.

Human organizations, and business enterprises in particular, are directed by men and women who claim to base their privileged position not on ascribed traits, such as race and social class, but on their superior ability. However, these individuals do not pretend to rely just on personal skills; most importantly, they are allegedly well versed in the discipline of management. Far from being one of the *arcana caelestia* and certainly not strictly modeled after the scientific method, this discipline, which allegedly allows those who master it to reach such privileged positions within organizations, supports its main tenets on not so rigorously gathered evidence. The findings and recommendations of the high priests of the discipline, aptly labeled management gurus, have been severely criticized on methodological grounds by academics. Reasoning that would hardly be tolerated in other social sciences is commonplace in many best-selling management books. For example, the methodological fallacy of finding the criteria by which some firms succeed while others do not upon the basis of a sample of 'successful firms', known as sampling on the dependent variable (Hannan and Freeman, 1989), is just one case in point. Other preferred methodological 'techniques' are anecdotal evidence and the stories — or worse, the hardly neutral self-reported stories — of successful individual managers or entrepreneurs. These methodological miseries aside, the distilled wisdom of the management pundits appears at best as common sense knowledge and in some cases as poor, misleading, or contradictory advice.[8]

The discipline of management, upon which the rationality of the capitalist enterprise is founded, enjoys a privileged status in contemporary society. However, it is difficult to understand why it is considered an authoritative source of the most valuable knowledge for organizations (how to direct them in an effective way), when even some popular management books openly contend that 'modern management theory is no more reliable than tribal medicine' (Micklethwait and Woolridge, 1997: 13). In comparison to the discourse of the social sciences, management, whatever its epistemic status, has a weaker form of supporting both its normative and descriptive assertions. This has led some authors to conclude that it is ideological and not scientific knowledge.[9] My definition of ideology has, however, a different meaning. For management to be considered an ideological discourse, the claims of management schools or traditions should be appropriately related to the legitimation of interests. Yet, the overwhelming evidence on the feeble methodology of most popular management books is an additional element that debilitates its argumentative power, thus helping to uncover its deceiving or mystifying character.

The study of managerial ideologies, although not much developed, is not a novelty in the social sciences. Therefore, I will attempt to clarify my concept of what is a managerial or administrative ideology.[10] Reinhard Bendix, who is usually credited as being the main pioneer of the research on this subject, used this expression to refer to 'all ideas which are espoused by or for those who exercise authority in economic enterprises, and which seek to explain and justify that authority' (1956: 2).[11] From a theoretical standpoint, Bendix's definition is too inclusive, since it may encompass not only management discourse, but also any kind of discourse that has something to say about the authority exercised by managers or entrepreneurs. Other authors have not paid much attention to definitional issues; instead, they have focused on management literature as ideological object. There has also been some debate on whether some ideologies, particularly social Darwinism, can be properly considered managerial ones as Bendix does. For Daniel Wren (1994), the effect of said ideology on the thought of the business leaders of the period was not significant. Nevertheless, whatever its real impact on the business world, it cannot be denied that social Darwinism was part of the cultural climate of its time, and it did provide a rationale for legitimating authority in business enterprises and, consequently, within society at large. For this reason, I include in this book the treatment, albeit brief, of this ideology. As a definitional stance, I consider that an administrative ideology is a set of beliefs mainly dealing with who should manage organizations and how.

The relationship between administrative ideologies and practices is strong, and some authors treat them as synonymous. Most management theory is based upon real practices and is typically inspired by the most successful ones. On the other hand, life within organizations determines in part how we perceive the world that surrounds us. Organizations help to construct and to inform the perceptual framework upon which those who inhabit them locate themselves in their own social reality (Thompson, 1980a; Salaman, 1980). In as much as organizations reproduce a certain social order and perform a function of integration and social construction, they also serve as transmission vehicles of managerial ideologies. However, it cannot be maintained that administrative theory and organizational practices necessarily go hand in hand. Not all theory or administrative ideology is massively adopted or even applied in real practice. So, although it can be affirmed that a relationship of mutual conditioning between administrative practices and managerial ideologies exists, the analysis of managerial ideologies does not allow one to draw conclusions about the ways in which the privileged classes of society exert control over other social strata through administrative practices.

Perspectives on the evolution of managerial ideologies

The prevailing approach in the consideration of the evolution of managerial ideologies suggests the existence of a process of progressive subtilization whereby control over the labor force is achieved in a less visible manner. The classic and pioneering study in this regard is that of Reinhard Bendix (1956), which culminates with the human relations ideology, but other authors have also observed this particular trend.[12] For Stephen Barley and Gideon Kunda (1992), this perspective can be characterized by three successive phases in dominant ideological views:
1. Coercive control, which lasted approximately until the late nineteenth century and centered on the discipline over the workers.
2. Rational control, which basically focuses on organizational and work-flow designs that are typically associated to Taylorism, whose engineering approach to management predominated until the emergence of the human relations school.
3. Normative control, which began precisely with this later line of thinking and aimed at securing the workers' compliance by resorting to their values and feelings.
    Other theorists have followed a similar line in their description of the phases of the evolution of managerial ideologies, although tying ideologies more closely to administrative practices, on the assumption that the latter were a faithful reflection of the recommendations at the theoretical-ideological level. Richard Edwards (1979) analyzed the existence of three strategies of control over the labor force that include both organizational ideologies and practices. While the three have a clear point of beginning and decline, they still coexist today in various types of organizations and according to firm size. Direct or simple control was the first to appear and was typical of nineteenth-century organizations, although it still may be found today in small enterprises. Then emerged technical control, associated to the assembly line and the scientific management movement. This was followed by bureaucratic control, which is embedded in the social structure of large organizations. James Barker (1993, 1999) added concertive control, which is based on self-managed teams, as the last stage of this evolution. Also drawing on Edwards's

work, Stewart Clegg (1981) discussed the simultaneity of the application of different forms of control within the same organization according to the organizational strata being considered. For him, control through technical rules is exerted over the workers, social-regulative rules are applied to supervisory personnel, while higher-level managers and professionals are subject to control through their socialization in business schools.

These issues of control, ideology, and surveillance were certainly attractive for a Foucaultian perspective.[13] This was attempted, among others, by Jean Paul de Gaudemar (1982), who mentioned several forms of disciplining the labor force and asked if we were not witnessing the inauguration of a new, subtler one: 'democratic surveillance'.[14] Coriat (1979) also dealt with the subject of managerial ideologies, establishing a relationship between Taylorism, which he analyzed in its double role of theory and set of practices, and the Fordist model of accumulation. This latter model's inherent tendencies toward crisis demanded the application of practices considering other aspects of the working conditions that had their ideological correlate in organizacional sociology and human relations. The decline of Fordism, as a result of technological evolution, made its administrative practices obsolete and gave way to the model of flexible production and, at the theoretical and ideological level, Japanese management style (Coriat, 1991).

All the aforementioned authors share a common perspective: the subtilization of the means of control over the labor force. This dominant vision was challenged by Barley and Kunda (1992), who developed a periodization of the evolution of managerial ideologies and identified a succession of cycles or phases between rational control (which privileges the appeal to the rational interests of the workers and the use of rationalist techniques of work organization) and normative control (which aims at manipulating the feelings and values of the workforce). They postulated the existence of five clearly distinctive stages. The first dates from 1870 to 1900 and corresponds to the 'industrial betterment' ideology, which emphasizes aspects of normative control. The second one, scientific management, lasts from 1900 to 1923 and is eminently rational. The third stage, again normative, is the human relations ideology and culminates in 1955. The fourth one, denominated 'systems rationalism' by Barley and Kunda, concludes in 1980; while the last stage, from that date onwards, is dominated by a normative emphasis on such issues as 'culture and quality'.

Recognizing the merit in the historical reconstruction of this framework, I believe that two aspects pertaining to this theory deserve a closer look. First, all historical periodization is to some extent ambiguous. Second, the sharp separation between a normative emphasis and a rational one cannot be easily established, especially at certain historical moments. Rational and normative elements always coexisted in the discourse of managerial ideologies from the beginning of the nineteenth century onwards. Although it is true that one could clearly surpass the other in some particular period (e.g., the cases of Taylorism in the early twentieth century and the human relations school in the 1940s), it is intrinsically difficult to delineate a clear divide. As Peter Drucker (1990, 1992a) noticed, some practices that seem to have a 'culturalist' (normative) emphasis, like Japanese Just-in-Time or Total Quality Management, are just a refinement of old (rational) Taylorism.

Nevertheless, the distinction between normative and rational control is central to Barley and Kunda's approach, because they correlate their periodization to the evolution of the long waves in the American economy. This allows them to find a relationship of correspondence between the expansion and contraction of the economy, on the one hand, and stages of normative and rational control, on the other. Working class turmoil, another potential explanatory variable for the cycles of normative and rational control, appears unrelated to them.[15] Barley and Kunda stated that the upswing phase of these economic cycles requires an increase in productivity, which is achieved through the application of the rational management methods proposed by the dominant ideologies of the period and the implementation of technological improvements. Both elements facilitate an increase in the rate of profit. Once the cycle demonstrates signals of exhaustion and recession, management resorts to a rhetoric focused on the other factor of production: labor.

Even authors who have written extensively about the long waves of the economy admitted that the acceptance of their existence is not free from controversy.[16] Nevertheless, a link between the long waves and the world of work is not something novel. Much has been written about such economic cycles and their relationship with technological innovations (Coombs, 1984) and the transformations undergone by the working class (Gordon et. al., 1982). More specifically, Clegg (1981) also related organizational practices to the long waves of the economy. His conclusion, however, differs from that of Barley and Kunda in some respects. Clegg associated the practices of the human relations movement to the post-World War II period of economic expansion, which contradicts Barley and Kunda's position. Although Clegg referred to administrative practices and Barley and Kunda only dealt with the discourse of management literature, it remains unexplained why the temporal dominance of the human relations ideology does not coincide with its impact over practices. No account is offered for this apparent lag in the practical implementation of this managerial discourse. Moreover, the periodization of the economic cycles made by these authors also differs; consequently, they arrive at conclusions that are incompatible and demonstrate the level of subjectivity in the periodization attempts. Hence, a double ambiguity exists: on the one hand, in the periodization of the economic cycles, and on the other hand, in the impact of each managerial ideology's rhetoric.

Acknowledging the persuasiveness of Barley and Kunda's theory and the unquestionable validity of some appreciations of the dominant or traditional view, I believe that a better understanding of how managerial ideologies have evolved can be obtained by focusing on their basic function as ideologies. If this function is to provide legitimation and not control methods, then the main theoretical task is to establish how the different managerial ideologies perform such function. Bendix's comparative analysis of managerial ideologies pointed precisely at identifying the arguments for the justification of authority in economic enterprises. Besides Bendix, several authors highlighted the legitimating role of management theory. John Child (1969), for example, observed that this discipline not only performs a technical function in relation to the improvement of organizational productivity and selected dependent variables, but a legitimating one as well. In a similar vein, William Scott (1992) considered that Chester Barnard's classic book *The*

Functions of the Executive, published in 1938, provided legitimation to the rising occupational strata of professional managers. More recently, and in a closer line to the one I pursue in this book, Yehouda Shenhav (1999: 196) claimed that the birth of the discipline in the United States served basically to legitimate the specific interests of the engineers in their pretension to be 'the new "authorized actors" to become managers'.

Management theorists have fulfilled since the very inception of the discipline, and even before it gained wide acceptance, two types of legitimation functions. The first is the legitimating support to the capitalist social order as a whole. The second involves a more subtle, but no less important, function: the legitimation of the access to privileged positions within the broader social order for certain interest groups, usually constituted along the lines of the professions to which the management thinkers belong (e.g., engineers, social scientist, management experts).[17] For the purpose of brevity, I will call the first function 'type 1 legitimation' and the second 'type 2 legitimation'.

At the turn of the nineteenth century, professional managers joined the ruling class, the owners of the means of production, in the ranks of the upper strata of society, which I denominate the structure of social privilege. In this book, I will refer to the privileged strata who hold control and authority in the workplace and whose composition varies through time as 'management'. This generic definition encompasses the typical entrepreneur of the early nineteenth century as well as the top executive of our present-day corporations.

Upon the assumption that ideologies legitimate the social order, it can be hypothesized that changes in this order might be associated to changes in ideologies. Therefore, it makes sense to relate managerial ideologies not to the economic cycles, but to the very evolution of the capitalist system. Much has been written on the periodization of capitalism. Different authors from several theoretical traditions have attempted the theoretical enterprise of identifying distinctive stages in the development of that system (e.g., Lenin, Baran and Sweezy, Mandel, Minsky, just to name a few). I have preferred to distinguish among liberal, organized, and disorganized capitalism, following the classification of Scott Lash and John Urry (1987, 1994). Of course, these stages are basically valid for advanced capitalist countries only, and even considering this scope condition, there are diverse national variants as well as complex transitions between the different stages. Three aspects are of particular importance to the establishment of this periodization: (1) the characteristics of organizations in terms of size and complexity, (2) the role of the state, and (3) the structure of social stratification.[18] Table 1.1 summarizes how these features varied in each phase of capitalism.

During liberal or free enterprise capitalism, which lasted from approximately the First Industrial Revolution to the end of the nineteenth century, organizations firms were typically small in size and many productive activities were carried out through independent contractors, as I will discuss in Chapter 3. The role of the state in the economy was minimal, in line with the 'night-watchman' model of classic economic liberalism. There was a polarized or dual social structure with marked inequality between the rich and the poor.

Table 1.1 Main aspects of three phases of capitalism

Phase of Capitalism	Role of the state	Social stratification	Characteristics of organizations
Liberal or free enterprise capitalism (1750–1900)	'Night-watchman'	Polarized society with increasing inequality in several core countries	Small firms in which production is sometimes carried out through independent contractors
Organized capitalism (1900–1980)	Active intervention as regulatory agent and direct producer of goods and services (especially welfare provider)	Growth of middle classes; inequality decreases	Bureaucratization of organizations; large, pyramidal organizational structures; ownership clearly separated from control
Disorganized or global capitalism (1980–onwards)	Intervention in the economy is more limited than in the previous stage (privatization and deregulation)	Increasing polarization of the social structure in many core countries	Large, bureaucratic organizations; limited experimentation with network forms of organizations

In the following stage, organized capitalism, large enterprises with increasingly complex and bureaucratized structures became dominant, and organizations in general experienced a process of increased bureaucratization. Oligopolies and cartels emerged in a process that led some authors to speak of monopoly capitalism. The state increasingly intervened in the economic realm, attempting to regulate the economy to preserve the order and rationality of the system. It was also involved in the direct provision of goods and services and acted as an active agent for improving the situation of the most unprotected sectors of society — a trend that ultimately resulted in the emergence of a 'full-blown' welfare state in the post-World War II years. The social structure also experienced transformations, and gradually a numerous middle class emerged, reducing the social polarization of the previous century. For many social scientists, this demonstrated that inequality tended to decrease in modern industrial societies.[19]

In the early 1980s, with the rise to power of conservative governments in the USA and the UK, a new stage emerged, which has been variously labeled as postmodern, global, and disorganized capitalism — an expression that I prefer. Some authors believe that one of its core features is the superseding of the so-called Fordist model of accumulation with new production techniques (e.g., Lipietz, 2001). However, I consider that the importance of such change has been overestimated and do not see much change in the internal structure of organizations, with the exception of limited attempts at new forms of work organization and the pursuit of more aggressive strategies of worldwide expansion. In this period, the former Soviet bloc crumbled, and the countries that integrated it embraced the capitalist social order, thus turning into propitious ground for the expansion of capital on a global scale. The state reduced its intervention in the economy as direct producer through a wave of privatizations worldwide. Its role as welfare provider became an object of attack and diminished in significance. Regarding the social structure, it can be affirmed that polarization rose in many core countries.

Although there were other changes in the cultural and economic realms between and within these stages, as we will later see, the three aspects considered represent processes significant enough to adequately identify distinctive stages of capitalism.[20] The first, liberal or free enterprise capitalism, was a period of unrestrained dominance of capital; the second, organized capitalism, a stage in which the state acted to counterbalance the power of individual capitalists and to introduce some form of general rationality in the economic order; and the third, disorganized capitalism, is in some aspects similar to the former, albeit with greater power for multinational corporations. With all the limitations inherent in any historical periodization, there is a relation of correspondence between these periods and the evolution of managerial ideologies, which is summarized in Figure 1.1.

To explore the relationships between managerial ideologies and the transformations in each phase of capitalism, particularly those pertaining to the structure of social privilege, is the object of this book. In my presentation of each ideology, I focus on the following questions: What are the main issues? Which rhetoric of control is emphasized? What is the image of workers and managers? I also analyze the significance of administrative ideologies in terms of their contribution to legitimate the social order (type 1) and the access of different groups to the structure of social privilege (type 2). When the ideologies indicate explicit prescriptions to improve organizational productivity, I review how they compare to the available empirical evidence. The reader will find that, in most cases, a blatant gap exists between the ideologies' claims and factual reality. This divergence helps to strengthen the concept of management theory as ideology since it precisely addresses the epistemological dimension of ideology, thus revealing its mystifying character.

The prebureaucratic management thinking of the nineteenth century constitutes a heterogeneous set of ideologies. First, I consider in chapter 2 the discourse of some utopian socialists who developed interesting theories about how the affairs of productive organizations should be conducted, but whose contribution has been largely neglected in most management history books. As a response to their criticism against the nascent industrial order, other voices rose to defend the social privilege of the enterprise owner-managers. In this regard, I focus my presentation on the theories of Andrew Ure and Samuel Smiles in England, who laid the foundations of what may be called the ideology of the entrepreneurs' superiority, and the discourses of social Darwinism and industrial betterment in the United

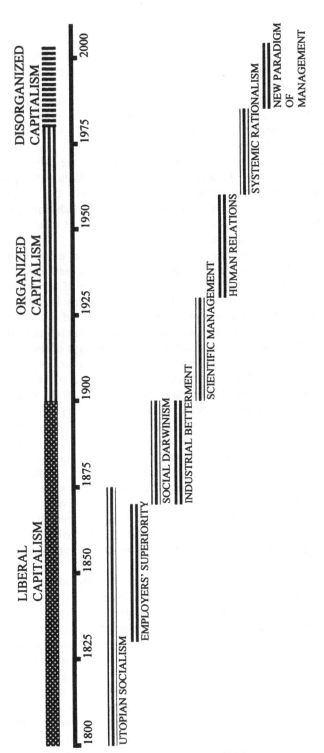

PHASES OF CAPITALISM

LIBERAL CAPITALISM

ORGANIZED CAPITALISM

DISORGANIZED CAPITALISM

1800 1825 1850 1875 1900 1925 1950 1975 2000

UTOPIAN SOCIALISM

EMPLOYERS' SUPERIORITY

SOCIAL DARWINISM

INDUSTRIAL BETTERMENT

SCIENTIFIC MANAGEMENT

HUMAN RELATIONS

SYSTEMIC RATIONALISM

NEW PARADIGM OF MANAGEMENT

MANAGERIAL IDEOLOGIES

Figure 1.1 Phases of capitalism and managerial ideologies

States (chapter 3). The legitimating role of both socialist and procapitalist nineteenth-century managerial ideologies is further discussed in chapter 4.

The ideologies of scientific management, human relations, and systemic rationalism (presented, respectively, in chapters 5 to 7) were the successive dominant managerial ideologies under organized capitalism. A central continuity united these three discourses: their adherence to a hierarchical and bureaucratic model of organization, which appears to be the implicit paradigm of management throughout that period. Each one of these ideologies legitimized the existing order and the access to the structure of social privilege of individuals with specific knowledge of diverse disciplines. However, in the same way that organized capitalism experienced several changes, the dominant managerial ideologies of the period showed distinctive emphasis and concerns in order to meet these changes, which is an issue that I deal with in chapter 8.

Simultaneously with the emergence of disorganized capitalism, a new ideological consensus, centered on flexible structures, self-direction, and the alleged obsolescence of bureaucracy begins to dominate the landscape of administrative thought. In chapter 9, I describe how the leading figures of this ideology characterize this new model of management represented by the rise of a new type of organization, which not only is more efficient but also releases the full potential of its members. Chapter 10 deals with the ideological representations of the world of work in this new paradigm, as well as with some of its alleged associated benefits, like an authentic meritocracy based on talent and intelligence and the end of alienation for the workers. Chapter 11 completes the analysis with the consideration of the significance and legitimating contribution of this discourse.

In chapter 12, I summarize the main points of this historical reconstruction of the evolution of management thought and discuss how the comparative analysis of managerial ideologies in relation with the three stages of capitalism contributes to improve our knowledge of the subject. One of the most interesting findings is the parallelism existing between liberal and disorganized capitalism, on the one hand, and some aspects of their respective managerial ideologies, on the other. Finally, I argue that, more than a subtilization of control, what can be perceived in the evolution of administrative thought is an exacerbation of its fictional or mystifying character. In the conclusion, I make some remarks on the current state of the discipline in the light of the preceding analysis.

The managerial ideologies considered in this work basically originated in the United States, with the exception of some nineteenth-century ideologies. This apparent bias in the managerial literature, my basic object of analysis, reflects the monopoly of American authors, who made of it one of the most successful American exports. A definite pattern of core-periphery transmission of ideas, with the core being the United States, is clearly observed in the processes of creation, diffusion, and consumption of management knowledge.[21] Although recent work reveals that the pattern is somewhat more complex,[22] American dominance has been a fact throughout the twentieth century. Not only the best selling books are from the United States, but also the local imitators (e.g., those in European countries) follow of the dominant ideologies advocated by their American peers.[23] American management theories have become the lingua franca of business elites worldwide. Although it must be acknowledged that certain variables, such as institutional factors, degree of economic development, and even foreign policy orientation played their role on the impact of management ideas and practices in specific countries (Guillén, 1994; Arias and Guillén, 1998), the American preponderance in managerial ideologies has been undisputed during the twentieth century. The validity of my argumentation, of course, is mainly limited to the core Western countries in which (1) the ideologies considered appeared or exerted a dominant influence and (2) the distinct types of capitalism, to which the birth of these ideologies was associated, have also been dominant.

Notes

1 Marx is perhaps the most conspicuous thinker who has contributed to this perspective. However, I must emphasize that a theory of social privilege is not exhausted in the Marxian tradition, since the bases for determining the access to social privilege are not only the property of the means of production, but also include other factors (e.g., sex, age, nationality, and psycho-physical attributes).

2 Eagleton (1991: 10) considered that 'to describe ideology as "interested" discourse, then, calls for the same qualifications as characterizing it as a question of power'. What makes the term 'forceful and informative', he contended, is whether the interests behind such discourse are 'fairly central to a whole social order'. To this, I would say that the definition of the criteria of centrality is also a controversial matter.

3 Abercrombie and Turner (1978) argued that the traditional Marxian model of the 'dominant ideology' assumes that the control of the 'means of mental production' held by the ruling class enables this class to impose a belief system to the dominated classes. However, according to these authors, there is no convincing evidence that the subordinated classes always accept the ideology of the ruling classes.

4 The term ideology is often confused with that of discourse. However, though sometimes they are used as synonymous, they are also employed in counterposed form, as Purvis and Hunt (1993) observed. For these authors, what transforms a discursive practice into ideological is its association with relations of domination. A similar reasoning that distinguishes between discourse and ideology has been put forward by Eagleton (1991). Ideology needs a vehicle to be transmitted, and such vehicle is the discursive practice. Although not all discourse is ideological, all ideology has a discourse.

5 When commenting David Ricardo's position before a request of workers unemployed because of mechanization, Klant (1988: 90) argued that the appeal to an inescapable natural order led to the logical and unquestionable conclusion — although not specified in such a crude way by Ricardo — that the unemployed, given the immovable order in which they lived, 'might improve their personal fate, and thus that of the nation, only by hanging themselves'.

6 For Marglin (1984: 482), 'The specificity of the capitalist mode of production is, as it were, too trivial a detail for neoclassical theory to bother with'. Precisely this lack of attention to such an important empirical aspect, 'in a world in which capitalism is, to say the least, controversial', cannot be interpreted 'other than as a defense of capitalism', he contended. The hegemony of neoclassical theory is not 'neutral ideologically', especially if 'that theory is not only increasingly esoteric, uncritical, and irrelevant but also supports the status quo by ensuring that the embarrassing questions do not get asked' (Marglin, 1984: 482).

7   For example, Farson (1996) defined management as the 'art of the absurd'.
8   For all its best selling success, recent managerial literature has been seriously criticized from within its own camp. In fact, some scholars have raised their voices against this apparent 'trivialization of management' in order to restore the rational foundations of the discipline. See, in particular, Hilmer and Donaldson (1996) and Eccles and Nohria (1992). Also related to this criticism phenomenon, which extends not only to the work of the management pundits but to the practices of the managerial consultocracy as well, is the idea of management literature as a commodity (Abrahamson and Eisenman, 2001; Carter and Crowther, 2000; Huczynski, 1993).
9   See, for example, Furusten (1998). Peter Anthony (1977: 261) also observed the discipline's faulty methodology, which is consistent with what he characterized as the 'theocratic' nature of management education. However, there is also a growing academic literature on management and organization studies that complies with the stringent canons of scientific methodology and is published in scholarly-refereed journals. Nevertheless, it seems as if this academic production, whose findings sometimes contradict the discourse of the popular management pundits, is considered unimportant or simply devoid of interest for the more mundane and pressing needs of the management practitioner (Alvesson and Willmott, 1996). As Nohria and Eccles pointed out (1998: 283), these academic publications 'rarely receive even a glance by managers'.
10 In this work I use interchangeably the expressions administrative and managerial ideologies, as usually seen in the literature.
11 James Burnham (1941) spoke about managerial ideologies before Bendix, but he did not devote a complete study to the subject. The work of Sutton et al. (1956) appeared in the same year as Bendix's and explored similar theoretical concerns.
12 See, for example, Mills (1953), Bell (1988 [1962]), Ray (1986), and Wilson (1999).
13 On the increasing influence of Foucault on organization studies, see McKinsey and Starkey (1998).
14 See also Sewell's (1998) conceptualization of chimerical control.
15 However, Abrahamson (1997) reported that the prevalence of normative managerial ideologies was indeed influenced by the degree of working class turmoil until 1954, a finding that he considers complementary to Barley and Kunda's pendulum theory.
16 See, for example, Wallerstein (1984) and Gordon et al. (1982). The debate not only pertains to the very existence of the waves, but also extends to its exact periodization.
17 Both functions were most often combined with the sole exception of early utopian socialist thinkers who aimed at changing the social order by piecemeal reform.
18 On indicators about inequality and its evolution in selected western countries, see Lindert (2000a, 2000b) and Morrisson (2000). The rise of the entrepreneurial state is discussed in Aharoni (1986) and Toninelli (2000), while the role of the state as welfare provider is analyzed in Ashford (1986) and Kohler et al. (1982).
19 See, for example, Lenski (1966) on the existence of a curvilinear relationship between the size of the social surplus and inequality.
20 These aspects, of course, are not independent between them (e.g., changes in public policies led to changes in social stratification; the growth of corporations and oligopolies prompted the action of the state, etc.).
21 Not without irony, Alvarez et al. (1997: 580) affirmed that management education might well be 'one of the last Wallersteinian worlds'.
22 See, for example, Üsdiken and Çetin (2001), Engwall (2000), and Guillén (1994).
23 American predominance not only includes popular management books, but academic management journals as well. For instance, in the period 1981-92, a scientometric

analysis of the main scholarly journals in the discipline shows that 86.4 per cent of academic production was written by North American authors (Engwall, 1996). This figure may rise significantly if we consider only articles published in American journals. Dannell (2000: 36) argued that the citation network constituted by management journals could be explained as a status-role system, 'structured in such a way that the European journals formed a periphery in relation to the American core journals'.

Chapter 2

Utopian Socialism as Administrative Ideology

In the eighteenth century, some economists made marginal remarks on the management function. Condillac, for example, emphasized the role of knowledge in entrepreneurial activity, and Turgot affirmed, in 1766, that those who supervise the work of others must have an intelligence or knowledge superior to them (Fontaine and Marco, 1993). These ideas were simply isolated appreciations of their time; however, when the phenomenon of industrialization became more visible in the nineteenth century, more specific discourses concerning the issues of management and authority in productive units can be clearly identified. The first administrative ideologies were conceived by the thinkers of the so-called utopian socialism, and F.A. Hayek observed that the generalized use of the term 'organization' appeared in France after the Revolution. This word referred to the idea of the reconstruction of 'society as a whole' until 'socialism' began to be used with this meaning (1973: 53). The great pioneer in this regard was the Count de Saint-Simon, whom Daniel Bell (1973) called 'the father of technocracy'. In fact, the Saint-Simonians aimed at replacing 'the rule of men over men' by 'the administration of things'. The rationalist philosophy of the Enlightenment exerted a powerful influence over Saint-Simon, whose education was supervised by D'Alembert (Wilson, 1972 [1940]). The goal of his work was the establishment of a rational social order opposed to the capitalist society of his time, which he perceived as unfair and inefficient.

Saint-Simon believed that society, in the same way as the natural world, obeyed certain laws that could be discovered through the study of human history. In the Middle Ages, the social order reflected the characteristics of a military society whose main figures were soldiers and clergymen, while the emerging industrial society was different and, in his opinion, had to be centered on the organized production of goods. According to Bell (1973), in the Saint-Simonian conception of society there were four distinctive features: (1) the centrality of production; (2) the new methods, which would be based on order and precision'; (3) the fact that it would be governed by individuals with technical expertise; and (4) the fundamental importance of knowledge. The basic principle upon which the organization of this new society had to rest was the hierarchy of merit. In his *Letter from an inhabitant of Geneve to his contemporaries*, published in 1802, Saint-Simon imagined a complicated institutional structure for the government of the new society. The 'spiritual power' would be in the hand of the wisest segment of the population: the scientists and the artists, those possessing some form of creative genius. They would integrate a body denominated the 'Council of Newton' whose functions would be primarily aimed at the enhancement of human intelligence. However, the temporal power, which included the administration of public affairs, should be in the hands of the property owners. In a clear statement of the principle of merit, Saint-Simon addressed the nonowners in the following terms: 'The owners, although less in number, possess more lights than you, and for the sake of the common good, domination should be distributed in proportion to the lights' (1832 [1802]: 40). His thought was very progressive, as he proclaimed that the objective of social institutions was the improvement of the physical, moral, and intellectual conditions of the poorest (Wilson, 1972 [1940]). Nevertheless, Saint-Simon's pretension of blending into a single class the capitalists with the proletarians has been criticized as naive and lacking realism (Buber, 1987 [1949]).

Saint-Simon was especially concerned about the legitimation of the authority of a social class composed of engineers, entrepreneurs, and planners in a new society that never came into being. It is obvious that authority differences do not disappear, but remain in the Saint-Simonian utopia, as the new society would be essentially meritocratic. Although Saint-Simon opposed the idle classes, he did not advocate a confrontation between workers and capitalists. On the contrary, he looked for a harmonic relationship between the two, whom he considered 'producers' — for Saint-Simon, a capitalist was not a parasite, but someone who managed his own enterprise. His term 'industrielle', which he used to refer to a sort of unique class of producers, included in its definition not only industrials, but also anyone directly in charge of a business (i.e., artisans, traders, bankers, and farmers). He estimated that in France at the time of his writings the number of 'industrielles' was 25 million. However, among them only the 'most important ones' would really govern society (Saint-Simon 1832 [1824]).

The appeal to the supreme authority of science in order to carry out a rational reconstruction of the social order and the concern for efficiency are also constant in the work of Saint-Simon. In recommending a social engineering of public administration, he was clearly a precursor of rationalism in management thought.[1] He affirmed that if his proposal were to be adopted, 'public affairs' would be 'directed by professors in industry or science, while at present they are conducted only by amateurs' (1832 [1824]: 238). In a clearly legitimating tone, he added, 'The truth is that the industrials are the only professors in administration, because they have learned sound management at their own expense'. The best and least expensive way to govern a society was, for him, to let it be ruled by the most capable men. In this regard, he wrote, 'the most important among the industrials . . . are those who, in short, will be necessarily in charge of the management of societal interests' (1832 [1824]: 50). It must be stressed that Saint-Simon's thought became the ideology of many bankers and industrials during the times of Louis Napoléon.[2] According to Harrington (1972), the French workers misunderstood Saint-Simon and erroneously interpreted his idea of a producers' association that would be directed by experts as a way of transferring the means of production to the labor force. Thus, what was an essentially technocratic theory was later considered an authentic socialist perspective. This was due, in part, to the reinterpretations that many of Saint-Simon's disciples made of his teachings.

The industrial system that presumably would develop as a result of the triumph of Saint-Simon's doctrine was one of associations of individuals in productive units. However, Saint-Simon did not advance much in the conception of how these productive associations would be internally organized; he just trusted in the wisdom of the industrials themselves. It was one of his compatriots, Charles Fourier, who discussed in detail the structure and operative characteristics of these associations. Fourier was in favor of a totally deductive science, centered on the human personality, upon which a total reconstruction of social institutions would be based. He devised a theory of passions and even a cosmological one, which, he claimed, would allow him to predict the future of the universe. His cosmogonic system is an interesting curiosity, as well as his methodological principles of the absolute doubt and distance, but what gave him fame was his system of social organization. He wrote several works, among them one suggestively entitled *Artifices and Quackery of the two sects of Saint-Simon and Owen, which promise association and progress; Means to organize in two months the real progress, the true association, or combination of the domestic and agricultural labors, giving quadruple product and elevating to 25,000 million the rents of France, limited today to 6,000 million and a third*. This fantastic promise would be fulfilled if his method of social organization, consisting in the generalization of productive units, which he termed 'phalanxes', were adopted.

What Fourier proposed was the suppression of the proletariat, transforming the day laborers into associates. The Fourierists communities were based on private property, and the annual earnings generated by their economic activity would be distributed according to three productive forces: capital, work, and talent. Fourier believed that this type of organization would lead to considerable savings in time and effort, which would represent a significant economic benefit. The 400 families who would compose each unit would require a single kitchen instead of 400; 400 barns would be replaced by one; and a majestic building (falanstery) would provide a magnificent lodging for all the phalanx's members.

The organization of work in these organizations was meticulously analyzed. Fourier remarked the importance of work groups and complained that their study was at that time a completely neglected aspect of scientific inquiry. Anticipating job-enlargement techniques by more than a century, he wrote,

> working in short sessions of one hour and a half or two, at most, anybody may perform in one day up to seven or eight types of pleasant tasks, vary the following day, and frequent groups other than those of the previous day. (Fourier 1971 [1829]: 67)

He grounded his method of job assignments on a theory of human motivation, which he called 'passionate series'. Each person would be assigned a set of tasks, selected from his/her own combination of passions and pleasures, and would avoid the monotony of a unique routine or occupation. There would be no reason for community members to be unsatisfied with their jobs, and according to its creator, this form of work organization would not only improve workers' satisfaction, but also enhance productivity and efficiency as well. These ideal communities were conceived as an answer to the bourgeois social order, which Fourier considered unjust and less productive. His disciples founded a falanstery in Condé-sur-Vesgres. The master himself was its director, but the result of this artificial community was negative, and it had to be abandoned.

The work of another leading figure of utopian socialism, Robert Owen, is of much greater importance for management thought. Although some of his ideas can be considered naive by today's standards, he is rightfully credited for developing pioneering contributions to the field of personnel administration. The career of Owen as entrepreneur is no less surprising. At the age of eighteen, he became a partner with the owner of a textile operation in Manchester and achieved good profits. His father-in-law transferred to him a cotton-spinning factory in New Lanark, Scotland, which he turned into a model community. Not only did he increase significantly the mill's economic yield, but he also improved the employees' living standard and education. He also founded there a school for children that excluded the idea of a system of rewards and punishments. According to Wilson (1972 [1940]: 109), 'Robert Owen in his factory played the role of a benevolent but omnipotent God'. Nevertheless, not all Owen's social experiments were successful. In the United States, he bought land in Indiana and founded the community of New Harmony, but the outcome was not positive. Upon his return to England, he tried two new communitarian experiments, first in the county of Lanark and later in Hampshire, yet they also ended in failure.

For Owen, the political economy of his time was a vulgar and ignorant form of governing society, and therefore, no general and substantial improvement of the living conditions of the people could take place without resorting to a superior way of wealth creation. His objective was absolute equality. In his 'Declaration of Mental Independence' — a speech he gave at New Harmony in 1826 — he stated that humanity should experience a 'mental revolution' to liberate itself from the 'three most monstrouos evils' that afflicted it: private property, religion, and marriage. Only then could rationality, virtue, and happiness reign in this world (Owen, 1970 [1826]: 70). His contribution to the discipline of management was, however, of another tenor. In his address 'To the Superintendants of Manufactories, and to those Individuals generally, who, by giving Employment to an aggregated Population, may easily adopt the Means to form the Sentiments and Manners of such a Population', he declared,

> Like you, I am a manufacturer for pecuniary profit. But having for many years acted on principles the reverse in many respects of those in which you have been instructed, and having found my procedure beneficial to others and to myself, even in a pecuniary point of view, I am anxious to explain such valuable principles, that you and those under your influence may equally partake of their advantages. (Owen, 1970 [1813]: 11)

Then, he drew a distinction between the inanimate machines and the 'living machines', which make up the 'system composed of many parts' that is the factory, to end up saying that:

> after experience of the beneficial effects from due care and attention to the mechanical implements, it became easy to a reflecting mind to conclude at once, that at least equal

advantages would arise from the application of similar care and attention to the living instruments. (1970 [1813]: 13)

Among the measures aimed at strengthening the 'living mechanisms', he mentioned: to treat them with courtesy, to regularly provide them with food, to avoid that their 'mental movements' undergo an 'irritating friction', and so on. Owen also emphasized that in British factories, since the massive introduction of machines, workers began to be treated as something of inferior quality, and he remarked the importance of reflecting on the subject since 'man, even as instrument for the creation of wealth, may be still greatly improved' (1970 [1813]: 14). His appeal aimed clearly at the calculative mentality of the public to whom he was addressing since he based his position on yield aspects, including an estimate of the rates of return that could derive from the application of his methods according to his own experience in New Lanark. He finally stressed that only the ignorance of their own interest can in the future prevent the industrials from paying greater attention to the 'living machines' they use, something that additionally would impede 'an accumulation of human misery, of which it is now difficult to form an adequate conception' (1970 [1813]: 14).

The importance of Owen's paternalistic practices and his discourse geared towards the greater well-being of the workers was mentioned by Bendix, who indicated that this way to face personnel management enjoyed certain diffusion at its time. This style reflected a type of relationship between the patron and the worker that was, at the same time, authoritarian and friendly, responding to 'a painstakingly elaborated model of the traditional relationship between master and servant' (Bendix, 1956: 49). According to Harrington (1972), Owen was an advocate of class harmony, who longed for the old times when the landowners had a common interest with the farmers, but his atheism earned him the dislike of the higher strata of the society of his time. Thus, the members of the underprivileged strata became his only public, who finally made a misguided but creative interpretation of his thought.

The industrial and commercial system, whose tendencies seemed cruel and inefficient to the first thinkers of utopian socialism, slowly became more powerful. New figures in the intellectual panorama appeared, and the debates focused on the organization of the working class as potential active agent of change. Nevertheless, besides the pioneers of utopian socialism, other authors committed to the critique of the capitalist system analyzed issues pertaining to administrative theory. In this regard, Piotr Kropotkin, a Russian aristocrat, disciple of the anarchist Bakunin, must be mentioned. Some of his most important works (e.g., *Fields, Factories and Workshops* and *The Conquest of Bread*), which date from the last quarter of the nineteenth century, deal with technical issues of production, as he championed the idea that people could enhance their living standard and work less time under a more rational organization of production. Kropotkin opposed the principle of integration of work to that of division and specialization, considering that the former would not produce a technical backward movement. In particular, he affirmed that there were real examples demonstrating that with an improvement in the organization of work at factories Fourier's dreams were no Utopia (Kropotkin, 1892).

During the nineteenth century, the practical attempts at building ideal communities were many. Karl Marx (1972 [1864]), in his Inaugural Address to the First International, emphasized that these social experiments demonstrated that large-scale production made according to modern science standards could be performed without the existence of a ruling class. However, reality later showed that the initial optimism around the associative way of production had been exaggerated. The analysis of these experiences is not the object of this book, although some of the lessons learned from them constitute perhaps forgotten but undeniable contributions to administrative theory. An interesting example in this respect is the work of John Humphrey Noyes, a prominent figure of American socialism. Noyes, who wrote a history of socialism in his country, studied the diverse communities and experiences that took place in the United States to explain the reasons of their repeated failures. For him, the most important point was the quality of the bond uniting all community members. It was necessary to count on a mysterious affective element, which he denominated 'afflatus', that would debilitate individual and family ties and create new ones around the community. According to Noyes, the idea of 'Communism' was a matter of degree: a small degree allowed Communism to take place in the 'limited sphere of familism', while increasing afflatus would create 'public institutions of harmony and benevolence' (1870: 198). Through inductive reasoning he concluded that afflatus might only be achieved by means of religion, yet he encouraged others to seek this normative inspiration in other ways. However, his analysis of several experiences also showed that economic aspects, such as community location and variety of income sources, should not be overlooked. He also recommended that the management of the community be in charge of the movement leaders, which meant that a separation between those who write great theories and utopian projects and those who enact them in practice should not exist. For him, too much devotion to theorizing and propagandism on the leader's part combined with a lesser concern for practical execution was a severe fault. The leader's daily presence may also be felt as inspiring by the followers. Noyes himself managed to make some of these conditions a reality at the Oneida community, which successfully functioned as such from 1848 until its transformation into a joint-stock company in 1881 (Rexroth, 1974).[3]

Noyes's writings clearly evidence that normative elements of control were already present in the protomanagement theory of the communitarian and utopian literature of the time, but there are also examples of the use of normative control at the level of administrative practices. In her study of the communitarian experiments in the United States during the nineteenth century, Rosabeth Moss Kanter noted the existence of what she denominated 'commitment mechanisms', which served to unite the individuals to the group. The more extensive use of these mechanisms took place in those communities that were more apt to endure over time. The first of these aspects, she indicated, was the act of monetary investment in the community. Other identified mechanisms were the isolation of the group with respect to the larger social environment, the frequent interaction between the members, and the enactment of group rituals (Kanter, 1972). In many successful experiences, the participants had a clear awareness of the 'mission' and importance of the community, which should be fostered by the leaders or founders. This particular feature is considered one of the most important aspects of leadership, if not the basic one, in contemporary writings on the topic.[4] However, this remote precedent in utopian communities is seldom acknowledged as such. In describing the practices occurring in this organizations, Kanter uses terms like 'sacrifice', 'renunciation', and 'deindividuation', which are indicative of the type of ideological control exerted over the members of some of these communities. It is noteworthy that the only personalities that could stand out were those of the leaders or founders (Kanter, 1972). This is, for instance, the recommendation of Charles Nordhoff, another contemporary observer of the development of socialist communities in the United States, who wrote that the failure of the Icarian experiment demonstrated 'how important, and indeed indispensable to the success of such an effort, it is to have an able leader, and to give to him almost unlimited power and absolute obedience' (1875: 339).

To sum up, the thought of the utopian socialists offers interesting notions about how organizations should be conducted, involving aspects of both normative and rational control. The most important contributions of this ideology took place in the first half of the nineteenth century, and by the mid-1870s, its appeal clearly declined as scientific socialism and Anarchism became more influential as antisystem discourses. With respect to its applications in actual practice, it is true that the successes of the communitarian experiments conducted in that century were few and generally short-lived. These artificial communities, created as germs to replace the capitalist economic system, disbanded as soon as the initial enthusiasm inspired by their founders came to an end. However, the reasons for the failure of the communitarian experiments are not necessarily related to their management model, but to the nature of the external environment. On the other hand, far from being ingenuous dreamers, many of the leading thinkers reflected largely upon their own negative experiences. Robert Owen, for example, discovered, after the failure of the New Harmony colony, that 'the habits of the individual system' were 'too powerful' and tended to debilitate the communitarian spirit (Buber, 1987 [1949]: 105). Conflicts of succession, as well as generational and economic problems, are also mentioned among the most common reasons leading to the dissolution of these organizations.

The capitalist form ultimately turned out to be more powerful than what the first socialists, and later the pioneers of Cooperativism, had imagined. In theory, it was possible to design more effective productive organizations, but in practice the illusory character of these proposals was clearly demonstrated. In fact, successful cases appeared to exemplify what Sidney and Beatrice Webb studied as the tendency to 'degeneration'. This meant that, typically, those cooperative organizations that had economic profits no longer operated as 'democracies of producers', becoming instead 'associations of capitalists' that obtained their benefit through the incorporation of salaried workers who were not associates (Webb and Webb, 1920: 29). For Marx, the experiences of the cooperative experiments from 1848 to 1864, although founded on noble principles and potentially useful, never could 'free the masses' nor 'perceptibly lighten the burden of their miseries'. Perhaps for this same reason, he added, kind philanthropists and even political economists praised enthusiastically such systems of cooperation, which they previously disqualified as utopian dreams or stigmatized as 'the sacrilege of the Socialist' (Marx 1972 [1864]: 380). However, those who considered the capitalist economic order perfectly legitimate also offered their own answers to the problems of management and legitimation of authority in productive units, which. is the topic of the next chapter.

Notes

1   In his later writings, Saint-Simon combined his rationalist stance with normative elements, by discussing a new form of Christianity. He realized that his rational design for governing society should not only be founded on scientific and moral beliefs but also on faith. This normative legacy extended to his disciples who spoke and wrote about the Saint-Simonian religion.

2   The Saint-Simonians performed an important role in the great economic expansion of the Second Empire, especially in the development of banks and railroads (Plessis, 1988). On the other hand, it must be pointed out that the Saint-Simonian principles of economic organization inspired the creation of financial institutions like the Crédit Mobilier, which funded, among others, the Companies of Gas and Omnibus of Paris, and the Crédit Foncier, dedicated to agriculture. Saint-Simon's influence crossed the Atlantic forty years after his death when these projects were imitated in the United States. Nevertheless, the Saint-Simonian program failed rapidly there (Montgomery, 1981).

3   An idea put in practice by Noyes during the last phase of the community (1869-79) is extremely noteworthy. He established a system of sexual union, denominated 'stirpiculture', by which a directive board selected sexual companions and prohibited some unions with the intention of producing better descendants (Wilson, 1972 [1940]).

4   See, for example, Nanus (1992) regarding the importance that leaders develop a vision and a sense of direction for their organizations.

Chapter 3

Procapitalist Managerial Ideologies of the Nineteenth Century in England and the United States

The British ideology of employers' superiority

In eighteenth-century England, the management of enterprises was characterized by the existence of a personal relationship between entrepreneurs and workers that generated tacit confidence (Bendix, 1956). This sort of paternalism has its antecedent in the bond that tied the master craftsman to his apprentices, but the emergence of mechanization brought about a change in industrial practices. However, Bendix admitted that this management style was still dominant in some industries during the nineteenth century.[1] A case frequently cited in the literature on the history of administrative thought is the factory of Boulton and Watt, considered a model of benevolent paternalism in many aspects akin to that of Owen in New Lanark. Boulton and Watt developed interesting management initiatives, such as the elaboration of detailed standards of operation for each machine according to the task to be performed, which anticipated Taylor by almost a century. But the most noteworthy of these initiatives was the personal considera-tion that workers received. For instance, the firm celebrated its employees' birthdays and made them gifts in Christmas in order to strengthen the bond between owners and personnel (George, 1968). James Montgomery, considered by some as the first management theorist (Bennet, 1990), also made recommendations in a paternalist line. His 1832 book *The Carding and Spinning Masters Account or The Theory and Practice of Cotton Spinning* made him very well known in England. He was invited to give lectures on the subject in the United States, but his trip did not have a major impact. Montgomery (1832) advised entrepreneurs that firmness was required in dealing with workers, but they should be treated with good manners, respect, and kindness, while avoiding too much familiarity. After Montgomery, few British authors contributed significantly to administrative thought in the nineteenth century.[2]

Beyond these minor attempts at normative control, the problem of the legitima-tion of the emergent dominant bourgeoisie in the face of the manifest unfairness of the economic order was a cornerstone for the British managerial ideology of the nineteenth century. It was necessary that the authority of the owner-manager to take any action he wished within his factory be perceived as legitimate. In order to dismiss the growing criticism against the nascent industrial order, the strategy of the legitimating discourse was twofold. On the one hand, to demonstrate that industrialism did not involve exploitation of the workers. On the other, to show that social inequalities were fair and, therefore, that the social privilege enjoyed by the ruling class was well deserved.

This legitimatory task was excellently accomplished by Andrew Ure in his book *The Philosophy of Manufactures*, written in 1835. Ure spoke about the union of capital and science, stressing the benefits to productive efficiency that technology would bring about, especially in terms of cost reduction. He argued that one of the blessings of mechanical science was that, contrary to unsupported claims stating that it put more pressure upon the workers of mechanized factories, it ameliorated considerably their fatigue and effort as compared to those experienced in a nonmechanized environment. He also found misguided the belief that children's work was harmful to their health. In particular, his writings had the merit of adequately portraying the image of the worker held by the members of the ruling class. Ure manifested his perplexity for not understanding why factory workers demanded less than ten-hour work days, and he contrasted this natural idleness on the part of the workers with the heavy duties inherent to the owners' management responsibility. Ignorant of 'the great operations of political economy, currency, and trade' and envious of the well earned prosperity of their employers, workers were 'easily persuaded by artful demagogues' that their work was worth a lot more than what was actually paid (Ure, 1861 [1835]: 279). Under that assumption and guided by 'the power of malefaction', some workers established associations that not only performed criminal acts against 'meritorious individuals', but often compelled others to join them by means of intimidation, thus limiting their own peers' individual freedom (1861 [1835]: 282). In sum, Ure's rhetoric offered a convincing vindication of the factory owners as job creators who facilitated the easiness of the tasks by means of mechanization and offered their employees the possibility of an improved living standard.[3]

Another thinker whose ideas were extremely popular in the third quarter of the nineteenth century was Samuel Smiles, who formulated, in Bendix's opinion, a 'new creed of the industrial class' (1956: 109). For Smiles, the key to success in life was hard work. The most admirable entrepreneurs earned their position thanks to their perseverance, diligence, effort, and assiduous dedication to their business activities. He based this theory on real life stories of successful men, and it can be inferred from his main arguments that those lacking will force and persistence justly deserve a lower social position. According to Bendix (1956: 110), Smiles 'continued the old theme that the workers were idle and dissolute'. Nevertheless, his doctrine is considered the 'gospel of work', as he maintained that the condition of poverty could be overcome. In this aspect, his discourse conveyed a message of hope, since he cogently argued that many admirable men were born in 'the humblest ranks' of society. He even affirmed that wealth acquired by birth might be an obstacle, instead of a blessing, to achieve a truly enduring reputation in life.

Smiles (1872) asserted that character was more important than genius. Among the virtues constituting character, so essential in the affairs of life as well as in those of business, he mentioned self-control, patience, and discipline. A man educated in the practice of self-watchfulness and self-control might by his force of will succeed in life, while one who just inherited his wealth, not having grown in the stern habits of self-discipline and personal sacrifice, might easily dilapidate his fortune. Smiles was a firm believer in free enterprise and individualism. For him, a nation's welfare was more dependent upon how well their citizens were stimulated to cultivate their personal development and independent action than upon the creation of new laws and institutions (Smiles, 1860). His writings constitute a catechism that taught that men were ultimately the masters of their own fate. In this latter aspect, his thought differs from Ure's, although both authors based their argumentations on the entrepreneurs' possession of singular traits that ultimately justified their social privilege. This view, which attributes valuable and esteemed traits to entrepreneurs, may be termed employer's superiority ideology and was the dominant legitimating ideology in England up to the 1870s. After this period, the discourse of social Darwinism achieved more prominence, granting scientific status to the belief that enterprise owners were superior to the rest of the people. This doctrine, mainly associated in England with the name of Herbert Spencer, was more fully developed in the United States where it was highly influential.[4]

Managerial ideologies in the United States: social Darwinism and industrial betterment

In the nineteenth century, the United States became one of the main industrial powers of the world, and the most important process in the evolution of its labor force was the transformation of artisans into workers. This meant that the craftsmanship culture of the small enterprise was displaced to the industrial periphery and paternalistic management gradually disappeared (Laurie, 1989). This process implied the appearance of novel organizational practices whose importance, however, has not been adequately addressed. At the beginning of the century, the craft master was still the owner in the typical factory, and the craftsmen who worked for him were proprietors of their tools (Pessen, 1983). Gradually, the masters began to act as contractors who were employed by the industrial capitalists under the system known as 'inside contracting'. For many entrepreneurs, who lacked the knowledge and the time necessary to acquire it, it was easier to decentralize specific production tasks or some parts of them to the craftsmen, who worked with their own workers in plants belonging to the capitalists.[5] This system constitutes one of the more interesting and often forgotten aspects of both the industrial development of the United States and business history (Englander, 1987).[6] Nevertheless, it characterized many American industries (e.g., sewing and agricultural machines, tools, etc.) from the first decades of the nineteenth century up to, in some cases, the first years of the twentieth century.

This management model emerged as a commitment between the enterprise owners and the craftsmen who needed each other. The capitalist lacked the capability to organize the production of articles like weapons, tools, and precision machines as well as the required ability to supervise the manual workforce. Hence, the association with the craftsmen became a necessity, since this complexity of the production process was precisely what called for decentralization. David Brody considered that the owner's capability to supervise the workers diminished as production volume increased, and this in turn compelled him to divide the labor force in smaller groups and let the traditional form of control operate through contractors. Therefore, it can be concluded that 'on the specific matter of managing workers, the nineteenth century manufacturer conceded the superiority of the close, personal supervision that characterized small-scale enterprise' (1980: 272). According to Englander (1987), there is some debate about the nature of the relationship between the contractors and their workers. For some authors, it had its tyrannical side, but for others, the own contractors' social status was dependent on securing the good will of their employees, with whom they shared the same neighborhood.

Unfortunately, the early administrative literature in the United States did not refer to this decentralized management model. Instead, in the third quarter of the nineteenth century, miscellaneous advice about how to treat workers and even how to succeed in the mercantile realm might be found in treatises addressing practical aspects of business, which mainly dealt with bookkeeping techniques and elementary finance topics.[7] Some of these manuals included reflections about the virtues and character of entrepreneurs. In a book that received much attention at its time, *Worth and Wealth*, Freeman Hunt, editor of the *Merchants' Magazine*, tried to exemplify the qualities of a successful businessman based on anecdotical evidence. He found it strange that 'no one has as yet attempted to construct the Science of Business' (1856: vi) and made suggestions about how such discipline would be composed, mentioning in this sense the need to develop a code of business ethics. His recipe for prospering in business did not differ much from Samuel Smiles's gospel of work. Above all, Hunt stressed the force of character (Jacques, 1996). In this respect, he wrote that those who made fortunes in business 'possessed an indomitable spirit of industry, perseverance and frugality', also underscoring the importance of having a strong moral basis of integrity, mercantile honor, intelligence, and good judgment (Hunt, 1856: 68). However, these claims about the elevated moral qualities of successful entrepreneurs, similar to those of the ideology of employers' superiority in England, were displaced as dominant managerial ideology in the United States in the 1870s.

After the Civil War, the modern American labor movement appeared, and the era of the big industrial company began. The new 'plutocracy' of the captains of industry adopted an ideology that was a fusion of Smiles's 'Gospel of Work' with the ideas of Herbert Spencer (Bendix, 1956). The winner in the struggle for existence was exalted, and the triumph in the business realm was considered the ultimate proof of success. For Bendix (1956: 258), 'this celebration of the businessman as hero went further than in England at the time of Samuel Smiles'. Although social Darwinism did not originate in the United States, it was there where it reached its widest diffusion (Hofstadfer, 1992 [1944]), especially in the last three decades of the nineteenth century. In his history of American sociology, Robert Bierstedt indicated that the doctrine of social Darwinism, in addition to its important consequences for social and political theory, 'achieved such dominance and potency that even its critics, so to speak, were members of the school' (1981: 5).[8]

The leading figure of social Darwinism in this country was William Graham Sumner, who in 1875 taught a course at Yale on Spencer's thought. In the animal kingdom, he argued, the strongest survive and the weakest die. This logic applies also to human affairs. The survival advantage, for him, was linked to economic wealth, to a prize that went to those who possess particular traits that enable them to obtain greater rewards in the struggle for existence. Nowhere was this clearer than in the realm of the commercial enterprise. Men and women who could obey orders were easy to find, but those who could aptly organize the productive activities and tell others what to do were rare. Consequently, it was quite reasonable that these latter individuals received much more income than ordinary workers (Sumner, 1883). For Sumner, wealthy entrepreneurs were not merely people gifted with special talent; most importantly, they were the product of 'natural selection'. Their success was proof of the law of the survival of the fittest. This natural law, he argued, was not the work of man, and therefore, could not be contradicted by him. Any interference with it would 'produce the survival of the unfittest' (1881: 311). He felt certain disdain for the lower strata of society, but he held in high esteem a social category that he denominated the 'forgotten man', whom he identified as the ordinary citizen who worked hard and paid his taxes without complaining. Unfortunately, and as a result of the mischievous conception of the state as welfare provider, this character was forced to contribute to alleviate the miseries of other less prudent individuals belonging to the lower social strata (Sumner, 1918). His conception of the 'forgotten man' could be understood as a nineteenth-century analogy to the 'silent majority' (Ruse, 1998).

Sumner seriously criticized the doctrines of the social reformers. He believed that the schemes for improving the condition of the workers interfered with the competitive dynamics of the struggle for existence, thus resulting in greater evils than those they attempted to repair or alleviate (Sumner, 1881). He did not deny that the living standard of the working class was deplorable, and he certainly cannot be accused of lacking realism in this respect; however, he deemed the socialist initiatives to escape the fierce discipline of nature as dangerous fallacies. He advised people to turn their backs on those fantastic projects for 'making everybody happy by setting those-who-have-not to rob those-who-have' (1882: 262). Echoing Smiles, he stated, 'the only two things which really tell on the welfare of a man on earth are hard work and self-denial', and he also stressed the importance of talent, skill, and training (1881: 318). The Darwinian landscape of society necessarily determined a widening gap between rich and poor, which was inevitable as a natural law. In this context, industrial virtues like energy, prudence, and sagacity were highly rewarded, while attributes such as folly and weakness were most severely penalized.

According to a classic study by Richard Hofstadter (1992 [1944]), many American entrepreneurs of the time adhered to the basics tenets of this ideology. For them, the struggle for survival constituted an individual competition in which there were winners and losers. The industrials, those triumphant in the fight, saw their authority over workers legitimized by virtue of their possession of some qualities allowing them to reach the highest social ranks. Workers, in contrast, were considered as individuals lacking those qualities. Such was the prevailing conception that the accommodated classes had regarding those from the lowest strata. For the rich, affirmed David Montgomery, the sufferings of the poor were due to their 'ignorance, indolence and immorality'. In the literature of the time, he added, workers were characterized as 'dullards or as dangerous, drunken louts' in a country portrayed as the land of the 'self-made man', where honest and persevering effort could lead any young person to climb the ladder of success (1983: 92).

The direct resistance to workers' collective action, sometimes contested by means of physical violence, and the ruthless individualism legitimized by social Darwinism constitute the evidence that supports the characterization of this period of American history as a stage of coercive control over the working class. Nevertheless, Barley and Kunda (1992) challenged this perspective through a reevaluation of the ideology of industrial betterment or 'welfare capitalism', which seems to have been overlooked in the historical reconstruction of Bendix and others who followed him despite having had significant diffusion in its time.[9] A relevant antecedent of this ideology is found in the works of Owen, Fourier, and Montgomery, but attempts at making their recommendations effective gained momentum in the 1870s, when a group of reformers spread such ideas as a way to align the interests of workers and capitalists.

Like social Darwinism, industrial betterment was born in Europe, and the most important experiences that inspired this movement were those of Sir Titus Salt in England and Jean Baptiste Godin in France.[10] Godin successfully ran a model factory at Guise and was also an important theorist who applied the Fourierist concept of phalanstery in the design of a magnificent building (the 'Social Palace' or *familistère*) for the lodging of his own workers and their families. Some of his writings were extremely influential in the United States, where his books *The association of capital with labor* and *Social Solutions* were translated and published in 1881 and 1886 respectively. Following the lead of these pioneers, the supporters of welfare capitalism installed in the American society the debate about the need to improve the condition of the working class. This managerial ideology originated as a result of the fear about the threat of socialism. The reformers looked for a solution to diminish social tensions without endangering free enterprise. Industrial betterment was based on the premise that cooperation between workers and owners was not only possible but also beneficial to both parts. However, the main reason behind industrial betterment as managerial ideology was economic profit, given that this movement's advocates underscored that the good will and disposition of the employees were advantageous from an economic viewpoint (Barley and Kunda, 1992; Mandell, 2002). As put by John Patterson, owner of the National Cash Register Company (NCR), which was deemed as a model organization within this management perspective, 'what benefits them [the workers] benefits us, while loss to them, in any way, means a corresponding loss to us' (quoted in Monroe 1898: 752).

Industrial betterment sought to materialize the harmonization of interests between workers and entrepreneurs through two basic instruments, often used in combination. The first one was profit-sharing, which is the idea of tying the income of the employees not only to a salary, but to the firms' earnings as well. In this line, one of the most conspicuous exponents of this movement, Washington

Gladden (1886), proclaimed that Christian entrepreneurs should associate their workers to their businesses offering them a fixed share in the profits. He was a priest who tried to link a certain religious morality to the business world, in what has been denominated the 'Social Gospel'. The second one was the betterment of the working conditions. This ranged from the improvement of the aesthetic and sanitary conditions of factories to the construction of educative, social, and recreational facilities for the workers and their families. The most ambitious developments were the building of whole communities for the employees, as illustrated by the cases of George Pullman and N.O. Nelson, both owners of large companies. Barley and Kunda (1992: 366) emphasized that, by the end of the century, industrial betterment was 'widely touted as the wave of the future', and the Universal Exhibition of Paris in 1900 displayed an exhibition of these kind of practices in American corporations. Some of the most important companies in the United States of that time applied welfare schemes.

This ideology has been characterized as an opposite to social Darwinism by authors like Guillén (1994) and Wren (1994), but this is not at all correct, since the rhetoric of social Darwinism also infiltrated the writings of some of its most representative advocates. One of them, Nicholas Gilman, asserted, 'nature . . . has strictly decreed that executive capacity in the conduct of large business shall be the possession of comparatively few persons' (1892: 128). Gilman was a fervent defender of profit sharing, but he warned that this type of cooperation between employers and employees should not advance too much because 'a limit is soon reached at which the inevitable claims of aristocracy make themselves felt' (1892: 127). N.O. Nelson, who founded one of the most important factories of its time and wrote articles in popular magazines about the necessity and convenience of improving the working conditions, also espoused a typical social Darwinist worldview. He claimed that 'the administration by one permanent head is a necessity, if the best results in manufacturing are to be obtained. Such heads, as a rule, will be an evolution of the fittest' (1887: 390).

The idea of private as opposed to public philanthropy was not a unique tenet of the welfare capitalism theorists, it is also found in the writings of many social Darwinists, including William Graham Sumner. A clear example in this regard was Andrew Carnegie, a steel industry millionaire and devoted disciple of Herbert Spencer. For him, the successful entrepreneurs should administer their fortunes for the benefit of the poor (Carnegie, 1889). He himself effectively practiced what he preached, donating huge amounts of money to museums, libraries, etc. throughout his lifetime. On the other hand, the negative image that the wealthy classes of the American society had about the workers was also present in the industrial betterment ideology. For example, in Gladden's opinion, the poor were somewhat responsible for their own situation. Not only did he believe that workers lacked the necessary talent to manage a business — a fact he considered key to the absence of sound attempts at cooperative experimentation in the United States — but he judged that their miseries were 'often due to extravagance and improvidence, rather than to insufficient incomes' (1876: 45).

However, in contrast to social Darwinism, the discourse of industrial better-ment presented a management model that proposed specific tools and strategies to run organizations. It is therefore relevant to see whether the practices associated to industrial betterment achieved their goals in terms of increasing the entrepreneurs' profits. There were some successful examples, like the NCR Company, but the evidences suggest that these were few.[11] For some authors (e.g., Shuey, 1900), welfare schemes generally paid off, while other researchers (e.g., Emmet, 1917) were skeptical about the alleged benefits of profit-sharing. In this latter aspect, the effect of profit-sharing as an economic incentive might have been null because, most often, what was offered to the employees amounted to a mere 'Christmas present'. The 'full-blown model', which was the construction of factories modeled after some utopic form of total institution, was dangerously similar to the communitarian experiments of socialist origin; therefore, few entrepreneurs were really interested in adopting it. Moreover, to sustain such an endeavor and still make an economic profit required enjoying a privileged market position, and thus, it could not attract many supporters within the ranks of the industrial capitalists. The negative side of these communities must also be highlighted. In this regard, Richard T. Ely, a respected economist of the epoch, made an interesting analysis of the Pullman case, which was one of the paradigmatic experiences of the movement. Although praising the community for its overall beauty and the quality of its facilities, he concluded that any type of marked individuality tended to be suppressed and that there were restraints to 'individual initiative' (1885: 465).[12]

By the end of the nineteenth century, both industrial betterment and social Darwinism began to lose importance as managerial ideologies. Although in the first decades of the twentieth century, some welfare-capitalism practices continued in many companies (Jacoby, 1997) and social Darwinism still influenced the beliefs of some prominent businessmen (Kidwell, 1995), a line of thought that was basically focused in the rational design of workflow operations rose to prominence in the 1900s. Its ascendance is associated with changes in the economic environment, which in turn affected the internal structural of organizations, and to the theoretical contributions that a new breed of experts began to develop.[13]

Contemporaneously with the emergence of industrial betterment in the decade of 1870, a new type of enterprise began to take shape in Europe and the United States. The first modern companies were created primarily in the railroad and communications industries (Chandler, 1977). By 1880, large enterprises in these industries generated a flow of goods and information in an unprecedented volume. This increase in the possibilities of business expansion caused, in turn, a wave of technological innovations in Western Europe and the United States in what is known as the Second Industrial Revolution. According to Alfred Chandler, the new companies differed from the older ones in their intense requirements of capital and their capacity to benefit from the introduction of scope and scale economies due to technological innovations. The operation of these companies called for greater coordination, which could not arise spontaneously, but 'demanded the constant attention of a managerial team or hierarchy' (1992: 81). This explained the emergence of a clearly identifiable management function that would be performed by people other than the enterprise owners. In this context, the inside contracting system began to lose ground, as entrepreneurs preferred to rely on internal experts rather than on outside contractors.[14]

Management theory registered a remarkable impulse from the contributions made by some of those who had managerial responsibilities in this new type of company. Daniel McCallum used administrative principles and procedures in American railroads, including organizational charts, and also spoke, by 1856, about the evaluation and discipline of managers and not only of workers (Chandler, 1977). Henry Poor edited the *American Railroad Magazine*, which included some articles on management. Moreover, in 1885, Captain Henry Metcalfe, administrator of an army arsenal, published a book entitled *The Cost of Manufactures and the Administration of Workshops, Public and Private*, in which he discussed the idea of the existence of a 'science of management' based on principles applicable to multiple cases. These pioneers were precursors of a rationalist approach to management that arrived at its definitive expression with the advent of Frederick Taylor's scientific management.

Notes

1 See also Burawoy's (1985) analysis of Lancashire mills.
2 However, it must be noted that some economists like Mill and Marshall mentioned in their works several aspects of business management. On the other hand, Charles Babbage, a mathematician who designed a precursor of the modern computer, argued in his book *On the Economy of Manufactures and Machinery*, published in 1832, that there were principles that guided the production of goods and services (e.g., the division of labor). Babbage dedicated a chapter of his book to discuss a system of profit-sharing that would bring about closer collaboration between owners and workers.
3 According to Wren (1994), Ure's work influenced the French economist and mathematician Charles Dupin. Nevertheless, though highly praising English industrial practices, Dupin did not subscribe to the ideology of employers' superiority espoused by Ure. Instead and on a clear normative tone, he commended Owen's experience in New Lanark and wrote that, despite his failure at New Harmony, 'it should not be forgotten the admirable example he has made, which must be imitated in the paternalist management of large manufacturing establishments' (Dupin, 1832: 227).
4 Spencer was the first to use the expressions 'struggle for existence' and 'survival of the fittest' in an essay published in 1852, expressions that later appeared as chapter titles in Darwin's *The origin of species*. His writings about management topics were few, but he was one of the first authors to speak about the intrinsic inability of public organizations for good administration. For him, this was due to the characteristics of their personnel because 'birth, age, back-stairs intrigue, and sycophancy, determine the selections, rather than merit'. Spencer contended that 'the man of capacity often finds that, in government offices, superiority is a hindrance — that his chiefs hate to be pestered with his proposed improvements, and are offended by his implied criticism', concluding that these organizations were thus 'made of inferior materials' (1873: 68). He opposed this characterization to that of private enterprise, which he considered more economically efficient, more capable of adapting to changing environmental circumstances, and less prone to corruption.
5 Indeed, this aspect differentiated inside contracting from the putting-out system, characteristic of England during the last decades of the eighteenth century and the first ones of the nineteenth century, since in the latter decentralized tasks were made in the addresses of the contractors.

6 For Englander, one of the reasons for it is that few records of the internal organization of work in the nineteenth-century enterprises are preserved. In addition, he noted that, 'paradoxically, 19th century observers apparently overlooked the system because it was *so* commonplace in key U.S. workplaces [emphasis in original]' (1987: 431).

7 This is illustrated by the work of Ira Mayhew (1866). In France, some writings of Courcielle de Seneuill offer a similar example. See Ribeill (1994).

8 The tenacious advocates of laissez-faire, who wanted to sacralize in the name of science the outcomes of a free market society, were not the only ones to apply Darwin's ideas or, more often, those of Spencer to the social world. Many thinkers favoring a socialist vision of the social order also advanced their own version of a progressive Darwinian worldview. Besides, Robert Bannister (1988) affirmed that the label 'social Darwinism' was basically an invention of some liberals in an attempt to caricature or otherwise attack the views of those who defended free enterprise.

9 Wren also referred to this set of ideas that, according to him, rose 'in counterpoint to social Darwinism' and 'came closer to grasping the policies and practices of the nineteenth-century business leader' (1994: 95).

10 See, for example, Towle (1872) and Howland (1872).

11 Regarding the example of NCR, I must point out that this company's success might not only be the result of its benevolent management model, but also of its aggressive policy towards the competition, which led the firm to be sued by the U.S. government under the Sherman Antitrust Act. See, in this last respect, Brevoort and Marvel (2001).

12 This led Ely to affirm that the 'the idea of Pullman' was 'un-American'. Therefore, he recommended to allow greater worker's participation in the government of the community in order 'to develop a democracy, or at least what might be called a constitutional monarchy, out of the despotism of Pullman' (1885: 465).

13 Litterer (1986) spoke about the management developments that occurred between 1870 and 1900 as the systematic management school. These included advances in cost accounting, shop-floor efficiency techniques, and the elaboration of labor compensation schemes.

14 For more details on the decline of inside contracting, see Clawson (1980).

Chapter 4

Managerial Ideologies and the Legitimation of Liberal Capitalism

In the nineteenth century, there were some attempts to systematize the dispersed knowledge on administrative practices, but the results were not important. According to Pollard (1965), this was due to three reasons: the difficulties to clearly differentiate a management function, the fact that the role of the manager, once isolated, was of a strictly individual nature, and finally, the existence of a dominant conception that viewed the labor force contemptuously. During this period, there was an extremely polarized social structure, and social privilege was based fundamentally on the individuals' position with respect to the ownership of the means of production. Organizational structures were fairly simple: the owner-manager at the top, a layer of foremen and supervisors to exert control and coordination in the middle, and finally the workers. Even complex productive tasks could be carried out by small organizations in the context of a network of independent firms, as illustrated by the case of inside contracting in the United States. The surveillance practices in productive units with a small number of people were predominantly those of direct or simple control (Edwards, 1979). Since the management function was neither clearly identifiable nor easily separable from the role of the factory owner and organizations were not so complex nor had a very large size, the existence of a discipline like management was not fundamental.

However, some discourses were articulated around the issues of the necessary rationalization of the emerging industrial order and the manifest unfairness of which the working class was the object. This led to the creation of productive organizations that were structured as cohesive collectives to avoid some of the costs of the capitalist system. Other discourses were elaborated from an opposite perspective, legitimating the authority exerted in the factories by their owners, justifying their rise to privileged social positions, and explaining the bad situation of the most unprotected sectors through a supposed inferiority or lack of positive qualities of their members. This period was distinguished by the direct control of the labor force and the existence of authoritarianism on the part of the owner-managers. Evidence of this may be found in many writings of the epoch, even permeating the works of authors sympathetic to the communitarian experiments (e.g., Nordhoff, 1875). But the recommendations of some theorists, like James Montgomery and Robert Owen, were also paternalist. It can therefore be concluded that the administrative ideologies of the nineteenth century endorsed a management model that can be denominated authoritarian paternalism.

This stage of capitalism was also characterized by the existence of a strong social conflict between capitalists and workers, motivated by the sharp inequality in the living conditions of the members of both classes. The managerial ideologies of the time made an issue of that. Table 4.1 summarizes the basic characteristics of these ideologies, distinguishing between antisystem (diverse utopian socialist theories) and prosystem ideologies (employers' superiority, social Darwinism, and industrial betterment) according to their basic stance towards the social order. Of course, the supposedly 'antisystem' managerial ideologies — e.g., those of Saint-Simon and Owen — were not so antisystemic after all, since they also allowed an interpretation favorable to the interests of the wealthiest classes. In fact, the Saint-Simonians had a remarkable influence in the industrial development of France during the time of Louis Napoléon. The real threats for the social privilege of the capitalist class were Marxism and Anarchism, while the administrative ideology of some collectivist thinkers, which inspired the sprouting of many utopian communities, was not a serious menace and only tried to alter the social order in a progressive and pacifist way.

The elimination of social unfairness was an objective of the socialist thinkers. For Saint-Simon, it was mainly a technical problem that could be solved through the application of reason to the economic organization of production. He was a hard detractor of the feudal regime, or what remained of it, and saw in industrialism a future of open possibilities for social justice. His objective was not to legitimize the order of his time, since he noticed the existence of flagrant injustices, but to construct a new society, molded on the basis of the rising industrialism. Although Saint-Simon is perhaps best known for his humanist vision, he is also considered the father of technocracy. By advocating a sort of illustrated 'state capitalism', he was the initiator of rationalism at the level of public management. His writings highlighted the importance of terminating with the parasites of the industrial system and of replacing the relations of power in society with the 'administration of things'. He was a humanist, but the social order he devised was strictly meritocratic. His proposal aimed at rationalizing capitalism, and the industrials, the authentic producers, were the class in charge of realizing it. However, Saint-Simon's ideology was antithetic to liberalism, despite his praise for the figure of the entrepreneur. According to him, managerial capacity was dependent upon the intelligence, personality, and business experience of the individuals, and the most able ones were those who should direct industrial activity. In this sense, his ideology legitimated the 'good industrial', although the maintenance of social privilege on the basis of heritage, a main institution of capitalism, was not legitimized.[1]

The concern with the rationalization of the economic order was also central to the thought of Charles Fourier, who believed in the spirit of association as a way to eliminate social miseries and in the improvement of organizational performance through the rational design of administrative structures and work processes. His approach was a failed attempt at organizational engineering, yet his idea of designing an organization on the basis of a cohesive collective is undoubtedly an example of administrative thinking ahead of his time. In England, Robert Owen also introduced new elements to management thought that were based on the

Table 4.1 Nineteenth-century managerial ideologies

Ideologies	Antisystem ideologies (utopian socialist thought)	Prosystem ideologies (employers' superiority, social Darwinism, industrial betterment)
Basic tenets	Search for a rational meritocratic society, ruled by experts in administration (Saint-Simon) Importance of attending to the workers' feelings and values (Owen) Rational design of organizations as communities; need to consider the preference of each person in the assignment of productive tasks (Fourier) Importance of the figure of the leader in these experimental communities (Nordhoff) Blend of rational with affective elements in order to increase the possibilities of the communities' survival and growth (Noyes)	The authority and social privilege of the entrepreneurs was justified on the basis of their superior moral or intellectual traits; this logic was elevated to the status of 'scientific law' in the discourse of social Darwinism Industrial betterment stressed the need of contemplating the workers' welfare as a means to improve organizational productivity and diminish social turmoil; specific organizational practices (e.g., construction of community infrastructure around factories and profit-sharing schemes) were advocated to achieve these goals
Image of the owner-manager	Not much an issue, except in Saint-Simon who considered the successful entrepreneurs as belonging to a strata of superior-minded people	Entrepreneurs were presented in a very positive light: persons gifted with superior abilities (e.g., intelligence, character) who constituted a 'natural aristocracy'
Image of the workers	Favorable and sympathetic image of the workers; they were not deemed as being responsible for their miseries.	Workers were basically depicted as idle and lacking the necessary qualities possessed by their bosses

Table 4.1 *(continued)*

Legitimated interests	Community founders and movement leaders In the case of Saint-Simon, there was also praise of the owners of industrial enterprises	Owner-managers
Main authors	Saint Simon Fourier Owen Noyes	Ure, Smiles (employers' superiority) Spencer, Summer, Carnegie (Social Darwinism) Gladden, Nelson, Gilman (industrial betterment)
Period of dominance	1810-1875	1830-1870 (employers' superiority) 1870-1900 (social Darwinism and industrial betterment)
Impact on administrative practices	Limited to experimental communities	Only the industrial betterment ideology dealt with administrative practices. The welfare programs advocated by the proponents of this ideology were actually adopted by several American firms

necessity to consider and 'give form' to the workers' feelings. His view that the employees' well-being also contributed to their employers' is a remarkable example of instrumental rationality.[2] Owen, however, did not want to legitimize the capitalist class, although some of his writings can be interpreted not from a humanist viewpoint but as a recommendation destined to improve business performance. A similar position, albeit with a more definite promanagement stance, can be seen in James Montgomery's contributions These two examples clearly demonstrate that the tendency to suggest the use of normative control in administrative thinking dates back to at least the first half of the nineteenth century.

In synthesis, Saint-Simon saw in the engineers and planners the solution to the problems of industrialism; Owen looked for the workers' well-being through paternalism; and Fourier appealed as much to rational as to normative elements by claiming that a cohesive collective, like an artificial community, would increase economic productivity and bring happiness to its members. Although the thought of these three authors fits within the category of administrative ideology, it is not a legitimating discourse of the social order. Yet, their ideologies can also be read as discourses aimed at fostering particular social interests, thus fulfilling what I have called type 2 legitimation functions. Basically, they served the interests of the members of their respective schools and, especially, those of the leaders of the utopian communities. Interestingly enough, Fourier (1831: 61) mounted part of his critics against the Saint Simonian discourse in the same line of thought, affirming that 'its dogmas' were 'the veils of personal interest'.

The social privilege of the ruling class was defended and legitimized by a heterogeneous assembly of managerial ideologies: employers' superiority, social Darwinism, and industrial betterment. The work of Andrew Ure clearly constitutes a legitimatory discourse of the social order (type 1), and it has recently been argued that his writings also involve what I identify as type 2 legitimation, aimed at associating technical experts, such as Ure himself, to privileged positions within the rising industrial order (Edwards, 2001). Ure vindicated mechanization and manufacturing discipline, and he was concerned with offering a clearly differentiated image about the dual society of his time: a dominant class composed by worthy individuals and a subordinated class made up by people of an inferior level. This type of description, also shared to some extent by other thinkers like Samuel Smiles, was widespread during the nineteenth century and influenced the cultural climate of the time. Social Darwinism also contributed to increase the plausibility of these characterizations, endowing them with scientific respectability, and thus increasing their force to legitimate the social privilege of the ruling class. This ideology changed the nature of the argument. The question was not merely that the possession of particular traits was what made entrepreneurs more worthy as individuals than the rest. Rather, it was emphasized that their rise to positions of privilege as a result of such traits was the consequence of a scientific law upon which depended the whole progress of the human race, and not just their own good fortune.

The ideology of industrial betterment was an answer to the social malaise that not only legitimized the privilege of a dominant 'natural aristocracy', but also aimed at creating adequate living conditions for the workers. With this purpose, in another example of normative control inspired by a definite instrumental rationality, it assimilated some proposals that had previously been an exclusive patrimony of the socialist thinkers, in particular the idea of building community infrastructures for the workers. The rhetoric of cooperation, as a response to that of 'irreconcilable conflict' sustained by Marxists and Anarchists, was a key feature of industrial betterment. Although its discourse proclaimed the need to care for the workers' well-being, the images of workers and entrepreneurs displayed in the writings of some of its most representative figures are similar to those portrayed by social Darwinism and the ideology of employers' superiority.

In the nineteenth-century management thought there were clear examples of the appeal to both elements of normative (Owen, Montgomery) and rational control (Saint-Simon, Fourier). But what Barley and Kunda (1992) considered as the dominant view on the evolution of managerial ideologies depicts this period as one of coercive control. Marx and Engels, for example, spoke in *The Communist Manifesto* about manufacturing discipline in terms of a military model, comparing the capitalist to the despotic leader of an industrial army.[3] Perhaps this could have been true at the level of administrative practices. Direct control surely had a negative side, especially considering the remarkable asymmetry between owners and workers. However, at the level of managerial ideologies, the rhetoric of despotism was minimal. As seen in the historical reconstruction outlined in chapters 2 and 3, elements of normative control were present in the benevolent recommendations of some theorists. The existence of a paternalist ideology for managing the workers falsifies the claims of those who see in all the administrative ideologies of the nineteenth century a discourse in favor of despotism in the capitalist enterprise. With this I do not pretend to deny the existence of coercive control over the labor force, whose nature and scope in administrative practices go beyond the object of the present work.[4] Simply, I want to emphasize that normative control aimed at giving form to the workers' feelings in benefit of the capitalist class dates back to managerial ideologies older than what is commonly acknowledged in the literature.

To sum up, this stage of capitalism, in which the state abstained from interfering in the economy and liberalism was still the source of economic policy, was characterized by:
1. Small-sized organizations with relatively flat hierarchies and, sometimes, with decentralization of some activities to outside firms.
2. A polarized and conflictive social structure.
3. A heterogeneous set of managerial ideologies that appealed to such diverse elements as the use of normative control to gain the workers' compliance, the rational design of communities and organizations, and the legitimation of the social privilege of the members of the dominant class on the basis of the alleged superiority of its members. This latter issue was the unifying theme behind all type 1 legitimating discourses and may be understood as the basic response to all the doctrines that questioned the social order.

The management literature of the period did not offer much in terms of prescriptive developments about specific organizational models, nor was there a need for it under the dominant model of authoritarian paternalism. However, there were some references to aspects that would be reinvented in later years (i.e., the adequate motivation of the employees, the need to gain their good will and disposition, the importance of a pleasant work climate, etc.).[5] The main concern of the legitimating ideologies, nonetheless, was to emphasize that the status differences between owner-managers and workers were perfectly legitimate, just, and even desirable. The predominance of a discursive rhetoric oriented to such aims was a logical outcome in the context of the dual society of the period.

Liberal capitalism started to change simultaneously with the appearance of a flood of technological innovations, in what has been called the Second Industrial Revolution. The passage from liberal capitalism to organized capitalism was gradual, and a transition phase existed, which extended from 1880 to the early twentieth century.[6] By that time, the demand for administrative jobs began to increase, facilitating the growth of a lower middle class in many core Western countries, and the big industrial enterprise achieved monopolistic presence in certain areas of the economy, drastically altering the operation of free competition. These transformations are associated with the displacement of the authoritarian-paternalist management model by the bureaucratic model, which was primarily applied in organizations of a certain size and complexity. In the realm of productive processes, industrial engineers carried out the first attempts at formalization, rationalization, and systematization. Such efforts finally culminated in the emergence of management as discipline with Taylorism, an ideology that legitimized authority in productive organizations on the basis of a neutral and impartial technology.

Notes

1   Saint Simon (1832c [1818]), in his *Views on property and legislation*, considered that the existence of society was dependent upon the conservation of the right of property, although he clearly stated that limitations to that right might be legislated. His disciples went further: Jean Reynaud (1964 [1877]), for example, condemned any inequality arisen from privileges of birth, including among them the inheritance of property.

2   By instrumental rationality I refer to means-end rationality. Here, the ends — the capitalist' profit maximization — is taken as data from the social system, and its evaluation is considered a process that escapes rational argumentation. Consequently, this view rejects the notion of a 'rationality of ends'. Herbert Simon (1957: 46) subscribed to this position by indicating that 'there is no way in which the correctness of ethical propositions can be empirically or rationally tested'. Nevertheless, the debate on the possibility of a rationality of ends remains open. In this regard, the positions of Apel (1979) and Habermas (1972), who both argued in favor of a philosophical foundation for a practical or ends rationality, are pertinent. In fact, the 'critical management school' appeals strongly to Habermas's contributions. See, for example, Alvesson and Willmott (1996).

3   One early German management theorist, G. Roesky, wrote in 1878 that industrials should imitate the Prussian army; however, this kind of suggestion was limited to German authors. See Guillén (1994).

4   By coercion, I understand the application of some type of physical or moral violence that goes beyond the fact that, in the capitalist system, workers are compelled to sell their labor force to the capitalists in order to secure their personal subsistence.

5   An undisputed precedent of employee involvement must also be mentioned: the case of NCR, a paradigm of the industrial betterment movement, whose practices of employee participation were described by Monroe (1898).

6   See, for example, Runciman (1993) on a subtype of British capitalism lasting from 1880 until 1914.

Chapter 5

Scientific Management

The thought of Frederick W. Taylor

Among those concerned with the application of rational methods to the management of organizational productive processes at the turn of the nineteenth century, the most outstanding figure was Frederick W. Taylor, the father of scientific management. He was an engineer who began working as a consultant for the improvement of manufacturing processes and ended up being recognized as a 'prophet' of a new managerial ideology (Kakar, 1970). His discourse emphasized the importance of cooperation between workers and entrepreneurs with respect to the application of a rational method of work organization whose result would be a greater yield for both parts. According to Daniel Bell (1973), Taylor was to Saint-Simon what Lenin was to Marx. In fact, the idea of rationalizing the industrial activity and founding the administration of economic units on the basis of scientific knowledge reached with Taylor its culminating point, although certainly Saint-Simonian humanism was alien to him. Urwick and Brech (1951) asserted that Taylor's main credit was not originality, but adequate synthesis and improvement of a method for optimizing production that had several antecedents.[1]

One of his first works published in 1903, *Shop Management*, gave him a popularity that he did not expect (Kakar, 1970). His system became object of analysis and application in several companies, and the news began to spread that the use of his method facilitated a remarkable increase in productivity and efficiency. The acceptance of 'scientific management', the name he later gave to his approach, grew remarkably as the industrial betterment managerial ideology lost its dominance. A group of disciples worked closely with Taylor. Among the most important ones were Frank Gilbreth and Henry Gantt, two of his oldest collaborators, and Morris L. Cooke, who is credited with writing part of the book *Principles of Scientific Management* (Wrege and Stotka 1978, Wrege 1995).

Taylor's goal was not only the design of a system for increasing organizational performance, but something much more ambitious: the solution to the 'labor problem' (Nelson, 1980). Actually, one of the basic elements emerging from the analysis of his writings is his focus on cooperation between management and workers as the only means to overcome the erroneous belief that an insuperable conflict existed between the two. The ultimate goal of capitalists and workers, to improve their living standard, could only be accomplished if the available wealth increased. If this happened, and the use of a cooperative strategy so assured, the benefits would accrue to both parties. To conceive the issue as a 'zero-sum game' in which the yield of one part derived from the loss of the other was socially perverse and deleterious, since it closed the doors to cooperation. Taylor eloquently exposed these ideas in several works.

In *Principles of Scientific Management*, he asserted that 'the principal object of management should be to secure the maximum prosperity for the employer, coupled with the maximum prosperity for each employé' (Taylor, 1947 [1911]: 9). His belief that the confrontation between workers and capitalists was a 'social error', based on the false premise of the 'zero-sum game' — an expression that he obviously did not use, but that perfectly represents what he wanted to indicate — was also expressed in a clear and forceful way in his 'Testimony before the Special Committee of the House of Representatives to investigate the Management System of Taylor and Others'.[2] In this opportunity, he indicated in January 1912 the following:

> I think that I am safe in saying that in the past it has been in the division of this surplus that the great labor troubles have come between employers and employees. Frequently, when the management have found the selling price going down they have turned towards a cut in the wages . . . as their way of getting out whole, preserving their profits intact. While the workman (and you can hardly blame him) rarely feels willing to relinquish a dollar of his wages . . . Thus, it is over this division of the surplus that most of the troubles have arisen . . . Gradually, the two sides have come to look upon one another as antagonists, and at times even as enemies . . . The great revolution that takes place in the mental attitude of the two parties under scientific management is that both sides take their eyes off the division of the surplus as the all-important matter, and together turn their attention toward increasing the size of the surplus until this surplus becomes so large that it is unnecessary to quarrel over how it shall be divided. (Taylor 1947 [1912]: 29-30)

The notion of a 'mental revolution' is what, in essence, defined scientific management, according to Taylor himself. In his testimony, Taylor admitted that this idea might sound like a 'bluff', but insisted that, without a drastic attitude change, scientific management could not take place. This notion entailed a different stance towards the workers on the part of management, but also on the part of workers towards their employers, their peers, and their jobs. In this respect, Taylor spoke about 'war' being replaced by 'peace' and pleaded in favor of the introduction of a climate of 'hearty brotherly cooperation' in the factories, which would substitute 'mutual confidence' for distrustfulness. For him, scientific management would not exist in reality 'until this new idea of cooperation and peace has been substituted for the old idea of discord and war' (Taylor 1947 [1912]: 31).

The necessity of cooperation was not the only essential element, as Taylor's major contribution to management was the introduction of scientific and systematic knowledge as a superior alternative to experience and personal knowledge. In this sense, what Taylor pursued was the abandonment of the traditional administrative practices and the adoption of his own system. This can be synthesized into four 'principles': (1) the development of scientific methods in substitution of the 'rule-of-thumb' practices to analyze the tasks to be performed by each worker; (2) the scientific selection and training of workers; (3) the cooperation with workers in the application of scientific methods for accomplishing the tasks; and (4) the fair distribution of responsibility between the worker and the manager, considering that management should assume all the responsibilities exceeding the workers' capacity. All these precepts constituted a differentiating element with the 'old type of management', in which 'almost all of the work and the greater part of the responsibility were thrown upon the men' (Taylor 1947 [1911]: 37).

For Taylor, the application of the scientific method would allow the detection of the 'one best way' to perform each job, which should not require abilities greater than those possessed by any normal worker. This was an exclusive responsibility of management and logically had to be trusted to experts. Once established the 'one best way' for each task, it must be taught to the workers, who would not have great problems in fulfilling their duties according to the established guidelines and standards. It was clear that the prevailing approach, in which workers learned by themselves the best way to perform a task on the sole basis of their talent and experience, was inefficient. The worker had to be guided by management, and the coordinated effort of both parts would result in the attainment of the optimal production output given the assigned material resources. It was essential to divide the tasks in their minimum operations, analyzing each of them through motion and time study. This would allow the total process to be reconstituted, eliminating idle times and unnecessary movements using the optimal standards that were determined considering the machinery and tools at hand, which could also be replaced in case of market availability of others that provided a superior use. The utilization of monetary incentives to motivate workers was also an integral part of Taylor's proposal.

Taylor criticized the 'old management methods' that based their success on obtaining the workers' initiative, something that according to him was rarely possible due a 'natural tendency to idleness' on their part. In this regard, he wrote in *Shop Management* the following:

> hardly a competent workman can be found in a large establishment, whether he works by the day or on piece work, contract work or under any of the ordinary systems of compensating labor, who does not devote a considerable part of his time to studying just how slowly he can work and still convince his employer that he is going at a good pace. (1947 [1903]: 33)

Therefore, it can be concluded that Taylor's concept of the worker is not very different than that of the dominant vision during the nineteenth century. What the Taylorist system vindicated as contribution is the method to by-pass this tendency and to increase the worker's productivity through an equation combining 'low costs' with 'high wages'.

To fully understand this ideology, one must delve further into the nature of Taylor's position, in particular into the roles that Taylorism assigned to managers and employees. The duties and responsibilities corresponding to each part were of course asymmetric. Management should provide employees with the supporting elements and training to perform the job, but instead of merely seeking the initiative of the workers, it should take a more active role. Managers should be in charge of the 'brain work', rigorously analyzing and planning all the operative and administrative tasks to be performed in the organization. The requested 'change of mentality' on the part of workers was, however, more problematic. It seemed quite unlikely that a spirit of cooperation with management would arise spontaneously in a time when social turmoil was particularly troublesome. Here enters the element of rational calculation that Taylor assumed would turn the table in his favor: the worker would willingly cooperate because an economic advantage was offered to him in return. The story of Schmidt, narrated by Taylor in *Principles of Scientific Management*, well illustrates this point, constituting a paradigmatic example of his method in action. There he described how he was successfully able to get a worker to almost quadruple his individual productivity by offering him a suitable economic incentive that was contingent upon his promise to dutifully follow the instructions indicated regarding the motions and pauses to be made during the tasks. The key to the mental revolution consisted in getting workers to understand that a conflict strategy was inappropriate for their own benefit. For the advocates of scientific management this was not only desirable, but also perfectly possible: 'If a square deal is assured, there is no doubt that labor will cooperate in every advance in the science of management affecting industry' (Gilbreth, 1970 [1923]: 258).

Despite the fact that Taylor's didactical examples mostly dealt with industrial production, scientific management should not be regarded as a contribution that solely centered on manufacturing processes. Gilbreth, one of Taylor's most prominent collaborators, considered that the methodology advocated by this school was also applicable to the office work. He indicated that this and 'other kinds of mental work can be done more efficiently, and are subject to the same laws as work in the shop' (1970 [1923]: 244).[3] Another management theorist who argued for the introduction of Taylorism in this area was Carl Parsons, though its actual application was the result of William Leffingwell's contribution, which included examples such as the elimination of unnecessary movements through the correct location of telephones and equipment in *Scientific Office Management*, published in 1917 (George, 1968).

Moreover, the scientific training and selection of workers, one of Taylor's main concerns, were also the focus of analysis by Hugo Münsterberg. A Harvard professor of psychology with a doctorate from the University of Leipzig, Münsterberg is considered the father of industrial psychology. He made interesting contributions in his 1913 book *Psychology and Industrial Efficiency*, which turned him into an epigone of Taylor, about whom he did not scrimp praises, in his own discipline.[4] He proposed a role for psychologists that consisted in (1) helping to select the most suitable individual for the job, (2) determining what were the psychological conditions by which greater employee productivity could be attained, and (3) producing 'the influences on human minds which are desired in the interest of business' (Münsterberg, 1913: 24). His objective was very clear: to obtain the control of the employees for the benefit of the entrepreneurs. This shows that industrial psychology was born with a very specific ideology, which in no way opposed to scientific management, but rather served as its complement.

For all its success, unsurpassed by any previous managerial ideology, Taylorism did not hold the absolute monopoly over the administrative thought of its time. Other authors must also be mentioned. Harrington Emerson, for example, emphasized in 1912 the importance of 'clearly defined ideals' for a company's success. Of course, he was not a rival of Taylor, as he was even considered one of the external members of his circle. Alexander Hamilton Church and Leon Pratt Alford underscored the importance of the 'leadership factor', while James Hartness maintained in his book *The Human Factor in Works Management*, published in 1912, that the Taylorist philosophy was very mechanicist since the industrial engineers ignored human nature. Oliver Sheldon, a British writer, affirmed in *The Philosophy of Management*, published in 1923, that management had to serve the community, a function that was independent of any socioeconomic system. Nevertheless, from the point of view of the contribution to administration as a discipline, only the work of the French Henri Fayol is considered of the same stature as Taylor's. However, despite the importance of his contributions, Fayol had only local repercussion. His main work, *Industrial and General Administration*, which appeared in 1916 in France, was 'virtually ignored in the United States' until its publication in 1949 (George, 1968:105).[5] In contrast, Fayol dedicated some pages to discuss Taylor's theory of scientific management

The significance of Taylorism

The main contribution of Taylorist ideology was the application of rationalization techniques to productive activity, aiming at the separation of execution from conception and endowing legitimacy to an ascending layer of managers who came to occupy a place in industrial enterprises previously reserved only for the owners. The engineers in the United States presented themselves as the key actors — the guardians of rationality — in the nascent industrial order (Kakar, 1970). These claims gained definite support with Taylorism, which demonstrated that an engineering approach to the issue of management was indeed correlated with increased productivity and profitability. Although there is still some debate about when and in which industries the rhetorical pretensions of Taylorism translated into a bottom-line effect, the historical evidence so far shows that increased productivity was associated with the application of scientific management methods — among them, not only the time-and-motion studies, but also the advances in cost accounting and budgeting techniques (Spender, 1996; Johnson and Kaplan, 1987). Taylorism made possible the introduction of the assembly line and is considered the framework on which the operation of the Fordist mass production was built (Heizer, 1998; Coriat, 1979).

It must be pointed out that despite Taylor's concern for the rigorous utilization of the scientific method, particularly regarding data collection and analysis, some researchers have demonstrated inaccuracies in his work.[6] The 'story of Schmidt', perhaps his most famous anecdote, was not quite real. The standards indicated in some of his experiments were based on the activities of two workers of extraordinary physical strength, something he never mentioned (Wrege and Perroni, 1974). Thus, what supposedly should be considered a reasonable time for an average worker was artificially inflated, a procedure not compatible with the scientific methodology that Taylor should indeed have used. A contemporary critic of scientific management, the economist Robert Hoxie, also questioned its character of 'scientificity', contending that no completely objective measures could ever be attained with the application of the system in actual practice. However, even Hoxie (1916) admitted that this approach could potentially achieve significant increases in productive efficiency and that it might even benefit the laboring classes by improving their living standard.

The ideological success of Taylorism surpassed its real practical application (Burawoy, 1978; Fleischman, 2000). During the two first decades of the twentieth century, the influence of Taylorism as managerial ideology was dominant and undisputed. Its diffusion extended beyond the borders of the United States, and by the end of World War I, it could already be considered 'an international movement independent of particular economic systems of political ideologies' (Kakar, 1970: 2).[7] In France, a memo of the Ministry of War, signed by Clemenceau, highlighted in February 1918 the importance of the application of methods based on Taylorism, establishing in each plant a planning department and recommending that those in charge of these areas become familiar with Taylor's writings. Lenin was also very interested in the results of the Taylor system regarding organizational productivity. The Pravda newspaper, in its 28 April, 1918 issue, published an article in which Lenin affirmed the following:

> the possibility of building socialism depends exactly upon our success in combining the Soviet power and the Soviet organization of administration with the up-to-date achievements of capitalism. We must organize in Russia the study and teaching of the Taylor system and systematically try it out and adapt it to our own ends. (1965 [1918]: 259)

For some theorists (e.g., Kakar, 1970; Merkle, 1980), the fact that Taylorism received such a wide acceptance in so dissimilar ideological environments can be explained by its presentation as technology with characteristics of universality and neutrality.

Taylor's technocratic ideal based on the application of science is what served to legitimate the role of the engineers and other practitioners of the new techniques. The social imagery of the epoch had a particularly positive view of the engineers, in contrast to that of the enterprise owners whom the American press described as 'robber barons'. Of course, Taylorism was not the only force behind this favorable image. It was also supported by the fascination with science and technology in the context of the nascent bureaucratic society, in which rationality became one of the ruling values. The economist Thorstein Veblen, an acute observer of the social reality of the epoch, even considered the possibility that the engineers develop some sort of class consciousness and rise to power in a silent revolution by which they constituted a 'Soviet of Technicians'. However, he deemed this as an unlikely event, since the engineers seemed quite comfortable in their role of lieutenants of the capitalist class (Veblen, 1921). They were particularly concerned with enhancing their status as an emerging professional group, a status that the scientific management movement greatly contributed to legitimate.

Taylorism sought to diminish the workers' discretion, separating planning from execution. For that reason, the term 'deskilling' is associated to the project of scientific management.[8] Clearly, Taylor left few doubts on this point. In one of his lectures, he declared, 'I want to say, brutally speaking, and I am purposely brutal in my presentation, our scheme does not ask any initiative in a man. We do not care for this initiative' (Taylor, 1995 [1907]: 8).[9] What scientific management aimed at was to centralize the knowledge about productive processes in the hands of a stratum of technocrats, loyal to the capitalist class. It is true that Taylor felt certain hostility towards some entrepreneurs, but despite his discourse in pro of harmonic relations between the owner-managers and the workers, he always exhibited a 'natural bias in favor of the employers' (Bendix, 1956: 281), with whom the technocratic strata he represented better identified itself.[10] This ideology consolidated the authority of the capitalists by founding the basis of their power not only on the ownership of the means of production, but also on the monopoly over production knowledge, which until that moment had belonged to the proletariat as a remnant of craft work (Coriat, 1979). With the advent of scientific management and its acceptance and massive use in the consolidation of the 'new industrial system', knowledge was taken away from the hands of the laboring classes and concentrated in a small group of experts whose allegiance to the entrepreneurial class was never in question.

Table 5.1 summarizes the most relevant aspects of this managerial ideology. I will not vindicate Taylor's philosophy, but I must point out some important aspects that, in my opinion, have been downplayed by many of the critics of scientific management. In particular, it must be emphasized that, as indicated by Alberto Guerreiro Ramos (1981), the belief that the human aspects of organizations did not receive any attention is inaccurate. Actually, a lengthy part of *Principles of Scientific Management* is dedicated to the problem of human motivation (Freedman, 1992). What mainly appears as discussion matter is Taylor's too materialistic conception of man, upon which the attack against his thought is mounted. In this critical position are aligned authors like Neil Smelser, who argued that scientific management 'more or less ignored the social-psychological determinants of morale and efficiency' (1968: 146), aspect against which the so-called human relations school would react. In opposition to such kind of statements, other voices were raised to defend the importance of Taylor and his legacy to administrative theory. No one better than Peter Drucker who, when receiving in 1967 the 'Taylor Key' from the Society for the Advancement of Management, maintained that those who underrated Taylor had the same stature as those who underestimated Newton for not discovering quantum mechanics.[11]

Regardless of the scope of Taylorism, through its direct or indirect influence on later schools of management thought, the decline of its ideological dominance can be dated to the late 1920s. An indicator of this was the proliferation of welfare policies for the workers, which marked a rebirth of industrial betterment practices (Barley and Kunda, 1992). By 1920, hundreds of companies implemented these practices; entrepreneurs no longer considered the practices of industrial betterment and scientific management as rivals. For Nelson (1980: 201), 'industrialists began to view them as compatible, even complementary movements'. Even some of

Table 5.1 Main aspects of scientific management

Basic tenets	Claims to be a solution to the problem of work
	Mental revolution requiring cooperation between management and workers
	Rationalization of production through the application of the scientific method
	The separation of conception from execution generates the need for a new strata of experts
Image of the worker	Naturally idle, must be told what to do. If offered an adequate incentive, the worker would be willing to collaborate with management
Image of the manager	The managers should be in charge of the 'brain work'. They, and not the workers, possess the relevant knowledge about how to organize productive activities
Legitimated interests	Capitalist class Experts who applied the recommended techniques (i. e., engineers, accountants)
Areas of application	Mainly industrial production, but the basic method could be extended to other areas of administrative activity
Main authors	Taylor Gilbreth Gantt
Period of dominance	1900-1930
Impact on practices	Significant international impact (e. G., France, Germany, Soviet Union, Japan)
	Existing research has shown that the adoption of practices inspired by scientific management led to increases in organizational productivity
Misrepresentations detected	It has been demonstrated that some examples reported by Taylor in his writings were not quite accurate

Taylor's disciples adopted a broader 'humanist' stance. Gantt (1970 [1919]), for instance, noticed that management had also a social responsibility towards the community that was essential for its own survival.

The scholarly literature became increasingly attentive to the problem of workers' turmoil, as strikes between the years 1906 and 1921 reached historical peaks (Jacoby, 2001). Beyond the industrial betterment practices and scientific management, some authors sought new ways to deal with labor turnover, which was perceived as a pressing issue. The emerging role of the personnel manager was first discussed; and the question of how to properly handle men was the subject of several books and articles, some of which criticized the apparent shortcomings of the administrative thought of the period in achieving cooperation in the industrial relations realm.[12] In this context, many companies created Personnel Departments where industrial psychologists and sociologists were employed, thus initiating their collaboration with management. One of the pioneers in this regard was Henry Ford, who in 1914 established a 'Sociological Department' in his namesake company. In a report of this department, dated in 1916, it is stated that the study of workers' behavior was, from the viewpoint of the owner's interest, 'the very best investment it has ever made' (Baritz, 1960: 33). This scenario anticipated that a change in the dominant managerial ideology was about to occur. Scientific management yielded its place to the 'human relations' school.

Notes

1   In this regard, it must be mentioned Charles Babbage, but there are also more distant precedents. Colbert, minister of Luis XIV during the second half of the seventeenth century, requested physicians and engineers to make the first experimental study of human work. Bernard de Belidor, a French military engineer, presented in his treatise *Architecture Hydraulique*, published in the mid-eighteenth century, an example of time and motion study akin to contemporary ones. Charles Coulomb in his *Memorandum on Human Strength*, dated in 1798, demonstrated that the unnecessary motions of the workers are one of the main causes of fatigue and considered that appropriate directives could eliminate them (Kakar, 1970).

2   The application of Taylorism was not viewed positively by some labor unions. In fact, the mentioned investigation by the U.S. Congress, in which Taylor had to testify, originated from a complaint raised by one of the unions.

3   In this, Gilbreth just followed the opinion of Taylor, who in the preface of *Principles of Scientific Management* indicated that, although his examples were of special interest for engineers and directors of companies, 'it will be clear to other readers that the same principles can be applied with equal force to all social activities: to the management of our homes; the management of our farms; the management of the business of our tradesmen, large and small; of our churches, our philanthropic institutions, our universities, and our governmental departments' (1947 [1911]: 8).

4   Gilbreth also championed the collaboration between engineers and psychologists. According to him, the problems of the administration of human work necessarily required the participation of professionals from both disciplines. On this matter, he considered that 'the psychologist, who has done so much not only in his own field but in cooperating with others . . . will doubtless prove not only an eloquent advocate but also an untiring participant in better management.' Gilbreth (1970 [1923]: 263).

5   There was an earlier English translation of that work in 1930, but its impact was negligible (Reid, 1995).

6   See, for example, Wrege and Perroni (1974) and Wrege and Hodgetts (2000).
7   There is an extensive bibliography on the worldwide impact of Taylorism. Its influence on selected European countries has been aptly summarized by Kipping (1997). Merkle (1980) described the positive reception of scientific management in the Soviet Union, which is also evident in some of Lenin's writings (Scoville, 2001). Even in Japan, a country in which authoritarian paternalist practices were rooted in old cultural traditions, Taylor's rhetoric and methods did not pass unnoticed (Tsutsui 1997, 1998). It has been argued that the doctrine of scientific management met with some resistance in England (Guillén 1994) where the adoption of its administrative practices showed a lag in relation to other countries (Urwick and Brech, 1953; Huczynski 1993). However, Boyns (1998) has recently suggested that some British firms adopted several accounting practices associated with this ideology, and Whitston (1997) demonstrated that Taylorism did receive some positive attention in leading professional journals.
8   Braverman's (1974) analysis is a classic exposition of the deskilling thesis. In this regard, see also the pioneering writings of Hoxie (1915, 1916). For an informed critique of this position, see Nelson (1991).
9   This does not mean that the unsolicited workers' collaboration was rejected. In this regard, Taylor affirmed the following: 'Every man that gives us a new idea in our establishment which supersedes our regular standard, we pay that man cash for it, and name it after him generally, so that our men have the greatest incentive to help us' (1995 [1907]: 9).
10 On Taylor's opinions about certain entrepreneurs and their financial managers, see Nelson (1980).
11 Drucker included among Taylor's legacy the contributions of 'Operations Research, Systems Analysis and, indeed, Human Relations' (Tarrant, 1976:17). Waring (1991) also emphasized the strong influence of Taylor on later developments in administrative thought, arguing that Taylorism must be understood as the ancestor of Simon, Drucker, and even of the theorists of 'corporativism', among whom he mentioned Deming and Ouchi.
12 See, among others, Slichter (1919a, 1919b) and Frankel and Fleisher (1920). On the qualifications and functions of the 'personnel manager', see Marshall (1920) and Tead (1921).

Chapter 6

The Human Relations Ideology

The thought of Elton Mayo

By the first decades of the twentieth century, many organizations had Personnel Departments, which initially only performed administrative tasks like recruiting, absenteeism control, transfers, dismissals, promotions, and the like (Stout, 1980; Jacoby 2001). The attention towards employees grew, and the dominance of the engineering approach to organizational problems gradually diminished. Consequently, an ideology whose main emphasis was the human element emerged, displacing Taylorism as the dominant managerial ideology at the beginning of the 1930s.

The first basic element in this approach, known as the human relations school, is its focus on the workers, who were considered as individuals within a group whose social processes should be scientifically studied. The objective was to improve the satisfaction of the group members, which in turn was supposed to have a positive effect on overall organizational productivity and, ultimately, on society as a whole. The second element, often overlooked in management and organizational behavior textbooks, is the recommendation for the creation of a managerial elite that can adequately understand and deal with the problems associated to human relations in organizations. This second aspect comes as a corollary to the first one: if the human relations issues are of paramount relevance, then it is essential to have appropriately trained managerial personnel to deal with them.

Elton Mayo, an Australian sociologist who settled in the United States and taught Industrial Relations at the Harvard Business School, became the predominant figure of this new approach to management, although Mary Parker Follett's works had already delineated the way in the late 1910s and early 1920s.[1] A series of experiments at the Hawthorne plant of the Western Electric Company, in which Mayo had a prominent participation, are considered the founding moment of this perspective. Several works are dedicated to the conclusions derived from these experiences, but Mayo's own books are the best source for analyzing this managerial ideology, since he not only explored specific aspects of human behavior in organizations, but also made a series of considerations regarding societal problems at large. Mayo elaborated a particular diagnosis about the causes of the social malaise and also offered his opinion about the direction that institutions should adopt in order to avoid their own future collapse.

According to Mayo (1945), in the primitive communities the codes of the social group determined the position of individuals and the direction of their lives. The interests of each person were subordinated to those of the group, which offered its members stability as well as a function to perform. In this respect, he noted, drawing on Frederic Le Play,

> The situation is not simply that the society exercises a powerful compulsion on the individual; on the contrary, the social code and the desires of the individuals are, for all practical purposes, identical. Every member of the group participates in social activities because it is his chief desire to do so. (Mayo, 1945: 5)

This social order persisted until the eighteenth century. This was a type of society that he referred to as an 'established society'. In contrast, the contemporary social order was based on a rupture with that 'communitarian solidarity' and, therefore, had a disruptive effect on people's lives. It constituted an 'adaptive society' in which most persons often switched organizational affiliations due to a variety of causes. Individuals suffered, according to Mayo, a difficulty in relating to other people, which brought them a solitary and unhappy life. In 1933, he claimed in his book *The Human Problems of an Industrial Civilization* that the 'new freedom' supposedly enjoyed by individuals in the society of his time entailed some costs. In particular, he stressed, 'any movement in the direction of this so-called freedom withdraws from the individual a measure of social understanding and support which he is usually unable to do without' (Mayo, 1946 [1933]: 123-4). Social disorganization was what caught Mayo's attention, who mentioned Le Play and Durkheim as the first ones to observe this alarming tendency. The fact that the work of the latter on suicide and the six volumes written by the former had not, until that moment, been translated into English was something he deeply deplored. The message to be learned from those works is not to yearn for returning to more traditional forms of organization, but to understand that '*collaboration in an industrial society cannot be left to chance* [emphasis in original]' (Mayo, 1945: 9).

Thus, the search for a solution to achieve effective collaboration in human organizations became, once again, an essential subject. The way Mayo proposed to attain this goal was different from that of Taylor, whose approach was object of passionate criticism. Mayo conceived the problem in these terms:

> Our administrative methods are all pointed at the materially effective; none, at the maintenance of cooperation. The amazing technical successes of these war years show that we — our engineers — do know how to organize for material efficiency. But problems of absenteeism, labor turnover, 'wildcat' strikes, show that we do not know how to ensure spontaneity of cooperation; that is, teamwork. (1945: 9-10)

The reasons he gave to account for the apparent ineffectiveness of the engineers deserve special consideration. Mayo believed that the high degree of technological advance of the society of his time contrasted with the negative consequences of a social order that produced a generalized anomie in large sectors of the population. He drew a clear distinction between technical skill, defined as the capability to manipulate objects, and social skill, understood as the capacity to communicate and to participate effectively in a common task with other people. In this regard, he indicated that an unbalance with deleterious consequences existed between both skills, affirming, '*If our social skills had advanced step by step with our technical skills, there would not have been another European war*: this is my recurrent theme [emphasis in original]' (1945: 23). The reasons for this disequilibrium were to be found in the education system, which favored logical reasoning and reflective and abstract thought over knowledge obtained from direct experience with facts and situations.

In the area of social skills, Mayo considered that possessing an extensive arsenal of personnel selection tests, which of course he deemed useful within limited margins, was not a convincing excuse. For him, these tests were focused on technical aspects and oblivious to those on human cooperation. The sociology of his time did not seem more effective, according to Mayo, but was merely an exercise of academic knowledge acquisition. Experimental work was little stimulated, and the result was that the graduates who left the universities were 'not well equipped for the task of bringing order into social chaos' (1945: 21). In particular, the study of the social sciences had to begin with something unfortunately ignored: the meticulous observation of the communication of feelings and ideas among individuals and groups. The main problems that civilization faced were indeed due to faults in these processes. The worldwide crisis was just a problem of communication between groups, Mayo insisted, adding, 'The outstanding instance of this defect is the group of acute issues between management and workers' (1945: 23). With this, he clearly exposed the governing idea of his thought about social conflict: it was a problem of ineffective cooperation because of deficient communication between both parts.

In order to strengthen his position, Mayo told an interesting personal anecdote about the resistance offered by six union members against an adult education initiative of the Workers' Educational Association in Australia. The greater opposition always came from a particular group of individuals, affiliated to a Leftist party, and Mayo affirmed that he came to know them well enough to be able to outline their psychological profile. According to him, they lacked friends, except at party level; they seemed unable to easily relate to other people; they lacked conversation skills; 'all action, like social relationship, was for them emergency action'; and finally, 'they regarded the world as a hostile place' (1945: 26) — in sum, a profile that matched Janet's characterization of neurotic individuals.[2] When one of these of union members received a psychological clinical treatment, 'he made a good recovery and discovered, to his astonishment, that his former political views had vanished' (1945: 27). For Mayo, this example offered a clear lesson that social adjustment was obtained at the expense of the abandonment of antisystem political ideas. Apparently, these types of political persuasions could only be adopted by individuals with neurotic tendencies who, after receiving psychological attention, would become happier and simultaneously more useful for the community interests.

It seems that Mayo regarded as highly unlikely the existence of healthy individuals who could be in favor of, or lead, organizations, parties, or groups with this type of ideology. An especially interesting fact for someone like Mayo, interested in the dynamics of social processes in human groups, is that individuals with so maladapted personalities sometimes occupy leadership positions. How can they obtain the adhesion and respect of the rest of the group members? How can people willingly accept the leadership of an ill-adjusted person? Do social mechanisms of rejection fail to operate in these cases? Mayo did not consider these questions, but limited himself to ask what were the ominous consequences that leaders with these personality disorders could produce upon mankind. He found no better example than Adolf Hitler to support his hypothesis that a deficiency of 'social skills' implied a potential danger of social crisis. It is true that Hitler's behavior was guided by a particularly ominous ideology, but this should not obscure the fact that he had certain personal conditions or skills that allowed him to be accepted as leader. Therefore, the psychologically pertinent questions were of another kind and were not raised by Mayo: How can someone like him be a leader? Where laid the fault? In his own person or in that of his followers? These issues were of no interest to Mayo. His 'scientific' position consisted in promoting the diffusion of social skills in order to make people less committed to ideological extremisms and thus more useful for the community.

Mayo delved into the intellectual developments leading to our deficit of social skills. Specifically, he examined the negative social effects produced by industrialism in the nineteenth century, namely, the passage from the established society to the adaptive society. His argument began with the analysis of economic liberalism, and although acknowledging that much of this doctrine was 'still important and still to be commended', he questioned the idea of the predominance of the individual interest, which he equated to 'the profit motive' (1945: 38). He focused his criticism against this motivating element, contending that it was insufficient as an explanatory factor of human behavior.[3] According to him, 'The desire to stand well with one's fellows, the so-called human instinct of association, easily outweighs the merely individual interest and the logical reasoning upon which so many spurious principles of management are based' (1945: 43). He used his own experiments at the Hawthorne plant to support his thesis that the economic interest as motivator was often overestimated. However, it must be pointed out that this perspective was already clearly outlined in his earlier writings in Australia; that is, much before it received the empirical support of the Hawthorne studies.[4] Therefore, the popular conception of these studies as an enlightening social experiment with unimagined theoretical consequences is a misleading image.

Mayo criticized David Ricardo's characterization of society as a disorganized horde of individuals acting in their own interest, which he denominated the rabble hypothesis. Then, he asserted that, based on such assumption, a Leviathan that could impose a unique authority on this herd if it became necessary. In this regard, he commented,

> This conception of an all-powerful State and a rabble of unrelated individuals is implied by economic theory, expressly stated by law and political science. It has given us a Mussolini and Hitler, and has confused the whole course of democratic politics. (Mayo, 1945: 55)

This argument implies an incomprehensible logical jump, since the own defenders of liberalism indeed maintained that governmental powers should diminish in order to avoid the ascent of totalitarianism.[5]

Mayo coincided with the socialist thinker Richard Tawney regarding the necessity of organizing the economy on what the latter denominated the functional principle. He accepted Tawney's formulation that opposed a functional society (i.e., one in which each individual knows his/her place and the value of his/her work for the community) to a disorganized society (i.e., one in which individuals lack a secure job and personal value). In *The Acquisitive Society*, Tawney sustained that success was judged from the acquisition of wealth rather than on any other criteria. That book, initially published by the Fabian Society, is an example of the English socialist thought of the time. Mayo found it interesting, but also pointed out that it contained deceptive aspects, especially the idea that the social deterioration was caused by certain people or groups, in particular the capitalist class. For him, that was 'the rhetoric of abuse' and had 'no serious value' (1946 [1933]: 146).

In order to arrive at a correct understanding of a functional society, one had to resort to anthropological research, which revealed how the solidarity of group norms creates firm bonds between the individuals, thereby guiding their actions towards the welfare of the community. The rupture of the social codes due to the development of industrialism was the source of the social malaise. According to Mayo, once people learn the social codes of behavior, they simply act by answering 'social signals'; hence, individual action is guided by nonlogical mechanisms. Social maladjustment, on the contrary, induces another type of action: irrational conduct. So, argued Mayo, 'If a specialist group develops scientific knowledge and applies it to technical practice at too high a speed for general social adjustment to the change, one effect is to transform nonlogical social organization into irrational social disorganization' (1946 [1933]: 158-9). This was what actually happened, he concluded, with the extinction of the cultural tradition of craftmanship, one of whose fundamental causes was the engineering approach to managerial and production problems.

For Mayo, the consequences derived from this transformation of the social order were serious and had political implications. Since his diagnosis of the social malaise blamed the ruling elite as responsible, it was suggested that its replacement by another one, better prepared in the key factor of social skills, was part of the solution. In *The Human Problems of an Industrial Civilization*, Mayo wrote the following:

> It is no longer possible for an administrator to concern himself narrowly with his special function and to assume that the controls established by a vigorous social code will continue to operate in other areas of human life and action. (1946 [1933]: 165)

Consequently, in Mayo's opinion, it was essential to pay special attention to the 'administrative problem' as the most important of the moment. On this point, he quoted Brooks Adams, a political scientist who thought that social revolutions resulted from the appearance of administrative problems. If the ruling class was not at the level of the circumstances, it was replaced by another one possessing a type of mentality capable of responding adequately to the demands of the moment. Mayo also relied heavily on Pareto's theory of the circulation of elites, which maintains that in a healthy society there is a continuous movement of ascending social mobility of the most capable people who belong to lower strata. For Mayo, this circulation process underwent a stagnation stage, and the challenge of the time was to find 'better methods for the discovery of an administrative *élite*, better methods of maintaining working morale' (1946 [1933]: 171).

In a certain sense, a common element between Mayo's conservatism and Marxist thought exists: the notion of social harmony in primitive communities and a quest for its recovery for the future society, but the similarities end there. In a passing reference to Communism and Marxism, Mayo suggested that these doctrines were possibly an expression of the 'workers' desire to recapture something of the lost human solidarity' (1946[1933]: 175). For him, the future would witness technological advances in production driven by the work of the engineers and even the 'proletariat'. In a clear anticipation of the rhetoric of the knowledge society, he wrote that the 'communist theories of revolution will be superseded by the profoundest revolution mankind has ever contemplated — the development of a society in which there will be no place for the illiterate or the ignorant' (1946 [1933]: 175). However, he deemed this panorama as too fantastic, given the pressing imperative to re-establish 'effective human cooperation'. The means to achieve this end consisted in training of a new class of leaders, understanding that the difficulties faced by humankind were social and not economic. He contended that the political and economic theories of the past were useless weapons in this battle, since the social codes that formerly regulated the organization of collaborative work were no longer in operation. Mayo's discourse served to legitimize a new cadre of managers educated in the social sciences, in the same way that Taylorism aimed at legitimating the social status of the engineers.

Mayo's ideology can be understood as a defense of the capitalist system that rejected liberal individualism and installed the notion of the social group as the basic social unit that gives sense to the lives of individuals, both inside and outside their roles of workers. Mayoism became an ideological answer to the decline of liberalism as well as to the menace of leftist extremism, which Mayo discredited, under the authoritative cloak of science, as being a manifestation of a pathological state of mind. His discourse with its emphasis on the social group to the detriment of the individual was consistent with the generalization of what William H. Whyte (1956) denominated 'social ethics'. The though of Mayo has a marked conservative character, aimed at reconstructing the lost spirit of community, without questioning at any moment the social privilege of the ruling class that benefits from the capitalist economic order. He was not worried about the issue of how to distribute the social product in a more equitable way among the people. For him, social inequality was not the problem, but rather the flood of individual anomie in a poorly administrated society. Consistently with the dominant political climate of his time, which was contrary to the idea of the state as 'night-watchman', Mayo criticized economic liberalism and its implicit concept of the individual. However, his doctrine was not merely a negative stance towards the former dominant political and economic ideology; it was also a contribution precisely aimed at preserving the social order under a new social and political environment.

The Hawthorne experiments

In his books, Mayo made numerous references to these experiments as proof of the correctness of his view on work and the social order. His conclusions received tremendous acceptance and are described as exemplary work in most of the introductory texts to the discipline of management. Surprisingly and despite such success, they have been the object of sharp criticism that clearly demonstrates the ideological character behind the veil of scientific objectivity of the human relations school's discourse. Alex Carey (1967) was right in affirming that there are few scientific disciplines in which only one series of studies or a single scholar has had as much relevance as Elton Mayo in management. Moreover, it is a reality that many students of sociology and business administration have been socialized in the tradition of the human relations school, judging by the coverage it has received, and still receives today, in textbooks. Paradoxically, the evidence available in support of these experiments seems to falsify the researchers' conclusions, especially regarding the preeminence of 'social rewards' relative to other types of behavioral determinants.

Carey developed a critical analysis in which he concluded that the findings of the Hawthorne studies, 'far from supporting the various components of the "human relations approach," are surprisingly consistent with a rather old-world view about the value of monetary incentives, driving leadership, and discipline' (1967: 416). On the other hand, he contended that, given the methodological shortcomings (e.g., the lack of an attempt to establish a representative sample of a population greater than the group under study, the fact that the conclusions derived from the observation of a group composed by only five people, etc.), the experiments could not be seriously taken as evidence for any kind of valid generalization. This being the case, one should add, they were much less capable of supporting a whole political and social theory. Carey (1967: 416) admitted that his analysis did not exhaust 'the gross error and the incompetence in the understanding and use of the scientific method which permeate the Hawthorne studies from beginning to end', but pointed out that the data needed to carry out a statistical interpretation were not available. The original observations were accessible later, and the first statistical analysis was performed by Richard Franke and James Kaul (1978). Interestingly enough, their conclusions also refuted the view of Mayo and its followers. Multiple regression analysis showed that three variables: the managerial discipline, the effect of the economic depression, and the rest pauses accounted for most of the productivity variation of both the group and the individual workers. They also indicated that the empirical evidence points at the positive influence of the system of material incentives.

For Carey, then, the relevant question is why most of the authors who write about the Hawthorne experiments in their introductory texts present a manifestly incorrect description of the real observations, in such a manner as to make these evidences consistent with the conclusions. Richard Gillespie (1991) considered that among the potential accounts or interpretations of these studies the preferred explanation was socially constructed by a complex set of actors and institutions, being welcome and actively supported by the members of the business community.

The capitalist class sought a new creed to counter the discourse of industrial democracy, advanced by some theorists of the period and considered dangerously closed to socialism; and the human relations movement seemed the perfect alternative. With its instrumental humanism, this movement offered the ruling strata a way to preserve their interests, while implementing a more benevolent attitude towards the workers (O'Connor 1999a). In this last respect, Franke and Kaul (1978:637) argued that the conclusions of Mayo arrived were received with approbation by people who were in favor of capitalism, but preferred social theories that 'could be seen as more useful, humane, and democratic'. The result of the diffusion of these findings determined that some practices advocated by scientific management (e.g., techniques to reduce workers' strain, the use of material incentives and managerial surveillance, etc.) were seen in a different light. However, 'it is precisely such factors to which we are directed by empirical analyses of the Hawthorne data' (1978: 638). For Franke and Kaul, neither these experiments nor the results of later investigations supported the idea that a better human relations climate necessarily generates an increase in productivity.

The influence of the human relations school: administrative practices and later developments

Although the Hawthorne experiments are of questionable scientific validity, their influence on the discipline of management has been remarkable. Regarding the acceptance of the human relations school's advice in real administrative practices, it must be indicated that companies like General Electric devised training programs based on some of the premises of Mayoism. A particularly interesting example of the application of Mayo's proposals is General Motors, a firm that used in some of its publications the symbols of the 'team' and the 'industrial family' (Bendix, 1956). In 1947 this company carried out a contest among its employees that consisted of writing an essay on 'My Job and Why I Like It', which Bendix (1956: 330) described as a 'major effort on the "ideological front"'. According to Alan Raucher, 174,854 employees, about 58.8 per cent of the eligible personnel, competed for 5,145 prizes estimated at about US$ 150,000. The contest's goal was to obtain an appreciation of the employees' feelings towards the company, and the sample was perhaps the largest survey of workers' attitudes. As Walter Reuther, a union representative, noted, there was a bias from the beginning, since the contest should have been called 'What I Like or What I Don't Like About My Job' in order to give opportunity for answers containing some criticism (Raucher, 1987).

The results from the analysis of both the 40 best essays and the essays in their entirety were similar, revealing that the participants often spoke in positive terms about their salaries and social benefits. The issue of job security also appeared among the most frequent ones, but other aspects, such as pride in the job and the positive feeling of psychological security produced by being part of this corporation, were also mentioned. However, it may be asked to what extent the essays were a sincere representation of the workers' attitudes towards the company. On the other hand, the company distributed before the contest a pamphlet of 11 pages suggesting aspects or elements that employees could value about their jobs. In spite of this, more than 7 per cent of the participants used the contest as a means to express negative feelings about their jobs. It must also be pointed out that there was an emphasis in material aspects (e.g., fringe benefits) and that some participants spoke about job satisfaction in terms of the pleasure and consumption activities that were conducted outside the job. Surprisingly, although the workers were satisfied with their jobs, positive references to teamwork were unimportant.[6]

Contemporaneously with this General Motors initiative, Ely Chinoy (1955) also did research on workers' attitudes in another plant of this company. His findings revealed that the workers felt alienated due to the monotony of their jobs and the labor discipline. Success for them had less to do with their jobs than with the life style they enjoyed as a result of their job — this was also something that could be inferred from certain responses expressed in the contest essays. It can be concluded that Mayo's advice was either not implemented correctly or did not have the desired effect. Alternatively, one could also think that economic or material rewards had a more important place than Mayo acknowledged or that he did not adequately understand the workers' hidden motivations.

Nevertheless, Mayo's work was a key factor influencing later developments that delved deeper into aspects of the 'human factor' in organizations. Mayo is credited as the initiator of the field of organizational behavior, but there are also other pioneers in this area that must be mentioned: Jacob Levy Moreno and Kurt Lewin. The former created the discipline of sociometry, which studied the relations of attraction and repulsion between individuals and became useful in personnel selection. The works of the latter gave way to two main currents. One was represented by a research group at the University of Michigan, and the other was developed at the National Training Laboratories, where a new method of human relations training was born in 1947: the training-group (Cornaton, 1969). The studies about leadership carried out by Lippit and White under the direction of Lewin in 1938-39 must be especially mentioned. They introduced a leadership typology that is still discussed today in management textbooks, distinguishing among three styles of leadership: permissive or laissez-faire, democratic, and authoritarian.[7] The work of Lewin not only dealt with the study of groups, but also with the broader issue of organizational change. Hence, he is indirectly considered the father of what is known as Organizational Development (Petit, 1979).

In addition, the themes raised by Elton Mayo and his disciples at the Graduate School of Business Administration of Harvard University were a starting point for other research issues related to the informal organization.[8] Human motivation is one of them. Mayo's criticism against the dominant idea of economic interest as the basic determinant of behavior led other scholars to conceive alternative theories of human motivation. Among the most cited theories of motivation, two must be mentioned: Abraham Maslow's needs theory, which dates from the 1940s, and Frederick Herzberg's two-factor theory, elaborated in the late 1950s. Another research line derived from the Hawthorne experiments depicts the job situation as a triangle of social relations that includes the worker, the group, and the job.[9] The success or failure of a worker was no longer perceived as depending solely on his or her individual productivity, but also on his or her performance regarding the work group. This led occupational psychologists to develop a series of techniques aimed at detecting the personality of individuals in order to evaluate their adjustment to the job situation.

The findings of the Hawthorne experiments also induced many researchers to explore the existence of a direct relationship between satisfaction at work and productivity. In this regard, the research efforts carried to test the validity of this hypothesis were many. Jean Guiot (1980) pointed out that the belief that satisfied workers would work more provoked great hopes, but he admitted that, based on the empirical evidence, it was demonstrated that high levels of satisfaction do not necessarily yield higher productivity.[10] Victor Vroom concluded, after an analysis of several studies on the matter, that a clear correlation between job satisfaction and job performance does not exist, indicating that 'correlations between these variables vary within an extremely large range and the median correlation of 0.14 has little theoretical or practical importance' (1964: 183). Raymond Katzell et al. claimed that the evidence linking increased productivity to those jobs that had been redesigned through job enlargement or job enrichment plans was 'sparse, at best' (1975: 153). More recently, Staw and Barsade (1993) asserted that the issue of the relationship between labor satisfaction and productivity must disappear from the agenda, since the existence of a positive correlation between both variables could not be adequately supported.[11] Consequently, what can be denominated the 'myth of the happy worker' is the most notorious misrepresentation of the human relations ideology.

What constitutes, in my opinion, the last important ideological contribution of this movement occurred in 1960 when a new view of the worker's nature appeared: McGregor's distinction between what he called Theory X and Theory Y. For him, 'many of our attempts to control behavior, far from representing selective adaptations, are in direct violation of human nature. They consist in trying to make people behave as we wish, without concern for natural law' (McGregor, 1960: 9). Theory X is the view of the worker sustained by most managers, claimed McGregor. The portrayal he offered resembles Bendix's description of the dominant conception about the worker in the nineteenth century. This is not surprising, given that Bendix's classic book on managerial ideologies is one of McGregor's few bibliographical references. Theory X's assumptions maintain that workers are, by nature, passive and indolent; thus, managers try to control them through the strategy of 'the stick and the carrot', which McGregor denominated 'management by direction and control'. In opposition to this erroneous vision, he introduced another set of assumptions, Theory Y, arguing that employees are not passive by nature, but that their passivity is a response to the dominant managerial style. Workers like their jobs and would always be willing to perform them should management create the basic conditions allowing this natural tendency to manifest itself. This could be obtained through what he called 'management by integration and self-control'.[12] Theory Y, explained McGregor, postulates that individuals will display this behavior in benefit of the organizational goals, insofar as management fosters their authentic commitment to accomplish these objectives. The solution is to let workers participate in the goal-setting process and to implement an adequate system of MBO (Management by Objectives).[13]

Even McGregor admitted that the initial interpretations of the human relations school were too simple because there is no direct correlation between productivity and job satisfaction. For him, it was important to understand that 'industrial democracy' cannot consist in 'permitting everybody to decide everything, that industrial health does not flow automatically from the elimination of dissatisfaction, disagreement, or even open conflict' (1960: 46). This marks a point of inflexion in the human relations ideology, as one of its basic tenets was called into question. However, the analysis of McGregor's thought suggests that, beyond his preoccupation for not seeming naive, he showed a strong adherence to Mayoism, especially when he criticized Whyte who affirmed that the group oppressed the individual. For McGregor, such a thesis was completely wrong. He even asserted that the study of group dynamics was received with hostility, without offering any type of evidence to corroborate, and insinuated that behind the critics to the human relations school there was often 'a deeper attitude associated with Theory X' (1960: 239-240).

The human relations ideology has a positive image of the worker, which reaches its most favorable characterization precisely in McGregor's Theory Y. First and consistently with an oversocialized conception of man, the worker was depicted has having a fundamental need of belonging. Later formulations advanced over this passive view of the worker without abandoning it, but adding further psychological attributes. So, employees were also portrayed as being intrinsically interested in their tasks and willing to participate and to collaborate with management. With respect to the image of the executive personnel, it was emphasized the necessity of possessing a strong and adaptable personality, in addition to adequate training in social and leadership skills. It must be pointed out that intelligence, as an attribute of both managers and workers, was not perceived as being fundamentally important. In fact, some authors (e.g. Basil, 1971) affirmed that a particularly elevated level of intelligence could be detrimental for the exercise of leadership. Mayo (1945) himself remarked especially that, in one of the Hawthorne experiments, the worker who ranked first in intelligence was the lowest in individual productivity while the one with the highest individual productivity ranked last in intelligence.

The significance of the human relations ideology

This ideology, whose main features are summarized in Table 6.1, turned the managerial attention away from the rationalization of manufacturing processes and towards the group dynamics occurring within organizations. When Mayo began his studies at Western Electric, a favorable climate to a sociological emphasis already existed. Actually, empirical investigations about the psychology of leadership date back to 1904, and besides, neither Gilbreth's recommendations about greater collaboration between psychologists and engineers nor Münsterberg's pioneering works should be forgotten.[14] However, there is a generalized consensus about the central role of Mayo, undisputed creator of the human relations school, as the main precursor of the discipline of organizational behavior (O'Connor, 1999b).

Table 6.1 Main aspects of the human relations ideology

Basic tenets	Search for reestablishing a bond of cooperation between management and the workers
	Oversocialized conception of man
	Emphasis on group processes
	Need to train an administrative elite well versed in the social sciences
Image of the worker	The worker is depicted has having a fundamental need of belonging
	Later developments also present workers as interested in their tasks and willing to participate and collaborate with management (McGregor's Theory Y)
Image of the manager	Managers need to have a strong and adaptable personality; they should also possess adequate social and leadership skills
	Intelligence was not perceived as fundamentally important in managers
Legitimated interests	Capitalist class
	Experts in the social sciences
Areas of application	Personnel Management
	General Management
Main authors	Mayo
	Maslow
	Lewin
	Herzberg
	McGregor
Period of dominance	1930-1960
Impact on practices	International diffusion, especially after World War II
	The new techniques inspired by this ideology changed significantly the practices related to personnel management
Misrepresentations detected	Myth of the happy worker

The interest of entrepreneurs and managers in 'human problems' as a result of the success of this ideology helped to promote the development of the social sciences through the funding of projects and research centers. The administrative practices related to human resources management changed substantially thanks to the influence of Mayo and his successors (Jacoby, 2001). This new managerial creed soon gained international relevance. With the aid of the Marshall Plan and through the intervention of specific administrative agencies, American managerial theories and techniques, among which Mayoism figured prominently, were diffused to several European countries (Carew, 1987). The acceptance of this ideology was not uniform in all of them, but we know it had a relevant impact in France, Spain, and the United Kingdom, where a local version associated to the research of the so-called Tavistock group appeared.[15]

The concern of the human relations ideology for reducing social tensions immediately led many authors to accuse its advocates of trying to reinvigorate the capitalist system. This is a correct appreciation since neither Mayo nor other thinkers within this perspective spoke about social conflict as a manifestation of relations of domination emerging from the economic order. Instead, they tried to solve the social problems within the framework of the existing order through the re-establishment of human cooperation. The personnel problems and the correct integration of workers to their organizations constituted the main agenda in the 1940s and 1950s. Management thus showed a more humanized face, which had little in common with the social Darwinism of the nineteenth century nor with the rationalism associated to the name of Frederick Taylor. There is a coincidence with the ideology of industrial betterment, as both considered the conflict between management and workers as a pathological manifestation (Barley and Kunda, 1992). Nevertheless, while the defenders of industrial betterment tried to socialize the worker through the communities in which they lived, those in favor of 'human relations' aimed at turning the organization itself into a cohesive collective, working with the feelings developed by the employees in their relations within their work group. This benevolent stance, however, was obviously interested. According to John Perry (1954), a human relations consultant and management writer, in the speeches of many businessmen it was frequent to talk about human relations in terms of 'clarified management' and 'humanitarianism', although in fact the goal they pursued was a more pragmatic and self-interested one.

Erich Fromm (1963) affirmed that the human relations movement originated from a desire to control the workers, and he even considered it as inhuman and cruel, arguing that it contributed to alienate the workers. This ideology and the practices adopted from it constitute an instance of normative control. Membership in a group may be used, and is actually used, as a control tool (Brown, 1980). The human relations school strongly promoted developments in leadership training to increase the interpersonal capabilities of managers at all hierarchical levels under the assumption that securing the employees' consent was the only way to build a healthy and productive organization. For Daniel Bell (1988 [1962]: 251), 'in the evident concern with understanding, communication, and participation, we find a change in the outlook of management, parallel to that which is occurring in the culture as a whole, from authority to manipulation as a means of exercising domination'. He was one of the first to acknowledge the normative turn in managerial ideologies by observing, in what is a clear statement of the dominant perspective about the subtilization of control in the evolution of management thinking, 'the old modes of overt coercion are now replaced by psychological persuasion'.

C. Wright Mills similarly interpreted the impact of this ideological transforma- tion and its correlate in the administrative practices of the bureaucratic enterprise. According to him, the nineteenth century was characterized by an explicit system of authority: 'the victim knew he was being victimized, the misery and discontent of the powerless were explicit'. In the twentieth century, however, 'manipulation replaces authority'. Domination is expressed by the 'engineering of consent', in which 'impersonal manipulation' exerts an influence more 'insidious' than coercion because it is less evident (1953: 110). A new form in the construction of worker's consent emerged through the manipulation of their feelings and attitudes, in the era of what Mills denominated 'the morale of the cheerful robots' (1953:233). For him, the ruling elite perceived itself as living in 'a small island in a politically hostile sea of propertyless employees' (1953: 234). Hence, it searched for 'symbols of justification' and the human relations discourse presented an elaborated conception to achieve this goal.

The human relations ideology in its quest for an improved workplace also had an impact on cultural changes. As a result of the advice of personnel experts arose what Mills denominated 'the market of the personality': 'With anonymous insincerity, the Successful Person thus makes an instrument of his own appearance and personality' (1953: 182). According to him, 'employers, again and again, demand the selection of men with personality' (1953: 186). An attractive physical appearance, the ability for teamwork, as well as good conversational skills became features much sought after in the world of work, given the new recommendations of the human relations experts. Furthermore, this went beyond the scope of public relations and reached the status of a life style, which spread as a result of the growth of the success and self-help literature (Mills, 1953).[16] David Riesman expressed similar ideas, when maintaining that what was more important in organizational settings was not the individual's achievements but his or her behavior in relation to the work group. He observed that solitary persons not only were unwelcome by their peers in informal groups at factories, but also were considered unfit for executive positions. The human relations experts tended to look for the 'other-directed personality' that was apparently more necessary for jobs than other types of qualities because what mattered in the American workplace was not so much productive capability or talent as social skills (Riesman, 1954).

It became essential to have an adaptable personality in a society in which there was an increasing tendency towards what Riesman denominated 'groupism'. William H. Whyte (1956) also maintained this in his classic book *The Organization Man*. He wrote about the emergence of a new 'social ethics', which he defined as a body of thought that endowed with moral legitimacy the pressures of society on the individual. As organizations became a central aspect in people's lives, the ideological primacy of the group over the individual marked the decline of the Protestant ethics of work, which nevertheless maintained its vigor regarding the value assigned to property and competition. This new ethics had three main tenets: the notion of the group as a source of creativity, the idea that individuals have a fundamental necessity of belonging, and the belief that the application of science was helpful in satisfying this necessity.[17] Whyte (1963) studied the expressions of groupism not only in organizations but also in his analysis of social life in a suburban district. He observed that adaptability had become a fundamental value, shared by all, and found that the main task of schools was, for the suburb inhabitants, to teach people to live with others, a thought with which Elton Mayo would absolutely agree. The relations among ideological, sociocultural, and economic processes are certainly complex, but undoubtedly there is a connection among the dominance of the human relations ideology, the emergence of groupism, and the consolidation of the bureaucratic organization. The diffusion of this ideology greatly contributed to legitimate groupism through its support of normative control practices in bureaucratic organizations.

Many social scientists of the time compared human relations with Taylorism and concurred that the role performed by sociologists and psychologist involved some sort of 'human engineering'. Speaking about the 'management demiurge' and his desire for control, Mills introduced the idea of a continuum between Taylorism and the human relations ideology, which he refers to as the 'the new (social) scientific management'. He argued that the realm of 'the world to be managed' extended to include 'the social setting, the human affairs, and the personality of man as a worker' (1953: 233), and this offered a new and privileged opportunity for professionals trained in the social sciences. In both discourses, the issue of cooperation appears in a conspicuous form. For Mayo, the cooperative spirit had to be reconstituted. In contrast to scientific management, however, he did not appeal to the rational spirit of workers and entrepreneurs but to the rise of a new elite, capable of assuring group consensus. The role of science was also paramount in Mayo's works, as it was in Taylor's, yet this was the time of the social sciences. Like Taylor at his moment, Mayo legitimated the access of men educated in his discipline to leadership positions.

In conclusion, with the rise of this ideology, social relations occurring within organizations became the central object of research and analysis. Although it is possible to detect the beginning of the preponderance of this discourse, the work of Elton Mayo and his associates, the moment when it began to decline cannot be easily established. While the original group of the Harvard Business School lost the monopoly in this area, the 'initial discoveries' generated an interest in the human factor and the informal organization that did not stop since then. If Mayo's great discovery consisted in stressing the importance of the human element in organizations, it may be deemed as a platitude, since the distinguishing features of the interaction of a group of workers, during prolonged periods of time and in the same physical location, must necessarily be considered in the analysis of the group's output resulting from such interaction. This was something that could not be ignored by later approaches to management. However, this perspective's oversocialized conception of man became the object of increased criticism. Barley and Kunda (1992) dated the turning point in the dominance of this managerial ideology to the mid 1950s. However, I prefer to speak of 1960, when McGregor's *The Human Side of Enterprise* was published. Yet, in the mid 1950s, there were attractive new options in the management ideas market. The center of attention in administrative thinking slowly moved away from group processes, which had previously displaced the technical-productive ones, towards broader aspects focused on the organization as a whole and nurtured by the latest advances in the hard sciences.

Notes

1   Follett dealt with leadership issues and coined expressions like 'group thinking' and 'togetherness', while also setting the stage for Mayo by affirming that teamwork would be the basis of the future industrial system (George, 1968). On Follett's contributions, see also Wren (1994) and Fry and Thomas (1996).

2   Mayo quoted a paragraph of Pierre Janet (1915: 357) from his book *Les Néuroses*, in which this latter author affirmed that philosophy becomes an 'object of devotion' for neurotics, turning them into enthusiastic devotes of metaphysics. For Janet, 'The spectacle of these unfortunates makes one ask sadly whether philosophical speculation is no more than a malady of the human mind' (Mayo's translation).

3   He even wrote the following: 'It is unfortunate for economic theory that it applies chiefly to persons of less, rather than greater, normality of social relationship' (Mayo 1945: 43).

4   See, for example, Gillespie (1991) and O'Connor (1999a).

5   For instance, Hayek (1944), in a work written almost contemporaneously to that of Mayo, contrasted liberalism against the fascist and nazi regimes, emphasizing the negative consequences derived from the expansion of the state's sphere of action.

6   Further details can be found in Raucher (1987).

7   The study of leadership constituted one of the most important avenues of research in organizational behavior. The main objective consisted in determining what differentiates a leader from its subordinates in order to use this knowledge to select and train leaders more efficiently and to identify the leadership style most favorable to group productivity. An historical account of the literature on the issue was carried out by Yago (1982). For a more exhaustive work on the subject, see Yukl (1981).

8   The study of the primary group in economic activity is to a great extent an American product, according to Smelser (1968). Most of the innovations in theory and practice, he affirmed, were carried out by American researchers.

9   See, for example, Neff (1968).

10 Similar appreciations were made by Carey (1967) and Franke and Kaul (1978).

11 Besides, in the few studies in which a limited direct correlation between performance and job satisfaction was found and the flow of causality was adequately contemplated in the research design, individual productivity appeared as a determinant of job satisfaction and not a result of it (Robbins, 1996).

12 The Scanlon Plan is often mentioned as a practical application of the assumptions of Theory Y. It can even be affirmed that Theory Y derives from the works made at the MIT by Joe Scanlon, with whom McGregor collaborated. This plan included an incentive system and aimed at favoring the participation of the workers to make them feel responsible for the result of their work and their contribution to the company (Frost et al., 1974).

13 Management by Objectives (MBO) was an original idea of Peter Drucker, whom Barley and Kunda (1992) did not consider a representative of the human relations ideology. Despite its good intentions, in actual practice MBO often served as a pressure instrument of management (Levinson, 1975).

14 See Terman (1904). Social psychologists in the early 1900s were interested in finding what Cooley (1922 [1902]: 317) defined as the 'rationale of personal ascendancy'.

15 See, for example, Cornaton (1969) on the diffusion of this perspective in France and Guillén (1994) in relation to its impact in Spain and the United Kingdom. About the Tavistock Group, which received the influenced of Kurt Lewin, see Trist and Murray (1990). Interestingly, ideas compatible with the spirit of Mayoism, but with even more collectivist connotations, were independently developed in the 1920s in Germany, gaining wider acceptance and being further elaborated during the Nazi period. For an analysis of the writings on leadership and the 'company community' of German management theorists of the epoch, see Larsen (2003). After the war, this line of administrative thinking 'merged' with the American human relations school.

16 The 'success literature' is, nevertheless, previous to the human relations school. Dale Carnegie's work is an example of this theme. His classic text, *How to win friends and influence people*, became an international best seller worldwide following its publication in 1936. However, it was originally written in 1926 under the title *Public Speaking and Influencing Men in Business* and was used as 'official text' by many important organizations of the period like the New York Telephone Company, for example (Bendix, 1956: 302).

17 The advancement of this social ethics, affirmed Ruitenbeck (1963), was more important in the United States, cradle of the human relations ideology, than in other Western countries.

Chapter 7

Systemic Rationalism

By 1960, the human relations ideology lost its predominance.[1] It was no more a novelty since the importance of the informal dimension in organizations had already been established as a fact. Management scholars perceived that the social interactions within organizations never conformed 'perfectly to official prescriptions' and that 'these departures from the formal blueprint' were what made organizations an interesting object for scientific inquiry (Blau, 1968: 56). If this were not the case, it would be sufficient to read the procedures manual and the organizational charts in order to know exactly what was happening. The formal dimension, nevertheless, would be object of increasing attention, especially in those aspects pertaining to the decision making processes of managers and the structural design of organizations. In this regard, the most important approaches were organization theory, operations research, and contingency theory. The interdisciplinary systems theory influenced all of them at varying degrees, strongly imprinting the language of management. In the next sections, I analyze this set of approaches that constitutes a new managerial ideology, which Barley and Kunda (1992) denominated 'systems rationalism'.[2]

The birth of operations research

This discipline was born in Great Britain when Professor P.M.S. Blackett, Nobel Prize of Physics, was hired by the British army in 1940 to lead a group of scientists whose mission was to solve some complex problems faced by this organization. The team was denominated 'operational research unit' — hence the name of the discipline that uses mathematical models to solve diverse kinds of problems. The application of this approach impressed the military because it could be used in questions of quite diverse sorts that nevertheless shared common structural characteristics (Emshoff, 1971). After the war, similar groups of operations research were formed in the United Kingdom as well as in the United States to transfer the techniques successfully developed in the military realm to the field of managerial decisions. During that time, a massive industrial expansion took place and the processes of decision making faced increasing complexity. The appearance of the digital computer in the postwar period also facilitated the development of operations research, which is also known as 'management science'. From that point forward, the interest in this knowledge area grew: diverse professional societies were formed, university courses on the subject were established, and the first academic journals appeared (Markland, 1983).

Linear and nonlinear programming, the application of stochastic simulation models, network analysis, queuing theory, and other aspects of operations research were used in the solution of organizational problems. For some authors, operations research can be considered 'a modern version of "scientific" management' (Stout, 1980:54). Barley and Kunda (1992) asserted that CPM and PERT, two classic tools of operations research, were direct derivatives of the Gantt chart. The advent of this discipline allowed a group of experts to introduce a new technical approach to management in large public and private organizations, where they gained managerial and consulting positions. The importance of the utilization of the quantitative techniques advocated by operations research did not reside solely in the area of problem solving. Operations research also modified the way in which managers began to understand and analyze problems: how they faced them, how they communicated with others about them, and how they obtained pertinent data to deal with them (Hayes, 1975).[3] It is difficult to assess the real impact of these developments, but it is clear that a change occurred in academic curricula by the late 1960s, with an unequivocal emphasis in quantitative aspects and decision making techniques (Barley and Kunda, 1992). This offered a new direction for the managerial elite, eclipsing the Mayoist concern for the human aspects of organizations. Moreover, the growing interest in managerial decision processes was also spawned by the 'organization theory' school.

Organization theory

Although published in 1938, when the human relations ideology was on the rise, the book *The Functions of the Executive*, authored by Chester Barnard, can be considered the starting point of the so-called organization theory school. Herbert Simon (1992), one of the most outstanding figures of management theory and the main thinker of this current of administrative thought, pointed out that Barnard's book was still as valid today as it was when first published. According to Barnard, organizations are cooperative systems that are guided by a purpose or objective. His interest in the organizational goals and the cognitive processes of the managers is what links him to later theorists who made the 'decision making dynamics' a central aspect of management theory. Simon's notion of 'bounded rationality' is also present in an embryonic state in Barnard, who observed that the 'power of choice' becomes 'paralyzed in human beings if the number of equal opportunities is large' (1976 [1938]: 14).

Besides incorporating the notion of the informal organization, Barnard also made interesting observations about what he defined as the 'economy of incentives'. In this respect, he considered not only the material (economic) incentives but also the nonmaterial (symbolic) ones; and he affirmed that the latter, such as the opportunities to gain prestige and personal power, were the most important. For Barnard, not all organizations can offer their personnel adequate incentives, and the failure to deliver them can mean the demise of the organization, unless it 'can by persuasion so change the desires of enough men that the incentives it can offer will be adequate' (1976 [1938]: 149). As persuasion methods, he mentioned the following: (1) coercion, as a way to generate a desired behavioral change by means of fear to a sanction; (2) rationalization of opportunities, defined as the propaganda destined to convince employees that collaborating with the organizational requirements was not only an obligation, but also something in their own interest; and (3) the inculcation of reasons, which he considered as the most important persuasion form, also based on education and propaganda. Thus, he explicitly recognized the role of manipulative processes to obtain consensus.

Barnard argued that authority depends on the acceptance of the individuals to whom it is directed, deeming it as 'another name for the willingness and capacity of individuals to submit to the necessities of co-operative systems' (1976[1938]: 184). This definition shows that the exercise of authority cannot be something 'bad' in any sense, since otherwise it would not be perceived as legitimate and therefore accepted. Barnard's notion of authority was favorably welcomed by Elton Mayo, who cited him as an authoritative source in *The Social Problems of an Industrial Civilization*. In fact, Barnard had many points in common with the human relations school.[4] He was not alien to the issues introduced by this ideology, but he integrated them into a more global vision of management that was further developed in the works of Simon, March, and others. In sum, Barnard was a precursor of the 'systemic rationalism' theorists, as much by his interest in decision-making managerial processes as by his focus on the organizational level, which is something that he considered as distinct from the individual and the group. His main objective, nevertheless, was quite pragmatic: to offer management practitioners valid elements to enhance organizational effectiveness.

Barnard's thought exerted a powerful influence on Herbert Simon, who acknowledged this in his influential book *Administrative Behavior*.[5] Simon took from Barnard the idea that the subordinate sets an acceptance area, within which he willingly accepts the decisions that his superordinate takes for him. Thus, authority appears as something neutral and necessary in Simon's discourse, as a sort of functional necessity of organizational life. By emphasizing that 'specialists' are needed in positions of authority in order to ensure better decision making, he advocated a sort of meritocracy based on what he called 'technical competence'. On the other hand, when speaking about the structure of organizations, he remarked not only the importance of horizontal specialization but also that of vertical specialization, which he considered essential in order to secure coordination among the organization's members.

One of Simon's greatest contributions is his thesis that 'administrative theory is peculiarly the theory of intended and bounded rationality — of the behavior of human beings who *satisfice* because they have not the wits to *maximize* [emphasis in original]' (Simon, 1957: xxiv). Rationality is bounded because the decision-maker's knowledge about possible alternatives and their probable consequences is imperfect. Rationality entails the elaboration of a mean-to-aims hierarchical chain, which in many instances of managerial decision making is incomplete or exhibits some degree of inconsistency. What is of the utmost importance in the Simonian concept of rationality is its strong instrumental character. Ultimate ends — if we even can speak about them — are excluded from rational analysis. For him, the idea of rationality is central to administration, inasmuch as rational processes are tied to daily decisions made within organizations. Within this scheme centered on rationality and decision making, he affirmed that the social sciences 'suffer from a case of acute schizophrenia in their treatment of rationality'. He thus criticized the omniscient rationality of economics, but also some tendencies of the psychology of his time that aimed at reducing 'all cognition to affect' (1957: xxiii).[6] The contrast between the Simonian perspective about organizations and the human relations approach is illustrated by his attitude towards one of the most important notions of that school: 'Personality! Truly a magical slogan to charm away the problems that our intellectual tools don't handle' (1957: xv). For Simon, personality does not arise in a vacuum, but is constructed within an organizational space that molds and constitutes it. The behavior of a manager, he argued, is a function of the organization in which he works: we cannot understand the former if we do not first understand the latter.

James March and Herbert Simon further specified the set of assumptions that inform this current of management thought in their classic book *Organizations*, published in 1958. They tried to differentiate organization theory from the human relations school, which for them dominated the discipline during the second quarter of the twentieth century and whose main limitation was that it paid scant attention to individuals as 'adaptive, reasoning beings' (1958: 210).[7] March and Simon did not ignore the contributions of earlier approaches to administration, but contemplated them in the light of a new theoretical framework. This school of management thought claimed that organizations are better understood as goal-oriented systems of collective action in which most relevant actions, as well as many irrelevant ones, emerge as outcomes from decisions. These, in turn, may come from a deliberation process (nonroutine, nonprogrammed decisions) or may be routinely embedded in the formal norms and procedures (programmed decisions).

This brief presentation by no means exhausts the theoretical contributions of the organization theory school, which include Simon's later works and Cyert and March's treatment of the existence of different coalitions of interests within organizations.[8] However, despite their relevance to the field, the writings of this group of scholars received some criticisms. For Tom Burns (1969), for example, the Simonian discourse marks a return to a pre-human relations thinking that considers organizations as composed of a unique, formal system and all behavior not framed within formally prescribed roles and procedures as being deviant. Nevertheless, and in relation to previous developments, it must be acknowledged that the organization theory school added a new dimension of scientific rigor to the management literature.

Contingency theory

The belief that there is a set of universally applicable best administrative practices was challenged by research carried out in England and first published in 1958.[9] In that pioneering study, Joan Woodward (1969 [1958]) concluded that the technical methods of production were the most important determinants of the organizational structure and of some aspects of the human relations climate of the firms. That work is credited as being the starting point of an approach that had remarkable acceptance in those years, also contributing to the displacement of the interest from human relations to the configuration of the organizational structure. This latter aspect was later considered a dependent variable of diverse types of internal and external factors; thus, the discipline reached a greater level of analytical sophistication. James Thompson (1967), an important theorist in this approach, conceptualized organizations as systems that have relations with an environment that includes and partly determines them. The basic task of organizations is, for Thompson, the reduction of environmental uncertainty.

In this approach, the human variable is not assigned the role of main determinant of organizational outcomes, but neither is it eliminated from the analysis. According to Lawrence and Lorsch (1967), conspicuous representatives of this school, the classic theory of the enterprise (e.g., Taylor, Fayol, etc.) tended to be more applicable in relatively stable environments whereas the theory of human relations was best suited for more dynamic situations.[10] This offered an explanation to the parallel existence of both theories, whose usefulness was considered dependent upon the characteristics of the organizational environment. A 'contingency theory' of the enterprise could now include both perspectives within a greater frame, indicated both authors. For Lorsch and Morse (1975), contingency theory had important management implications. They pointed out that managerial action should be aimed at obtaining the most adequate fit among personnel, task, and organization. This called into question McGregor's dichotomy between Theory X and Theory Y because he ignored the existing complexity in organizational reality. The right question is not which perspective is superior, whether the classic one (theory X) or the participative one (theory Y), but rather, what approach is most effective under a particular set of conditions (e.g., the task, the people, the market, etc.).

The knowledge that contingency theory made available to management was aimed at the determination of the most adequate organizational design vis-à-vis the environment faced by the organization and the specificity of the core technology utilized. The manipulation of structure and operating procedures was perceived as a possible strategy to increase organizational performance. As Barley and Kunda (1992: 378) indicated, this theory suggested that 'there might be no "one best way", as Taylor had proposed, but some ways were clearly better than others'. The search for worker's satisfaction was not the key of productivity. Instead, contingency theory advocates postulated that the existing complexity of the organizational realm demanded that the managers' attention be directed towards several different and simultaneous fronts.[11]

The integrators

Some authors whose works enjoyed ample diffusion among management students and practitioners alike cannot be located as belonging to any of the previously presented perspectives. Harold Koontz, for example, is one of these authors. In a classic textbook, written in collaboration with Cyril O'Donnell, he synthesized the recent developments in the discipline, emphasizing the existence of the 'management theory jungle', given the diversity of approaches and the confusion that this generated. In order to develop their formulation, Koontz and O'Donnell (1976) often resorted to the language of systems theory, treating organizations as open systems composed by interrelated subunits. Their objective was to improve the practice of administration by summarizing the most relevant aspects of the diverse approaches to the discipline and by trying to establish an ordered body of knowledge to help managers in rational decision making processes. The systems approach to management was further elaborated by many authors of the period in works that were influenced by such diverse thinkers as Ludwig von Bertalanffy, Norbert Wiener, W. Ross Ashby, and Jay Forrester.[12]

More interesting, personal, provocative, and novel is the work of Peter Drucker, whose trajectory has unquestionably turned him into the most influential 'management philosopher'. His first writings, especially *The Concept of the Corporation* published in 1946, were very close to Mayoism. In that book, Drucker sustained that corporations were institutions that would give workers a sense of dignity and a place in society. In later years, he became more interested in societal changes and the broader perspectives that managers should adopt in order to direct organizations effectively. For Drucker, the society of his time was no longer capitalist, and in the 1950s, he suggested that the stratification between 'capitalists' and 'workers' was an anachronism. The 'poor' were not the majority of the people, rather they were those who had difficulties in ascending to the middle class, a strata he deemed as the most numerous at that time. In *Landmarks of Tomorrow*, which appeared in 1959, he affirmed that workers were no longer proletarians, but part of the middle class, since they had adopted its preferences and way of life. In relation to the management of business enterprises, Drucker argued that the government of corporations was not legitimate; but he added, breaking away from Aristotelian logic, that neither was it illegitimate. With a clear legitimating stance towards the corporate order, he contended that the managers of corporations did not use their power to benefit themselves nor the workers, but rather in favor of society and the organization's goals through a sort of 'benevolent managerialism' (Tarrant, 1976).

In *The Age of Discontinuity*, Drucker (1969) observed the growing importance of knowledge for society, which led him to identify a new category of worker: the 'knowledge worker'. Although he received some attention for this, it was not until the late 1980s and early 1990s that this concept gained momentum in management thought. In 1974, he wrote what became one of the discipline's leading texts, *Management: Tasks, Responsibilities, Practices*, in which he presented his views about how a business should be managed, combining insights from different strands of management theory. Following the basic tenets of the ideology of systemic rationalism, he dealt with the most important issues that should concern the managers: goals, purposes, priorities, decisions, structures, performance, results, and control. He also included an analysis of his most personal themes: the relevance of knowledge for organizations and the nature and importance of management itself, in its double meaning of discipline and occupational group. In this respect, he stated, 'The emergence of management may be the pivotal event of our time' (Drucker, 1993 [1974]: 10). For him, American society was enjoying a level of prosperity that was unprecedented in human history, and precisely, management was to some extent responsible for it.

According to Tarrant (1976: 57), the Druckerian philosophy contended that in the new economic order that would overcome capitalism, the most humble employee should have to be intellectually equipped with a 'managerial attitude'. This would allow anyone in the organization to perceive the jobs and tasks in the same way that management does. If this way of thinking were widespread, workers would perfectly understand the necessity of the existence of profits and the reason why higher executive positions are remunerated with extremely elevated wages. For Waring (1991), Drucker tried to reunite in a synthesis the collectivist spirit of European political theory with the individualistic tradition of American entrepreneurship. Most importantly, the Druckerian ideology tried to legitimate capitalism by denying or understating its negative consequences, while also affirming that the Marxian perspective could not be taken seriously, since factual reality had already falsified its predictions.

Strategic Management

Another important current of thought within systemic rationalism is strategic management. For Igor Ansoff (1979), the conception of this approach can be dated back to 1965, the year that his book *Corporate Strategy* was published. The strategic behavior of organizations is generally understood as a deliberate interaction process with the environment, which also involves changes in the configuration and dynamics of internal operations. The development of strategic management was influenced by previous developments within the systemic rationalism tradition.[13] Several key thinkers in this approach, such as Ansoff and Ackoff, consistently framed their normative and descriptive schemes in terms of systems theory. The goal of strategic management is to offer the organizations' top management tools to devise higher-level objectives and effectively perform long term planning, under the assumption that organizations face a 'turbulent environment'.

During the 1970s and 1980s, the literature on strategic management grew, and specialized journals appeared. In order to have an idea of its importance, the identification of ten schools of strategic management by Henry Mintzberg (1990) is a clear example. Commenting on the history of this line of administrative thought, Mintzberg affirmed that in the mid 1960s the 'corporate leaders' considered it to be the new 'one best way'. Moreover, the relation with Taylor is not accidental, 'this one best way involved separating thinking from doing and creating a new function staffed by specialists: strategic planners' (1994: 107). Strategic management tried to equip managers with rational and effective tools to direct organizations, not only regarding their relations to a broader environment (i.e., clients, competitors, suppliers, government, unions, and so on), but also, albeit to a lesser extent, to those pertaining to their own members. It helped the experts in the new techniques and approaches (e.g., systems theory, decision theory, and operations research), which required a background in the hard sciences, to attain privileged positions, either as higher management personnel or as specialized consultants. In fact, many economists joined the higher ranks of the managerial elite due to their supporting role on issues of strategic nature, and one of them, Michael Porter (1980, 1985), wrote a series of books about strategy that turned him into one of the most influential management gurus.

The significance of systemic rationalism

It must be acknowledged that even during the years in which systemic rationalism can be considered as a dominant ideology, it was not the only perspective that addressed management issues. Some authors developed models inspired in Weberian sociology,[14] while there were also new approaches in the line of the human relations ideology. In fact, the change of dominant ideology did not occur as a 'sudden permutation' of one belief system for another, rather, it was quite gradual. The ideology of the human relations school did not disappear completely; its attraction was progressively eclipsed by systemic rationalism in a process whereby both coexisted on an approximately equal basis during the second half of the 1950s. In the 1960s, Herzberg continued writing about personnel motivation, Likert (1961) developed a typology of management models based on the characteristics of supervision (authoritarian or participative), and Slater and Bennis (1990 [1964]) wrote about the 'inevitability' of the adoption of more 'democratic' organizational forms.

Nevertheless, the language, the techniques, and the issues put forward by systemic rationalism were the most visible in the managerial literature discourse during the years between 1960 and 1985. During this period, the MBA model, first inaugurated in American universities at the beginning of the century and later diffused to other parts of the world, was heavily oriented to the set of approaches that make up this ideology (Locke, 1989), whose main features are summarized in Table 7.1. Its impact on administrative practices, basically achieved through a series of techniques and tools utilized by 'boardroom' consultants and top managers in formal activities of planning and design, was also very important. The increased role of information technology in office and administrative work was a leading factor behind the influence of systemic rationalism, both in the ubiquitous presence of its discourse and in the possibility of applying its analytical prescriptions and procedures.

Perhaps the most important contribution of systemic rationalism is the construction of the 'rational manager': an individual who makes informed decisions based on expert knowledge and relevant data. The emphasis on the processes of problem formulation and solving as well as the specific university training received by those who would be part of the managerial elite contributed to the diffusion of this image.[15] What do managers do? They decide, following a rational analytical process. They establish objectives and participate in a struggle against competitors and other environmental forces. Their authority resides in their superior knowledge and talent to perform the functions entrusted to them. The fact

Table 7.1   Main aspects of systemic rationalism

Basic tenets	Use of systems theory and language
	Emphasis on decision making and problem formulation and solving
	Concept of the organization as an open system in relation to a broader environment
	Instead of focusing on workers-management industrial conflict like previous ideologies, the emphasis was placed on the opposition between organization and environment
Image of the manager	The manager was depicted as a rational decision maker who possessed a fair amount of specialized knowledge that justified his authority
Image of the worker	The worker was perceived as one more decision maker, a rational actor; workers were not seen as proletariats, but as part of the middle class
Legitimated interests	Capitalist class Top managers Experts in the new management approaches
Areas of application	Mostly general management (i.e., long-term planning, organizational design) but also other areas (e.g., operations management)
Main authors	Simon Drucker Ansoff Ackoff Thompson
Period of dominance	1960-1985
Impact on practices	Some of the tools and elements offered by this line of thought were applied worldwide to many general management issues
	Strategic management, in particular, had strong importance for managerial consulting
Misrepresentations detected	Myth of the rational manager

that they occupy a position of authority is precisely the demonstration of their ability, for they have already passed several tests in their ascent up the 'hierarchical ladder'. Those who are at the lower levels of the organizational chart must imitate them, endorse their decisions, and use their own responsibility in the best possible way.

It should be emphasized that this ideology 'lacked an explicit model of the workforce' (Barley and Kunda, 1992: 380). Its discourse dealt extensively with the managers and the techniques that they must use to arrive at optimal or merely 'satisfycing' decisions, and the issue of the workers ceased to be an important concern. We are far from Taylor, who tried to solve the 'labor problem', and from Mayo, who aimed at healing the cultural malaise of industrial society. For systemic rationalism, potential noncompliance actions on the part of workers did not seem a threat. Employees were perceived as 'manageable', as a mere 'organizational resource'. For Barnard and Simon, solving the equation that balanced the employees' individual objectives with the goals of the organization was fundamental, and this was something that a capable manager could achieve without problems. On the other hand, management could always resort to persuasion techniques. In addition, during the 1960s, the theories of motivation inspired by a hierarchy of needs, such as Maslow's, were challenged by the appearance of new approaches that emphasized the character of the individuals' cognitive evaluation processes.[16] Thus, the worker appeared as one more decision maker. The increasing bureaucratization of organizations led to the establishment of a bond between the company and its personnel based on mutual convenience. Employees traded loyalty in return for lifetime employment. This is one of the aspects of what has been conceptualized as the 'psychological contract', which assumes that the workers' behavior can be influenced by management through a 'contractual' interchange beneficial for both parts.[17]

Another important aspect of this ideology is the key role assigned to the environment. Sherwin recalled a discussion maintained with a personnel manager who insinuated that employees could not be treated according to the recommendations of Theory Y because 'they were Theory X'. For Sherwin (1975), environment determined behavior: organizations established that their personnel were Theory X. Only by changing the general organizational environment and, consequently, the work atmosphere, could it be hoped that workforce behavior would conform to the assumptions of Theory Y. In addition, there was an abandonment of a dichotomous opposition characteristic of previous ideological discourses. In the cases of Taylorism and, to a lesser extent, the human relations movement, an opposition — not regarded as an overt conflict, but as a situation that could be understood as potentially conflictive — was recognized: the owner-manager versus the employees. Hence, the emphasis was then put on cooperation; while with systemic rationalism, a new opposition emerged: the organization versus its environment.[18]

Empirical studies (e.g., Kotter, 1982; Mintzberg, 1973) demonstrated that the model of the 'rational manager' popularized by systemic rationalism did not correspond with the real behavior of managers at successful companies. In actual practice, managers did not spend their time elaborating formal models, but rather established relations with their peers, networking, and talking about subjects not directly related — and, in many cases, without any relation whatsoever — to the administrative issues that required decisions or actions on their part. These informal contacts appeared, however, most important for the management of their companies. This shows the character of ideological construction, divorced from reality, of the image of the rational manager. Moreover, formal analysis in organizations often serves a symbolic purpose in order to convince others to support decisions that have been taken beforehand or to justify the existence of those who are responsible for these analytical tasks (Langley, 1989).[19] Interestingly enough, research on managerial work also cast serious doubts about the usefulness — for managers themselves — of emulating the image of the rational manager. As shown by Fred Luthans et al. (1988), those managers who spent more time analyzing information and completing task related activities, although efficient in their jobs, did not reach the organization's higher ranks faster than those managers who spent their time on networking and social activities. Their analysis revealed that 'successful' managers, as measured by their advancement within their companies, were not 'efficient' managers: the profiles of both types of managers appeared to have 'little in common' (Luthans, 1988: 127).

The rational techniques espoused by systemic rationalism may not have been so widely adopted adoption because managers themselves are not as rational as they seem in textbooks and other sources. However, it is pertinent to consider whether these techniques effectively deliver the promised results. In this regard, it should be stressed that often very popular tools like strategic management proved less useful than expected when applied in practice. Mintzberg acknowledged this point and stated, 'While certainly not dead, strategic planning has long since fallen from its pedestal' (1994: 107).[20] Operations research, one of the pillars of systemic rationalism, has been similarly criticized by one of its most outstanding figures, Russell L. Ackoff. For him, the mathematical models of the discipline are sometimes inappropriate to formalize the complex and hardly structured problems and situations faced by managers in contemporary organizations. Instead of a means to the end of improving the quality of decision making, these models have become ends in themselves. The experts who incessantly used these quantitative techniques in such a manner transformed them into an absurd 'mathematical masturbation' (Ackoff, 1979: 95). The application of such methods in order to solve questions for which they are manifestly inadequate discredited the discipline in the eyes of management practitioners.

According to Barley and Kunda's (1992) scientometric analysis of articles indexed in the Business Periodicals Index, systemic rationalism began to wane in the early 1980s.[21] The remarkable growth of the Japanese economy meant that many scholars started to carefully watch the administrative techniques applied in that country. Also the increasing globalization of the world economy, which spawned a ferocious competition, induced some theorists to believe that the economic problems of the United States could be solved through more 'flexible' organizational forms. Meanwhile, the concept of organizational culture was popularized by several management best sellers that associated some informal features of organizations to superior performance, as illustrated by the huge success achieved by Tom Peters and Robert Waterman's (1982) *In Search of Excellence*. However, it was not merely a problem of finding new formulas, either by emulating earlier American recipes transformed by the Japanese like Total

Quality or by eliciting the employees' emotional commitment through the deliberate construction of cultural norms. Rather, the bureaucratic model itself, the cornerstone of management under organized capitalism, was called into question. In this context, the conditions were given for the rise of a new ideology. This time, the change was fundamental: a new paradigm that promised to make many basic notions of management completely obsolete had emerged.

Notes

1. The dates that delimit the periods of dominance enjoyed by the different managerial ideologies can be interpreted rather loosely. For instance, according to Barley and Kunda, the human relations ideology was superseded by systems rationalism in the mid-1950s.
2. Guillén (1994) also considered that these diverse approaches were a coherent and homogeneous set, which he termed the 'structural analysis paradigm'.
3. Problems involving human behavior were also approached from this perspective. Emshoff (1971), for example, described several experiences conducted at the Center of Training for Conflict of the University of Pennsylvania in which operations research models were used.
4. Along with Elton Mayo, Barnard was also a member of the Harvard 'Pareto circle' (Keller, 1984).
5. See, for example, the correspondence between both authors in Wolf (1995).
6. Simon continued defending the same line of thought and became deeply interested in cognitive psychology, to which he also contributed (e.g., Newell and Simon, 1972).
7. In his later works, March (1976) adopted a modified perspective, emphasizing the irrational aspects of organizational behavior.
8. See, for example, Simon (1960) and Cyert and March (1963).
9. Russell Robb can be considered a precursor of this approach. At the beginning of the twentieth century, he put in doubt the existence of universal principles of management in one of the chapters of his *Lectures on organization* entitled 'Organizations as Affected by Purpose and Condition' (Robb, 1970 [1910]). Barnard also pointed out that decision-making processes vary according to the type of organization in question.
10. Burns and Stalker (1961), leading figures of this approach, raised a similar point, introducing the concepts of the mechanic and organic types of organization, whose efficiency was contingent upon certain environmental conditions.
11. Some authors (e.g., Donaldson, 1996a; 1996b) still develop this line of inquiry, although it has lost much of its appeal.
12. See, for example, Johnson et al. (1963), Timms (1966), and Beer (1972).
13. Drucker (1954), for example, was one of the first authors to speak about strategy in *The Practice of Management*.
14. This school began in the 1940s when Weberian thought spread in the United States as a result of Talcott Parsons's translation of some of Weber's works. Among its leading names are Merton, Gouldner, Etzioni, and Crozier. Weber's influence can also be found in March and Simon, according to Perrow who labeled them as neo-Weberians and considered that they formulated an 'expanded bureaucratic model' (1986: 131).
15. On the desired profile of education for managers, see Buckingham (1961).
16. For example, goal setting theory (Locke, 1968) and expectancy theory (Vroom, 1964).
17. This is not a real contract, but a theoretical construct referring to the mutual set of expectations between employee and employer during a labor relationship (Schein,

1980). The genesis of this concept, first used by Argyris, owes much to the Barnard-Simon 'organizational equilibrium' theory (Roehling, 1997).

18 This can be seen not only in strategic management, but also in some approaches of organizational sociology, with organizational ecology (Hannan and Freeman, 1977) being the most noteworthy.

19 Pfeffer made a similar appreciation when speaking about the 'need for the appearance of rationality'. For him, 'using rational, or seemingly rational, processes of analysis helps to render the use of power and influence less obvious' (1992: 249).

20 Strategic management, however, appears to have outlived its alleged fall, since the issue of strategy is still one of the most popular topics in the management literature. In addition, there is also limited evidence that strategic planning activities have a positive, albeit small, influence on financial results (Capon et al., 1994).

21 The decline began in 1981, and by 1985 the number of articles related to organizational culture issues exceeded that of articles associated with systemic rationalism.

Chapter 8

The Legitimating Contribution of Managerial Ideologies to Organized Capitalism

Scientific knowledge changes over time. Perspectives and traditions succeed one another, and likewise, so do administrative theories. Traditional histories of management thought explain these developments on the basis of cognitive progress. Whether by solving more adequately old challenges encountered in the management of organizations or by facing totally new problems in the economic, political, and social dimensions of the business environment, each new theory is depicted as increasing the knowledge base of the discipline, thus contributing to effectiveness and efficiency.[1] This is an idyllic case for rational scientific progress. In contrast, researchers working within a Marxist theoretical framework (e.g., Edwards, 1979) concluded that the search for efficiency could not account for the development of administrative practices and theories. Rather, as also recognized by non-Marxist theorists of organization like Hannan and Freeman (1989), these analyses served to show that organizations were not rationally managed. For Marxist scholars, the capitalists' main concern was not efficiency, but control. Hence, the relevance of studying the coercive, rational, and normative rhetorics of control in the evolution of managerial ideologies. Acknowledging the value of this approach, I adopt a different position. Since the legitimating function is what defines an ideology, I will analyze in this chapter how the different ideologies legitimated organized capitalism.

By the turn of the nineteenth century, Taylorism emerged as the dominant managerial ideology, marking the birth of management as a discipline. In the first decades of the twentieth century, Weber wrote about bureaucratic domination, and Fayol, who developed his professional career at a typical bureaucratic enterprise, tried to systematize the basic principles of administration. As these developments occurred, the formalization of work procedures and organizational structures in large organizations became commonplace in many core Western countries. Scientific management was central to this process, and its success as an ideology required a certain business environment that was nonexistent in earlier years. The positive reception of Taylor's creed was linked to the rise of mass production in many American industries. This productive model, in turn, was greatly enhanced through the contribution made by scientific management to the emergence of the Fordist assembly line. In a classic study, Braverman (1974) argued that Taylorism, centered on the rationalization of productive processes, could not be widely adopted until the size of organizations allowed the rationalization efforts to yield benefits superior to their implementation costs. But the great ideological success that this discourse achieved cannot be explained solely by technological or economic determinism. For Michael Burawoy, the free market ideology could not adequately legitimate a social order in which the state progressively intervened in the economy, as was the case in the first decades of the twentieth century. A new source of legitimation was needed, and in this respect, he affirmed that scientific management accomplished more than the expansion of the forces of production,

> [it] simultaneously laid the basis for a new ideology in which the preservation of capitalist relations was presented as a technical matter to be removed from political discourse. The pursuit of 'efficiency' became the basis of a new ideology, a new form of domination. (1978: 281)

The spontaneous order of the free market rested upon the assumption of the existence of a Walrasian universe, under whose inescapable logic entrepreneurs maximized their wealth and that of society. Taylor added a new twist to this abstract conception: there was no automatic profit maximization without the application of sound, rigorous management techniques. No 'invisible hand', except for the one present in his engineering approach, could ensure the rationalization of the economic order. This view legitimated the deliberate action taken by the state in the national economy as long as it was guided by the minds of professional experts.

However, besides providing an ideology that legitimated the capitalist order (type 1 legitimation), Taylorism served to legitimize the access to privileged positions within the social order of a stratum of professional managers (type 2 legitimation).[2] Several strata compose the social privilege structure of a society, and with Taylorism, professional managers became one of them. Their basis of social privilege was not the property of these means, but their possession — or rather, their claim of possession — of the technical knowledge required to direct organizations in an effective and efficient way. Their specialized knowledge qualified them to act as privileged agents of the capitalist class.

This change in the structure of social privilege questions lead us to consider some questions about the nature of the ruling class under organized capitalism. Were the new cadre of managers just servants of the capitalists, or did they aspire to something more? During liberal capitalism, the composition of the dominant class was not a theoretical problem. Although authors like Marx acknowledged the analytical difference between the role of the capitalist and that of the manager, the typical industrial firm of the period was basically controlled by the owner-manager.[3] Like in today's family enterprises, the relatives of the owner most often carried out what we now identify as managerial or executive positions (Bendix, 1956).[4] However, with the rise of large enterprises and joint-stock companies, the separation between property and control became an object of scholarly interest. By the turn of the nineteenth century, some observers pointed out that the operation of large firms was a complicated matter, which wealthy capitalists preferred to leave in the hands of expert personnel. The French socialist Paul Lafargue (1900) argued that the capitalists trusted the management of large enterprises to highly salaried intellectuals, who would never join a revolutionary cause because their own interests were aligned with those of their employers. Thorstein Veblen also noted the existence of the separation between managers and owners, while not dismissing as a possibility the 'revolt of the engineers' (respectively in Veblen 1923, 1921). But in the early 1930s, Berle and Means raised with greater clarity the issue of the divorce between ownership and control of the means of production. In this regard, they indicated that the elimination of the exclusive interest of the capitalists put 'the community in a position to demand that the modern corporation serve not alone the owners or the control but all society' (1968 [1932]: 312). Burnham's (1941) theory about the 'managerial revolution' was even more audacious, since he argued that the managers would become the new ruling class in a society that would replace the bourgeois or capitalist order. For him, the means of production would finally pass to the property of the state and the managers of corporations would conquer social dominance.

Despite these speculations, the managers did not displace the capitalists as the ruling class; instead, a mutation in the structure of social privilege occurred. Managers became a stratum 'associated' to the social privilege of the owners of the means of production. Neither Burnham's pessimistic predictions nor the advent of some sort of 'benevolent managerialism', as depicted by Berle and Means, have occurred. Rather, managers have acted as perfect agents of the capitalist class, internalizing a basic principle of capitalist rationality: the search of the shareholder's profit. In his exhaustive analysis of the available empirical evidence, Herman came to the conclusion that the managers of large corporations 'seem as devoted to profitable growth as are the leaders of entrepreneurial and owner-dominated companies, past and present' (1981: 113).

In addition, it must be taken into account that those belonging to the managerial strata, since they have became part of the privileged sectors of society, tend to be recruited among the members of the ruling class. Thus, many members of the capitalist class, their descendants, and other relatives also become members of the managerial strata. The replacement of a dominant class by another, except in the case of violent social revolutions, does not take place through a mere permutation of their members. Instead, the members of the old ruling class, by means of their social privilege, accede to merge with those of the emergent elite (e.g., by marriage). Robert Michels demonstrated this in a study of the 'disappearance' of feudal nobility, in which he analyzed the genealogical records of families of this class. In that work, he elaborated a complement to Pareto's theory of the circulation of elites. According to Michels (1949 [1927]), the old aristocracy of a given social order does not disappear or become 'proletarized', but manages to join the new ruling class.[5] This thesis suggests that the social privilege of the old ruling class allows it to 'infiltrate' its members into the new one. Regarding the access to positions in the managerial strata, it is clear that members of a bourgeois family have a significant comparative advantage. The similarity in the composition of the capitalist and managerial elites is further shown by the fact that many successful managers gain the status of owners or capitalists as a result of investing their income in public corporations or receiving equity of the companies they direct. In sum, both strata overlap to a certain degree and are basically composed by people of the same social origin.[6]

Not only did the structure of social privilege change in this stage of capitalism, but the wider social structure itself also changed with the appearance of a more numerous middle class. The dual society of the preceding stage of capitalism turned into a different, more diamond-like structure (Tezanos, 1992). In addition, life at bureaucratic, pyramidal organizations affected the individuals' perception about the image of society, and an important proportion of workers began to view society as a progressive order (Popitz et al., 1969 [1957]). In Dahrendorf's (1959) opinion, a hierarchic stratification system supports a vision of society as an integrated order, whereas a dichotomous structure supposes the existence of antagonism and conflict. Middle class individuals who experience their organizational lives in job positions in which there are people both above and below them tend to have an integrated image of society.

The growth of the middle class and the intervention of the state in the disputes between entrepreneurs and workers through specific legislation, as well as its active role as welfare provider, appeared to attenuate social unrest. For Dahrendorf, class conflict could be controlled within the existing institutional framework of the advanced Western countries, and this removed the fear of a social revolution against the continuity of the capitalist order. These societal transformations had an impact on the writings of management thinkers. In the administrative ideologies that followed Taylorism, social conflict did not figure as a pressing issue. In fact, as Dahrendorf (1959) observed, the irresolvable antagonism of class conflict, did not exist for Mayo and Drucker; however, the stance of both ideologies towards this subject was different. Mayo stated that the idea of the existence of social conflict was scientifically erroneous and attributable to the hatred professed by Marx towards the bourgeoisie, and he considered that many union leaders firmly believed this false notion simply because of their sick personalities. Nevertheless, he did write extensively on the topic of social unrest. In the case of systemic rationalism, class conflict almost disappeared from the discourse, and only a few authors wrote about social issues. Among these, Drucker stressed the idea that workers had substantially improved their living conditions and, consequently, became part of the middle class. Thus, there was no reason for them to ask for more. This logic was in part supported by the fact that income distribution in the United States reached its height of fairness in the period of systemic rationalism.

The human relations ideology endowed legitimation to the experts in social sciences, who gradually joined the engineers in the management of the companies (type 2 legitimation) and achieved their own place in the structure of social privilege. With the discourse of these new 'humanists', the thesis of the progressive subtilization of ideological control acquires certain plausibility. The employee was portrayed in a more favorable light than in previous ideologies; in particular, Theory Y's assumptions regarding the nature of the workers contrast noticeably with Taylorist and older conceptions. The human relations school also fulfilled a legitimating role for the existing order (type 1) since it discarded the notion that social conflict was intrinsic to capitalism, by depicting society as a stable order in which individual and social pathologies were reduced, moderated, and even eliminated. Moreover, this ideology played a central role in the integration of workers into the capitalist system as consumers.

According to Alberto Guerreiro Ramos (1981:72-73), the rise of 'the human relations school was triggered by the imperatives of a business structure demanding emphasis upon consumption rather than upon saving', something that was also observed by other authors like David Riesman and W.H. Whyte. What actually was emerging was a consumer society in which the media incited people 'to diversify their wants and to express them in such specific terms that only through buying specific commodities can they be satisfied' (1981: 84). While it can be argued that the processes leading to the rise of the consumer society in the United States date back to earlier decades, there is general agreement that its consolidation occurred in the period between 1930 and 1960, which also marks the preeminence of this 'humanist' approach to management.[7]

Riesman's concept of 'groupism' and the consumer society are inextricably linked. One of the salient features of the consumer society is the phenomenon of the dissolution of individualism. As noted by Herbert Marcuse, in this stage of capitalism, the traditional concept of the individual has turned obsolete, 'canceled (*aufgehoben*) by the historical development of productivity' (2001 [1966]: 80). In this context, Marcuse indicated that the human relation ideology had become closely associated to the American way of life. If groupism, so accurately described by David Riesman, is a basic cultural characteristic of this stage of capitalist development in the advanced countries — and mainly in the United States — then the importance of the human relations ideology must be acknowledged. This discourse, beyond type 1 legitimation, can also be considered as performing a constitutive ideological function. The consumer society has been to a large extent constructed by the social ethics that this ideology has helped to imbue in the minds of the men and women of bureaucratic organizations. Groups press towards homogeneity, and in order to be accepted, one has to conform to a certain model of behavior socially dictated, which includes consumption patterns deemed as desirable and normal. The other-directed personality, ever seeking approval from peers and society at large, is a fertile ground for the seed of consumerism to be sown. The human relations ideology nurtures this type of personality; marketing and advertising techniques further mold it; and the resulting final product is the average worker-consumer. While the importance of the latter techniques has been largely recognized, the constitutive role of the former has been often downplayed.

Once the consumer society was firmly established as a characteristic of the social order, the predominance of the human relations ideology decreased. Another managerial ideology gained center stage: systemic rationalism. The instrumental 'pseudohumanism' of the human relations ideology was not sufficient to manage organizations effectively. For this reason, several theorists began to elaborate a new perspective, moving the emphasis from the psychological to the organizational. To a certain extent, the approaches outlined under the denomination of systemic rationalism (e.g., operations research, organization theory, etc.) are a return to Taylor's rationalism. Management theory did not abandon the study of the informal dimension, but focused more on the improvement of formal aspects. Thinkers like Herbert Simon, James March, and Peter Drucker developed approaches integrating both the formal and informal dimensions. Systemic rationalism contributed to reify the notion of organization. Its discourse was apparently neutral with respect to the economic order within which organizations act and not much concerned with broader social or political issues, which was equivalent to an implicit support to the prevailing status quo. Since there was nothing wrong with the social order, management theorists had nothing to add. One exception in this regard was Peter Drucker, who actively vindicated capitalism through the simple argument that it made possible an improvement in the situation of the workers. Thus, this ideology, guided by a technical, neutral, and instrumental rationality, contributed to legitimize the social order (type 1 legitimation).

New developments in science (the rise of systems theory) and technology (the introduction of the digital computer in the world of work) allowed for the introduction of new managerial tools and conceptions. The discourse of systemic rationalism presented organizations and their environment as being subject to increasing complexity, with which managers could only cope by means of specific analytical techniques. This led a new stratum of technocrats and professionals, educated in the new approaches at business schools, to reach managerial positions and, therefore, a place in the structure of social privilege. This ideology endowed a quota of legitimation to those who comprise this stratum through the figure of the 'rational manager', icon of a society of efficiency and technological progress (type 2 legitimation).

To sum up, I have tried to show that each of the dominant managerial ideologies under organized capitalism contributed to legitimate the existing order and the access to the structure of social privilege of those with knowledge of specific disciplines.[8] Moreover, during organized capitalism, several factors can explain the evolution of managerial ideologies: (1) the emergence of the bureaucratic model and the rise of mass production, which were both associated to Taylorism; (2) the consolidation of the consumer society, which was clearly reflected in, and even fueled by, the human relations ideology; and (3) the apparition of new technological developments, which was closely related to systemic rationalism (see Table 8.1). Yet, despite these discontinuities, a central theme unites the three ideologies analyzed in this chapter: their commitment to a hierarchical and bureaucratic model of management. With its emphasis on formal and complex authority structures, hierarchical as opposed to participative decision making, and abundance of impersonal rules and procedures, this model can be considered one of the basic features of this phase of capitalism.

Scientific management signaled the first relevant attempt at formalizing in detail the productive operations of industrial enterprises. The human relations introduced the study of the 'informal organization', but the theorists of this school did not criticize the existing bureaucratic structures and procedures.[9] On the contrary, they were responsible for adding a further level of bureaucratization, since they variously tried to formalize the informal. They sought to identify and add to the manuals of administrative procedures the more adequate ways to both select individuals with 'leadership potential' and deal properly with superiors, subordinates, and customers. Systemic rationalism also contributed to support the bureaucratic model of management with its focus on aspects such as the need to

Table 8.1 Aspects of organized capitalism and associated arguments of the managerial ideologies

Ideologies	Aspects of organized capitalism	Associated arguments
Scientific Management	Generalization of the bureaucratic model of management; rise of mass production	Expert knowledge considered as a basis of authority and also as the only possible way to rationalize administrative processes
Human Relations	Consolidation of the consumer society	Emphasis on groupism: priority of the group over the individual
Systemic rationalism	Scientific and technological developments, in particular introduction of the digital computer	Increased emphasis on formal aspects like planning and organizational design; construction of the figure of the rational manager

carefully document administrative processes; the emphasis on hierarchy and authority; the so-called programmed decisions; and the incipient use of information technology, which resulted in further formalization of administrative work. However, in the mid 1980s, the consensus regarding the bureaucratic model was widely questioned as a new paradigm, whose emergence was associated to significant transformations in the capitalist order, gained predominance as managerial ideology.

Notes

1   See, for example, Wren (1994).
2   For a similar view on the role of the management literature of the period, see Shenhav (1999) and Shenhav and Weitz (2000).
3   For a review of Marx's reflections on this issue, see Duménil and Lévy (1993).
4   See also Useem (1984) on early forms of 'family capitalism'.
5   Andrle (2001) provides another interesting illustration regarding this thesis: the case of the emergent Czech business elite and its relations to the ruling class under the Communist regime.
6   In this regard, see for example Lenski (1966) and Beder (2000). Several self-made successful managers or entrepreneurs have fulfilled the American dream of ascending socially from lower social strata. Yet these isolated examples of upward social mobility do not invalidate the main argument about the social origins of the managerial elite.

7   On the periodization of the development of the consumer society in the U. S., see Cross (2002).
8   The evolution of the management consulting industry mirrors the access to privileged managerial positions of professionals from the disciplines that the successive dominant administrative ideologies espoused. The first consultants were engineers (the shop-floor consultants) and accountants. Then came the social scientists (the personnel experts); and finally, the experts in operations research, information, strategic management, and marketing (the 'boardroom advisors'). Of course, this pattern may differ in specific national contexts. See, for example, Kipping (1996, 1999), Wright (2000), and McKenna (2001).
9   Some exponents of the human relations ideology spoke about libertarian forms of organization (Slater and Bennis, 1990 [1964]), but these were isolated examples.

Chapter 9

The New Paradigm of Management

The management literature from the mid-1980s onwards shows a strong interest in new organizacional forms. In particular, the bureaucratic model is displayed as dysfunctional in relation to the challenges posed by a complex and ever changing environment. Robert Waterman (1987: xii) affirmed that 'the only constant is change', an opinion, often repeated as a mantra, that is shared by other specialists in the field. Many of the tiles of best-selling management books insinuate a sense of radical change of perspective. Among these, the following can be mentioned: *Thriving on Chaos* by Tom Peters, published in 1987, whose subtitle *Handbook for a Management Revolution* is an especial example; *Reengineering the Corporation: A Manifest for a Management Revolution*, the 1993 best-seller by Michael Hammer and James Champy; *Corporate Revolution*, authored by Roger Hayes and Reginald Watts and published in 1986; and *Workplace 2000: The Revolution Reshaping American Business* by Joseph Boyett and Henry Conn, which appeared in 1991. They are all indicative of supposedly new ideas that imply a rupture with previous thinking. This 'rupture', however, is not so drastic: Bennis and Slater (1968) called for more participative organizational forms in the 1960s, and the philosophy of the Scanlon Plan must also be considered a precedent. Moreover, although rediscovered in the 1980s due to its extensive application in Japan, a country that was regarded as a model for administrative theory,[1] Total Quality Management, an important management fad within this new ideology, was introduced in the 1950s. In many aspects, certain elements of the human relations ideology were slowly seen in a much more favorable light, especially the emphasis placed on the importance of the human group and the informal organization.

Diverse approaches exist and there are some differences, or points of friction, between different authors; nonetheless, the reference to a new model of management, which supersedes bureaucracy, is an indicator that there is a consensus with respect to several issues pertaining to the organization of work and a new image of society. Recent tendencies in scientific discourse (the paradigm of chaos and complexity) and the influence of information technology, involving the possibility of introducing substantial modifications in the routines of administrative work, are mentioned as key elements in the adoption of a 'new paradigm of management'.[2] This paradigm is based on the crisis of the bureaucratic model, whose emergency dates back to the time of Taylor and Fayol, and the interest for new, more horizontal, 'democratic', and 'participative' organizational forms in which formal authority is diluted.[3] In turn, this generates a new appreciation of the labor force, whose importance had been obscured during systemic rationalism and which now returns to center stage as the most vital organizational resource. In the next sections, I review three of the main aspects of this managerial ideology: (1) the technological changes and the cultural as well as scientific conceptions associated with its appearance, (2) the characterization of the knowledge society and its impact on organizations, and (3) the emerging new organizational forms. I will then discuss, in the following two chapters, the implications of the postbureaucratic management model for the world of work and the significance and legitimating contribution of this new paradigm.

Technology, postmodernity, and complexity

Technology, IT in particular, is unanimously considered as a determining factor in the transformations of the world of work. It is celebrated the coming of a 'third industrial revolution' (Wriston, 1992), which has made possible the rise of a new type of organization, the virtual corporation (Davidow and Malone, 1992), and even the emergence of a new society (Drucker, 1992b; 1992c; 1993a). Since the invention of the digital computer, much has been speculated about its consequences for the organizational world. Herbert Simon already discussed this point with certain detail in the 1960s, but it was not until the 1980s, with new developments in the area of telecommunications and the introduction of the personal computer, that these effects gained wide visibility. It is argued that such advances are affecting, and will substantially affect, the organization of work. According to Paul Strassman (1985), the most important transformation would be the advent of the 'paperless office', and the 'electronic message' would become the medium of information par excellence of the service society. Moreover, the cost of information transmission by unit of time and distance has diminished drastically, laying the groundwork for a dramatic change in the economy and functionality of coordination processes. This led Michael Scott Morton (1991) to suggest that the structure of organizations, which is to a great extent determined by these processes, will also be the object of severe transformations.

The emphasis on innovation and change as well as the extensive panegyric expressed about these technological advances were the elements that enable the affirmation of the existence of an axiological assumption that characterizes the new paradigm of management: cyberphrenia. This means that, although technology does not appear as an end in itself, it is increasingly considered an ideal means of releasing mankind from performing unpleasant tasks and of offering individuals the authentic possibility of self-realization. According to Michael McGill,

> the cyberphrenics argue that technology will bring the true age of enlightenment, freeing
> workers and managers from the mundane, the trivial, the boring, and the stressful work
> in organizations, tapping into rather than destroying human creativity, and creating new
> jobs in the process. (1988: 181)

In line with this discourse, many authors stressed the liberating power of technology. William Halal, for example, with great optimism affirmed the following:

Information technology is spreading like wildfire to ignite an enormously higher level of social complexity, and the need to handle this turbulence is creating one of most significant but less understood imperatives of our time: the startling discovery is dawning that democratic participation and entrepreneurial freedom are no longer luxuries or moral niceties but the most essential ingredients for survival, especially in the high-tech fields of the future, because they are *productive*. Thus, a quiet economic transformation seems to be underway as the demands of information technology relentlessly drive these two powerful ideals to new heights and unite them into an unusual alliance [emphasis in original]. (1986: 7)

Nevertheless, some effects of the computer science revolution, ignored or minimized by the discourse of the new paradigm of management, are negative. For Tom Bottomore (1992), technological advances have produced two categories of workers: those whose occupations have a scientific and engineering nature, thus reporting a high degree of autonomy for them, and those whose jobs basically involve tedious routine tasks requiring the intensive use of computers. Hence, the liberating effects of technology, if any, do not affect the latter. The problem of unemployment, associated to the substitution of one factor of production (labor) by another (high technology equipment, that is to say, capital) cannot also be overlooked. In fact, the hypothesis, or rather, the prognosis of a significant increase in the unemployment rate has gained an image of plausibility. The central argument used to counter this criticism is that the present crisis will be solved in the same way as previous crises: on the basis of spontaneous market mechanisms, which eventually manage to overcome the problems. However, this position is somewhat naive. To suppose by incomplete induction that all crisis have solution is dangerous, unless one firmly believes in what can be termed 'catalactic infallibility' (Gantman, 1994). In any case, the panorama does not seem so optimistic as posed by those who align themselves with the new paradigm of management.

The rhetoric about the effects of technology centers on the emergence of organizational forms based on a horizontal model and the obsolescence of bureaucracy. As Halal (1986: 31) affirmed, 'The old form of management did not suddenly turn bad, it is simply no longer appropriate'. Thus, 'the most damning thing one can say about an organization today is to call it a "bureaucracy"' (1986: 39). However, it must be indicated that the thought of the new paradigm is not only based on the dysfunctionality of the old model to meet technological change, but it is also related to the cultural climate of the so-called postmodernity and to new developments in the hard sciences. Both tendencies point at the necessity of more flexible, 'democratic' organizations, with greater participation on the part of employees to face the challenges posed by constant innovation and fierce competition.

The topic of postmodernity is associated to technological and economic changes. In this sense, the meaning of the postmodern is related to terms like postindustrial, service, or information economy (Borgmann, 1992). A very deep connection between recent economic developments and the postmodern movement exists (Harvey, 1989). Several authors have tried to define the 'postmodern organization', assimilating it to a form that results from the techniques of flexible specialization, which is presented as an antithetical model to mass production, commonly denominated 'Post-Fordism' (Bergquist, 1993).[4] The sense of 'newness', of epochal change marking 'the end of modernity', constitutes a legitimating element of the new ideology, since postmodernism buries in the past old narratives that defied the social order, in particular Marxism.[5] Everything that could be negative or perverse in liberal capitalism is associated to 'modernity', whose demise suggests that something different occupies its place. Authoritarian and bureaucratic organizational structures, also associated to modernity, are part of a heritage that Western thought is willing to disregard. The new organizational forms are allegedly based on another philosophy and will raise a more authentic sense of freedom. This new philosophical current is thus perceived as a source of legitimation for the new paradigm and the 'new society' whose advent is heralded.

The discipline of management has always pretended to be based on science, and certain ideas associated to the conception of chaos and complexity in the hard sciences have been rapidly embraced by some management thinkers to endow the discipline with a renewed image of scientificity. In the same way as managers permanently worry about 'the volatility of the business environment, scientists have become preoccupied with the inherent volatility of nature and with the dynamics of unpredictable and unstable systems in the natural world' (Freedman 1992: 26). Ilya Prigogine's discovery of the so-called dissipative structures could have a correlate in the social sciences, since it is reasonable to expect a higher instability in the phenomena with which they deal. In this respect, David Freedman, in an article published in the *Harvard Business Review*, observed that 'chaos theorists and complexity scientists may not be studying business organizations, but their perspective has already shaped recent managerial literature' (1992: 33). A particularly representative example is Peter Senge's best-selling book *The Fifth Discipline*. According to Senge (1990), organizations must be analyzed from the vantage point of living systems. He attacked Taylor's reductionist thought and advocated the use of 'systems thinking' as the most adequate way to understand organizational behavior in a holistic form and create an authentic 'learning organization'.[6] Senge distinguishes himself from other authors of systemic rationalism, though he is to some extent undoubtedly indebted to them, because he adopts the paradigm of complexity associated with the developments of what is usually known as 'second cybernetics'. Science changes, hence management theory must also change if it still claims to have a scientific foundation. The new techniques of the postbureaucratic model can be 'scientifically' justified if necessary. Tom Peters, for example, did not hesitate in resorting to analogies between administration and quantum mechanics in *Thriving on Chaos* and *Liberation Management*.[7]

In sum, the new paradigm of management was born in the midst of a 'technological revolution' that is considered its determining factor and to which it displays a definitely positive axiologic position. In addition, the rhetoric of the literature aims at gaining greater legitimacy by underscoring the idea of a cultural rupture, postmodernity and being in line with a new perspective born in hard sciences.[8] Both strategies are consistently used to support a conception that emphasizes the idea of leaving aside hierarchic control. However, some theorists of the new paradigm were not satisfied with just offering management techniques or models. Consequently, they devoted a major part of their writings to argue about the insertion of these models within a new type of society, itself the result of the transcendental change of which we are witnesses. Many authors presented the technological, economic and social transformations of the last quarter of the twentieth century as indicating the coming of a new social order, to which I turn to next.

The knowledge society and its impact on organizations

In a world where technology has acquired a preeminent role, and services constitutes a privileged sector of the economy, a tendency seems to have emerged: the growth of activities and occupations that are knowledge intensive. This lends plausibility to the hypothesis that a new type of society in which knowledge is more important and necessary has appeared. While the topic of the superseding of capitalism by something qualitatively different is not quite new, the theorists of the new paradigm of management consider the relevance of knowledge as a core element.[9] Peter Drucker reintroduced some ideas from previous works to develop his conception of the new society, emphasizing that he did not intend to formulate a prediction but to comment on changes that were currently happening. His book *Post-capitalist Society* is a true manifesto about the characterization of the new society. Other authors like William Halal (1986) and Richard Crawford (1991) offered similar views. However, Drucker deserves especial attention by virtue of his remarkable influence as a management guru, based on his extended career beginning in the late 1930s that turned him into the most important living philosopher of management. The prestige and authority of his word among management theorists and practitioners alike is, therefore, an element that grants him a leading role as spokesman of the new paradigm.

According to Drucker (1992c), knowledge is the main resource for individuals, organizations, and countries in the new society. In this regard, he claimed that the developed countries have 'already moved into post-capitalism with new "classes" and a new central "resource"' (1992b: 92). Today, the new decisive factor of production is knowledge, overcoming in this sense capital, land, and labor. For him, these last three factors cannot guarantee an authentic competitive advantage. 'Rather, *management* has become the decisive factor of production [emphasis in original]' (1992a: 8), he maintained, establishing a sort of equivalence between management and knowledge. Instead of capitalists and proletariat, the relevant classes of post-capitalist society are the 'knowledge workers' and the 'service workers' (Drucker, 1992b). The same forces that caused the collapse of Communism as regime and of Marxism as an ideology making capitalism obsolete as a social system. Nevertheless, the society that will replace it will not be 'anticapitalist': the institutions of capitalism will live on, he affirmed. The ruling elite will consist of the knowledge workers (i.e., executives, professionals, and entrepreneurs), who possess 'the insight to allocate knowledge to productive use,

94 *Capitalism, Social Privilege and Managerial Ideologies*

the way the "capitalists" knew how to allocate capital to productive use' (1992b: 94). Knowledge workers develop their activities within organizations, but unlike traditional employees they are proprietors of their own knowledge, which becomes the new 'means of production'. This allows them to easily transfer this intellectual capital to where they please (1992a, 1992b). The figure of the Druckerian knowledge worker is, in certain aspects, analogous to Robert Reich's 'symbolic analyst', who manipulates oral and visual symbols (data, words, and representations) in a task of problem identification and solving. Although Reich does not use Drucker's incisive rhetoric, he also argued about the relevance of this type of workers, by concluding that 'the only true competitive advantage lies in skill in solving, identifying, and brokering new problems' (1991: 184).

Walter Wriston also agreed with Drucker. He posited that the 'drama of economic production', once dominated 'by the brute force of industry' will now depend on 'products and processes that consist more of mind than of matter' (1992: 7). Similarly, Richard Crawford spoke about the emergency of talent, intelligence, and knowledge as an economic force on a worldwide scale. In a typical 'good versus evil' comparison, he asserted that the knowledge society will have values opposed to those of the industrial society, which emphasize: equality instead of hierarchy, individuality and creativity instead of conformity, diversity in lieu of standardization, preoccupation for the quality of life and the preservation of the environment as opposed to the maximization of material wealth, quality instead of quantity, self-actualization prevailing over security, and the like (1991). Given such statements, also common in other books (e.g., Harris, 1985; Clarke and Clegg, 1998), the axiological orientation of the new paradigm thus appears to lack precedent in relation to previous management thought. While authors like Mayo and Taylor exhibited in their discourse a concern for solving social problems, the advocates of this new ideology have more ambitious goals: bringing paradise to earth. In the coming society, they argue, the role of capital will be limited to release the potential of the knowledge workers and to assure their productivity.

The category of the knowledge worker, as presented in the recent administrative literature, is key to the understanding of both the contemporary organizational developments and those that, according to the same sources, will take place in the future. This has brought about a noticeable concern for education at all levels, but especially for higher education. If, as Hayes and Watts argued in their book *Corporate Revolution*, 'intellectual and knowledge-based skills should permeate every part of the corporate structure' (1986: 106), then it is clear why advanced countries pay much attention to the issue of their citizens' education. The importance of education was also emphasized by Arthur Wirth, who affirmed in *Education and Work for the Year 2000* that corporate leaders 'are convinced that a viable labor force depends on having employees who have strong number and literacy skills — and above all the ability to learn, to think abstractly and contextually, and to collaborate in problem solving' (1992: 42). It cannot be otherwise, since the identified tendencies point to a redefinition of the nature of work: 'more high-order thinking, less nine to five' (Kiechel, 1993: 39).

The centrality of the idea of learning not only refers to individuals, but also to 'organizacional learning', which became a largely discussed issue within the new paradigm of management. Moreover, the recurrence of themes like the new cognitive models and the fact that consulting companies, allegedly populated by knowledge workers, are portrayed as the model for tomorrow's successful organizations constitute one more form of emphasizing the importance that the new paradigm assigns to knowledge in contemporary society. The interest for knowledge in the business world grew dramatically in the 1990s.[10] Friso den Hertog (1998) commented, in order to illustrate this 'knowledge mania', that his publisher believed that adding the word 'knowledge' to a book title would double its sales.

The rhetoric about the new society and the sweeping technological advances contributed to the emergence of knowledge management (KM) as a central theme in the managerial literature. This approach basically deals with two questions, which are respectively related to information technology and the behavioral sciences: (1) how organizations capture, store, and retrieve knowledge for later use, and (2) how to socialize or make 'explicit' to the whole organization the knowledge that individuals acquire through their working experience but do not share with their peers. In association with KM appeared the concept of intellectual capital, according to which the knowledge embodied in people is a strategic organizational asset. Thomas Stewart (1997) noticed in his best-selling book *Intellectual Capital: The New Wealth of Organizations* that, as knowledge became the most important factor of production, the management of intellectual assets has turned into the most relevant task in organizations.[11] Beyond this declamatory assertion, most theorists of intellectual capital try to measure objectively its value for business firms.[12]

Knowledge Management is a clear example of rational control. It tries to codify or formalize every piece of information considered relevant for organizational purposes, not only the information routinely gathered and not exploited, but also the workers' tacit or personal knowledge. The organizational structures more apt for this kind of management practices, and within which knowledge workers must act, differ from the traditional ones (Stewart, 1997). For Halal, the information era generates an obvious pressure towards organizational change, given that the new jobs 'are quasi-scientific in nature, and scientists are notorious for resisting authority, because their work cannot be dictated but requires independence of thought and action' (1986: 177). Thus, the traditional hierarchical model is not advisable. In conclusion, more flexible models, in which knowledge, initiative, and even power flow down, up, and throughout the organization, are very often recommended as the most adequate and, in the last instance, as the only functional ones in the new knowledge society.

The postbureaucratic organization and the twilight of hierarchy

According to Harlan Clevellan, a 'revolution' in the organizational world was under way: the 'twilight of hierarchy'. The cause behind such a dramatic change is found in information technology. In the 'new knowledge environment', it is necessary 'to rethink the very nature of rule, power, and authority' (1989: 122).

Greater participation in decision making on the part of all employees becomes a basic condition for good organizational performance. This implies 'more openness, not as ideological preference but as a technological imperative' (1989: 123). As a result, the nature of management undergoes a very important change. This argument is characteristic of the thesis that links the evolution of technology to two distinguishing features of this new managerial ideology: the knowledge society and the obsolescence of the bureaucratic model.

For Rosabeth Moss Kanter, another recognized expert in the field, 'As work units become more participative and team oriented, and as professionals and knowledge workers become more prominent, the distinction between manager and nonmanager begins to erode' (1989a: 88). The bases of power suffer a mutation, she argued, because formal authority and its associated prerogatives are no longer appropriate in a world in which workers are pushed to think by themselves and work within organizations takes place under the imperative of synergetic action among different areas. In her opinion, we are witnessing the demise of hierarchy, as the bureaucratic stance towards order is being replaced by an 'entrepreneurial' drive towards creativity (Kanter, 1989b).[13]

As several theorists have affirmed, the organizations of the future will not resemble their predecessors. William Davidow and Michael Malone resorted to the notion of virtual reality, extending it 'one step further to reflect what is going on around us today' in the business world (1992: 4). Thus, they used the term 'virtual corporation' to describe the progressive dematerialization of organizations. For an external observer, they explained, the corporation will appear as having permeable borders and being in permanent change regarding its relations with customers and suppliers. Internally, it will be 'no less amorphous'. Departments and lines of authority will be in constant reform, and the 'very definition of employee' will have to be reviewed as some of the firm's clients and suppliers will be physically present at its offices and plants more often than its own workers (1992: 6). Therefore, the internal and external frontiers of organizations become diffuse, sparking the notion of a 'networked organization'. The supporters of this approach to deal with the multiple interrelations that bind companies and their subunits to each other considered that it allows organizations to maintain a flexible and rapid response capability, usually associated to the small enterprise, while simultaneously increasing their scope and complexity (Rockart and Short, 1991). During the first half of the 1990s, there was a flood of articles in business magazines about these issues, under such banners as 'modular organizations', 'network organizations', and the like (Tully, 1993).[14]

The organizations of the future will be flatter and more flexible. Gareth Morgan, a well known organizational theorist, summarized this tendency thus: 'Strong holographic tendencies are also being created in modern organizations through the introduction of microprocessing technologies that diffuse information, communication, and control' (1986: 105). This new technology allows for the appearance of communication networks whose effect, according to him, render unnecessary the controls of the hierarchical line. So, in his best-selling textbook *Images of Organizations*, Morgan affirmed, 'we need to break the hold of bureaucratic thinking and to move toward newer, less exploitative, more equal modes of interaction in organizations' (1986: 383). In order to achieve this, enterprises must strongly invest in human resources, redesign their structures, and put in practice new managerial processes. The proposal of several management theorists, from different perspectives, suggested leaving aside the traditional forms characterized by hierarchical authority, centralization, and well-delimited structures. Instead, managers should resort to 'designs that rely upon work teams, decentralized decision making, and informal networks crosscutting formal boundaries' (Useem and Kochan 1992: 399).

In many cases, the traditional dividing lines among authority, task, and function will simply be blurred until almost disappearing. In this regard, Larry Hirschhorn and Thomas Gilmore spoke about the 'borderless company'. The management of these organizations constitutes a true challenge that must nevertheless be confronted. The responsibilities of each organizational member are clearly defined in the traditional model; in contrast, new boundaries exist in the borderless company that will have their locus in the employees' minds and not in the organizational chart, which might potentially result in increased tensions in the workplace. Hirschhorn and Gilmore recognized that even in these organizations 'some people lead and others follow, some provide the direction while others have responsibility for execution' (1992: 107). The fact that traditional lines of command and function disappear does not imply, according to them, that the differences between authority, talent, and knowledge cease to exist. Simply, new strategies must be developed to manage the 'new borders' of authority, task, politics, and identity.

The diagnosis of the new paradigm is very emphatic with respect to the criticism to the hierarchic model. Paul Adler observed that there was a generalized consensus according to which hierarchy asphyxiates learning. Ideas like this, he noted,

> are becoming the new conventional wisdom about work. This new gospel sets up Frederick Winston Taylor and his time-and-motion studies as the villain . . . It insists that detailed standards, implemented with great discipline in a hierarchical organization will inevitably alienate employees, poison labor relations, stifle initiative and innovation, and hobble an organization's capacity to change and to learn. (1993:97)

Nevertheless, Adler presented evidence from the experience at the NUMMI plant of GM-Toyota that supported the hypothesis that Taylorist time-and-motion methods as well as bureaucratic work designs are both functional to the efficiency of certain productive tasks. However, he acknowledged that this was not the dominant position.

This strong consensus against hierarchy and formal bureaucratic controls has a correlate in the importance assigned to informal organizational dynamics, in line with the new organizational model. Groups constitute the wave of the future, according to Charles Manz and Henry Sims (1993). In a similar vein, Richard Wellins et al. deemed the coming of empowered teams as a 'workplace revolution' (1991: 1). For Manz and Sims, the adoption of teamwork is sometimes motivated by a humanistic intention associated to an increase in workers satisfaction, but they considered that the most important determinants are the issues of productivity and quality. The emphasis on teamwork has also arrived to public administration, through David Osborne and Ted Gaebler's (1992) best-selling book *Reinventing Government*, which makes a call for decentralization and the displacement of hierarchy by participation and teamwork.

Very popular approaches like Total Quality during the 1980s and reengineering in the 1990s also contain an important component of participation and teamwork. Total Quality is considered more a philosophy than a set of techniques (Gamache and Kuhn, 1989) and is strongly associated to the perception of the success of Japanese organizational schemes.[15] Although this method has American origin and dates back several decades ago, its massive application in the Western world was prompted by the interest for Japanese management, where the techniques of Deming, Juran, and others have been used for decades (Garvin, 1988). Barley and Kunda (1992) related it to a broader topic: the emphasis in organizational culture. Similarly, Donald Gamache and Robert Kuhn affirmed that TQM change initiatives are 'a lot less statistics and a lot more culture and operational philosophy than is generally recognized' (1989: 23). However, as noticed by Peter Drucker, Statistical Quality Control (SQC) has a potential integrating effect, since it combines Taylor's engineering approach with that of the human relations movement. Both perspectives, Drucker indicated, were traditionally considered as antithetic and 'mutually exclusive', but in Total Quality they go hand in hand (1990: 96). Taylor and Henry Ford, he argued, opposed controls by inspection in the past as much as Deming's followers at present, but the rigorous methodology of SQC was necessary to achieve that control be built into the process itself.[16] Thus, the rational aspects underpinning Total Quality are actually as important as the normative ones, which nevertheless appear as more popular.

Reengineering has some points in common with Total Quality, like its emphasis on processes and customers, but its radical divergence is based on the fact that it aims at redesigning everything from scratch, whereas Total Quality, in Michael Hammers's words, 'is about improving something that is basically okay' (1993: 29). Hammer and Champy, the fathers of this approach, insisted on the issue of self-managed groups, but Hammer admitted that the implementation of their proposal was 'a very top-down, very autocratic, very nondemocratic process' (1993: 33). In their book *Reengineering the Corporation*, Hammer and Champy (1993) declared that reengineering required the presence of a czar. Evidently, this recognition demonstrates that some allegedly democratic and participative models entail certain undesirable aspects, at least during their implementation.

In the tradition of the human relations school, the work of Edward G. Lawler stands out. His model tries to advance beyond the traditional participative practices of quality circles. In the 'high-involvement organization' (his neologism), the structure is constituted by 'minienterprises' that sell services and products to each other in a scheme of high decentralization. The organization is based upon teamwork, and according to Lawler, this requires particular attitudes on the part of those who integrate it. Hence, he concluded, 'Clearly, this type of organization is not for all individuals' (1986: 206). For him, the conditions were set for many companies to massively apply employee-involvement plans; but he later revised this opinion and stated that he was 'probably too optimistic, in retrospect' (1993: 27). The materialization of his participative model does not seem easily replicable, since even in companies like Motorola, which has been using advanced techniques of participative management for many years, the managers are 'still basically trapped in the command-and-control model' (1993: 26).

Other advocates of the new paradigm had more optimistic appreciations. Boyett and Conn, in *Workplace 2000: The Revolution Reshaping American Business*, also analyzed these tendencies. The companies of the future will be flatter, more flexible and aggressive, they claimed, following the dominant line of thinking. In addition, they emphasized that all the employees in an organization will be part of a team. They harshly criticized 'scientific management', which they held responsible for the tedious and uninspiring tasks that the American worker was required to perform. For them, the influence of Taylor and his disciples survived under other names until the 1970s. Boyett and Conn vindicated the Hawthorne experiments, concluding that if the results of these experiences 'had been fully understood and applied, America might have reached *Workplace 2000* half a century earlier' (1991: 87). According to their prognosis, in the organizations of the twenty-first century, 'rigid hierarchies will be dismantled' in order to bring about 'harmony and unity' between management and workers. In this regard, the following comment is a clear illustration of normative control: 'More importantly, the goal will be to attach people mentally and emotionally to the workplace — to make them feel intimately connected to the corporation even if in reality that connection is transitory' (1991: 109).

In synthesis, the literature analyzed so far presents a discourse that suggests more flexible models of organization as successors of bureaucracy. Quality circles, 'empowerment' of the existing human resources, flatter structures, and greater employee participation and involvement are some of its central themes. The new organizational forms are depicted as embodying basically positive values. Depending on the author in question, this portrayal may vary from moderate praise to overt panegyric. However, it is again pertinent to quote Drucker, who, perhaps against the current, contended that although people will manage themselves in the organizations of the future,

> this does not mean we all shall be working in free-form organizations. That is nonsense. A land animal on this earth cannot be more than six inches in size without having a skeleton. Companies are the same. Above a very small size, every company needs the skeleton of a formal command structure. (1992a: 348)

This argument points out the limits of this 'democratic' and 'egalitarian' new organizational model. Undoubtedly, power and differences between people will continue in organizations, although new guises may be adopted for masking them. In this regard, the new paradigm of management, which pretends to have a revolutionary character, provides new ideological representations about the world of work, some of which I discuss in the next chapter.

Notes

1 See, for example, Ouchi's (1981) best-seller *Theory Z*.
2 Redman (1991) indicated that the term 'paradigm' has been used in a multiplicity of ways: economists, for example, associated it to a sort of weltanschauung. Here, I conceptualize paradigm as a set of assumptions about the nature of the world and, in particular, about the functioning of organizations that are shared by the management professional and academic communities. When using the term paradigm, my emphasis is on the consensual element of scientific knowledge, which is central to Kuhn.
3 This ideology has even been characterized as the new 'spirit' of contemporary capitalism (Boltanski and Chiapello, 1999; Chiapello and Fairclough, 2002).
4 Postfordism has been defined as 'a new model of capitalist development, of a rather progressive type' (Leborgne and Lipietz, 1994: 32).
5 For postmodern philosophers, one of this movement's central characteristics is the death of the 'great narratives'. When Lyotard (1992 [1986]: 31) asked rhetorically, 'how can the great stories of legitimation continue being credible?', he announced the disappearance of the need for the existence of ideologies to legitimize a social order. In postmodern society, the social order (or disorder) does not demand an ideological legitimation.
6 The first mention of the idea of 'organizational learning' is, however, much older. It dates back to the 1960s and is rooted in previous work in aerospace engineering (Huber, 1996).
7 The list is endless. Many 'respectable' management thinkers or gurus raised this kind of analogies as justification for their rhetoric. Some of them base their work entirely upon them, like Margaret Wheatley (1992) in *Leadership and the New Science*.
8 In fact, both legitimatory rhetorical artifacts usually come together. Of course, this is not strange, since postmodern theorist often support or justify their claims upon the discourse of chaos and complexity theory. See, for example, Cilliers (1998).
9 In the 1950s, Dahrendorf (1959) used the term post-capitalism to talk about the society of his time and to describe its class structure, emphasizing that the social conflict that Marz spoke of was now contained and had been institutionalized. Bell (1973) also dealt with the knowledge society in his book *The Coming of Post-Industrial Society*.
10 On average, the number of published articles on knowledge management indexed in ABI/INFORM database increased more than 100 per cent each year from 1988 to 1999 (Despres and Chauvel, 1999).
11 In this work, Stewart (1997) deplored management fads (i.e., reengineering, the virtual corporation, the learning organization, etc.) and even spoke about a 'fad denouncing fads'. Although in a quite faddish style, he declared to offer, in lieu of managerial fads, 'understanding' in a turbulent business environment.
12 See, for example, Sveiby (1997), Liebowitz and Suen (2000), and Petty and Guthrie (2000). Intellectual capital is not limited to the knowledge possessed by employees, also known as human capital, but includes other elements as well.
13 One may certainly ask how is it possible to mention an 'entrepreneurial emphasis' within a 'post-entrepreneurial society' — Kanter's own term for disorganized capitalism. This can be explained by the urge of many management theorists to coin and give ample diffusion to their neologisms.
14 Nevertheless, some executives did not seem affected by these developments. For example, Andrew Grove, Chairman of Intel and a management writer as well, affirmed that the virtual corporation was a 'business buzz phrase' that was 'meaningless' (Business Week, 1993: 40).

15 Total Quality has had a huge impact, and the literature on the subject multiplied in the 1980s. The approach advocated by Deming and Juran has been applied to public administration with certain modifications (Swiss, 1992) and even to the management of personal life (Roberts and Sergesketter, 1993). For a historical description of this management approach, see Garvin (1988) and Huggins (1998).

16 According to Drucker (1990), quality circles, characterized by the workers' participation, enjoyed wide success in Japan and accounted for the massive adoption of Total Quality in that country. He pointed out that the failure of attempts to install quality circles in American companies was due to the fact that they were established without its counterpart of SQC, that is to say, they lacked the accurate information feedback that was available in Japan.

Chapter 10

The World of Work under Disorganized Capitalism

The postbureaucratic model of management reflects important changes in the ideological representations of the rulers and the ruled in the realm of organizations. In this chapter, I discuss the most important ones. In the first place, I analyze the new image of workers and managers. Then, I consider how a new social Darwinism in the social sciences, which emerged almost contemporarily to the ideology of the new paradigm, depicts the transformations in the world of work and somewhat influences management thinking. Finally, I present two conceptions related to the alleged generalization of the postbureaucratic model: the advent of meritocracy and the end of alienation.

The new image of workers and managers

In a world increasingly dominated by corporations, as capitalism continues its expansion on a planetary scale, the ruling elite appears redeemed from its bad reputation of the late nineteenth and early twentieth centuries (the time of the 'robbers barons').[1] Now, the management of corporations proudly exhibits a more ethical image, which coincides with the growing concern for business ethics in the managerial literature of the 1980s and 1990s (e.g.: Harmon, 1996; Badaracco, 1997; Dalla Costa, 1998). Strategic alliances between companies, their clients, and their suppliers to develop activities or projects in common are regarded as a core feature of the business world of the future. This has interesting consequences for the behavior of top managers, since dealing with these 'new associates' requires a special capability to gain their confidence and respect. Consequently, Rosabeth Moss Kanter wrote about the importance that the managerial elite of the future, the 'business athletes' as she defined them, be guided by the 'highest ethical standards' (1989b: 362). Alan Webber (1993) tackled the same problem by indicating that the creation of trust among the members of corporate networks is a central aspect that managers will have to face in the knowledge society. This 'new ethics', however, seems inspired by a clearly instrumental rationality: the world of the future demands the establishment of conditions of trust between parts engaged in a commercial relationship in order for it to endure. The morality of the contractors and, consequently, the mutual confidence they have in each other lead to greater profits in their operations. Thus, the reduction of moral behavior to economic profit is here demonstrated in a fascinating form.[2] Nevertheless, the ethical aspects of business management do not only refer to the commercial relationships among corporations, but also to issues pertaining to workers, management, and the community at large.[3]

This new positive image is further demonstrated by the increasing interest that organizational leaders, at least at the discursive level of the management literature, show for other 'politically correct' ideas that received little or no attention in previous ideologies. Sensitivity to the communitarian and ecological environment is an attitude that Philip Harris identified as a characteristic of the new management style of 'the post-industrial work culture'.[4] He also indicated that organizations must advocate the strengthening of a 'wellness lifestyle' among their employees (1985: 298). The 'new age business climate' and some aspects of spirituality, one of the latest managerial fads, are also in line with this managerial philosophy.

The transformations in the world of work during the 1980s have had an evident influence on the new image of management. The word 'entrepreneur', which in the 1950s when Whyte wrote *The Organization Man* was 'almost a dirty word' (Bennet, 1990: 226), regains an honorable and positive meaning. Thus, the figure of the capitalist owner, depicted as an innovating entrepreneur, receives a renewed aura of respectability. On the other hand, as the example of John Cage's (1992) book *From the Ground Up* shows, the small and medium enterprises are portrayed as the dynamic force behind the American economy, which contributes to emphasize the positive characterization of the small entrepreneur. This tendency is also present in the work of Peter Block (1987), who severely criticized the figure of the manager-bureaucrat and suggested that its replacement should be the 'empowered manager', worth praising for his or her creativity, thrust, and dedication to work, almost like an entrepreneur. In a similar vein, Gifford Pinchot (1985) introduced the neologism 'intrapreneur' to refer to employees who are empowered to create new products at their companies without being subject to bureaucratic constraints. These persons, gifted with 'entrepreneurial traits', may help to significantly improve the profitability of their organizations if allowed to follow the instinct of their 'animal spirits', to borrow from Keynes's expression, within their companies.

In a context in which the traditional distinction between worker and manager appears complex, since formal authority becomes diluted within the framework of a postbureaucratic model, the rhetoric of leadership acquires growing relevance when analyzing the image of the manager. It should be noted that leader and manager continue being different concepts (Kotter, 1990), but some authors do not respect this distinction and try to overcome it, affirming that the manager of the future must have strong leadership skills. The new leader will necessarily be more democratic, as Laumann et al. pointed out, asserting that the processes of technological change, which many organizations will have to implement, require a new role for management: 'Managers give up control and become resources encouraging cooperation and trust rather than authoritarian guards' (1991: 14). In synthesis, managers at all levels are depicted in a positive light, though the term 'manager' itself has lost part of its appeal. Managers are no longer 'bureaucratic robots'; instead, they have to possess dynamic leadership capability and a strong aptitude for acquiring knowledge if they pretend to remain at privileged positions.

The ideological change brought about by the new paradigm was also accompanied by real phenomena of organizational change during the last two decades. I refer to the fever of mergers and acquisitions that implied in many cases the necessity to dramatically diminish the size and manpower level of many companies (downsizing). Massive dismissals at all the levels, but especially at middle management, entailed the 'death of the organization man' (Bennet, 1990).[5] During the height of the bureaucratic model, a 'psychological contract' existed between the organizations and their employees under which the latter traded loyalty and experience for a secure guarantee to remain employed and to enjoy a predictable career in the company. However, 'with layoffs and downsizing, the old contract has been broken' (Duck, 1993: 115).[6] Not only did the promise of an organizational career within the company disappear, as observed by Drucker (1993b) who acknowledged that the managerial ladder had ceased to exist, but also the assurance of job stability. Thus, some theorists indicated that labor stability yielded its place to 'job resilience'. So, it became fashionable to speak about a new psychological contract under which 'the employer and the employee share responsibility for maintaining — even enhancing — the individual's employability inside *and outside* the company [emphasis in original]' (Waterman and Waterman 1994: 87-88). In this context, the image of the worker changed, and the problem of employee motivation, after the rupture of the traditional psychological contract associated to the organization man of the 1950s, returned to the center of attention.

Part of the recent managerial literature focuses on self-actualization and the name of Abraham Maslow has regained prestige among those who speak about 'new age business' (Nichols, 1994). In the postindustrial era, however, some authors postulated the exhaustion of the motivation theories that were inherited from the human relations school. Such is the case of Michael Maccoby (1988), a Harvard psychologist, who criticized the framework of Maslow's needs scale and suggested that a 'theory of social character' becomes more adequate to explain the motivational processes of present-day workers. As organizations undergo mutations towards more flexible, flatter forms, the opportunities to obtain promotions reduce drastically. For Maccoby, the psychological rewards derived from a social relationship carried out according to the expectations of the role that each actor prefers constitute his or her main motivation for action. A person can be fitted within a classification of ideal types that define his or her 'social character', and the principal motivating factor for individuals within organizations is the ability to work in a position according to the ideal type that corresponds to each one of them. Hence, it is assumed that successful role performance satisfies a personal necessity that is of an intrinsically social character.

The job plays the most important role in this theory of human motivation by making it possible for individuals to develop the role they wish. To motivate somebody becomes a minor problem for management, since according to Maccoby's scheme, it is just enough to give employees the opportunity to carry out the role that motivates each of them. Maccoby's theory relates, in some way, to the self-realization concept because the effective performance of a job role is what gives satisfaction per se. Both conceptions, leaving terminological aspects aside, are very similar. Though Maccoby is critical in his appreciation of Maslow's contribution, his own formulation does not differ significantly from the position of those who recommend helping individuals to pursue self-development. For Maccoby, the maximization of self-development takes place as a result of a successful social-role performance within a job situation, but this makes his approach a subspecies of, and not a different species from, previous human relations theories.

Maccoby wrote about a new generation of Americans, typically composed of couples in which both spouses work, that is defined not by their age but by their values and whose 'main goal at work is self-development'. These individuals, whom he denominated self-developers, 'are motivated to solve problems cooperatively with co-workers, customers, and clients. They are ready to learn and succeed in the new workplace, which demands a combination of technical knowledge and teamwork' (1988: 20). Maccoby not only devised a theory of motivation, but also presented a new image of the employee. For him, the motivational structure of the worker, mainly oriented to professional self-development, is different from that of the nineteenth-century worker. The self-realization derived from the satisfaction of professional aspirations, so important for today's workers, appears as the central element.[7] The loss of job security will have to be compensated by organizations with the offer of employment positions that provide a professional challenge and an opportunity to acquire new knowledge. In the knowledge society, increased training and the opportunity to gain new experience and skills are an intangible remuneration that will have a positive effect on workers. The mere provision of a demanding job will be a sufficient motivating element for their self-development. This new emphasis on worker motivation is quite noteworthy, as it suggests that providing jobs, in a world in which a shortage of employment positions is apparently forthcoming, is considered by itself a powerful motivating element.

In the presentation of the new image of the worker, it is also necessary to analyze the conception about the workforce control characterizing the new paradigm. Richard Walton, an organizational behavior professor from the Harvard Business School, was one of the first authors who wrote about a new strategy for managing the labor force. He asserted that the old strategy of control, inherited from Taylor's thought, should be replaced by a strategy of commitment based on a nontraditional view of the worker's nature. Successful companies, assured Walton (1985), nurture and foster their workers' involvement and participation through empowerment and freer supervision methods. These organizations use ample job descriptions, a drastic reduction of managerial levels, and the task responsibility rests not in individuals but in teams, which are all practices recommended by the new paradigm theorists. 'At the center of this philosophy is a belief that eliciting employee commitment will lead to enhanced performance', indicated Walton (1985: 80), adding that the evidence obtained at some plants of General Motors, Procter & Gamble, and others, supported this conclusion. In this new conception, power descends from the peak of the managerial hierarchy and flows throughout the organization, releasing its members from their constraints. The principal point of this strategy responds to a change in the basic assumptions about 'the nature of employees'. McKersie and Walton maintained that the managerial beliefs on this subject could hinder or facilitate the transit towards the learning organization. 'Are employees thought of as cogs in a machine who have to be told precisely what to do, or are they people who can be trusted to think for themselves and the organization?' they asked (1991: 244). If organizations do not adopt this latter perspective about the nature of the worker, it is unlikely that programs destined to improve productivity have a positive and lasting effect.

Walton's strategies of control and commitment are quite similar to McGregor's Theory X and Theory Y. Both authors claimed that there is a set of basic assumptions that determine management's stance towards the labor force (whether we call them Theory X and Y, strategies of control and commitment, or whatever). Therefore, it seems that this is another case of 'old wine in new bottles'. The only difference lies in the emphasis on the construction of an organizacional culture that incorporates the new assumptions about the nature of the worker as one of its constituent elements. One of the aspects that makes possible to draw a distinction between the new paradigm and the human relations ideology regarding the management of the labor force is the utilization of organizational culture as a form of control. For instance, Terrence Deal and Allan Kennedy (1982: 16) pointed out that 'a strong culture enables people to feel better about what they do, so they are more likely to work harder'. According to these authors, in the organizations of the future, middle management will disappear and 'will be replaced by mechanisms of social influence — by emphasis on culture'. Their term for the postbureaucratic model is the 'atomized organization', whose characteristic will be 'the no-boss business', and they considered that for it to be effective, 'strong cultural ties and a new kind of symbolic management will be required' (1982: 177).

The advocates of the new paradigm coincide in emphasizing the turn from external control by direct supervision to self-control. These are indeed the recommendations of Henry Sims and Peter Lorenzi: 'The self-managed employee is the natural, ultimate expression of the new leadership paradigm' (1992: 197). Waterman (1987: 75) denominated this 'directed autonomy', which is a truly accurate expression because it stresses that the goals of the workers' actions are not their own, but those of management. Consequently, this 'autonomy' has actually important limits. If this form of control is effectively achieved, it will obviously bring great advantages to management since each control action, each surveillance action, implies a cost, which is thus reduced. The effectiveness of control over the employees can increase if the workers themselves perform it and, therefore, become docile agents of management by internalizing the objectives and values taught to them through a strategy of organizational culture indoctrination. According to many management theorists (e.g., Kilmann et al., 1995; Cameron and Quinn, 1999), organizational culture can be successful manipulated and designed, which is a goal that reflects a purely instrumental purpose: to increase economic profits.

The new conceptions of management and workers are framed in a context in which the very notion of job is subject to a drastic reconsideration. One of the most audacious speculations, but not for that reason devoid of logic, is that of William

Bridges (1994), who claimed that the end of the job was imminent.[8] For him, the noteworthy fact is not the massive loss of jobs, but 'what is disappearing is the very thing itself: the job' (1994: 47). This 'much maligned social entity', in Bridges's words, is a species whose time of extinction has arrived. Humanity will soon experience a 'huge leap in creativity and productivity', but the notion of job is not going to accompany such development (1994: 48). The social conditions that created the appearance of the job have disappeared, and hence the job must also disappear with them. Some solutions currently being adopted by organizations or recommended by the new paradigm advocates, like flexible working time (Bailyn, 1992; Jamieson and O'Mara, 1991) and the hiring of temporary manual labor (Fierman, 1994), are examples of this tendency. However, the change will be even deeper. So indicated Bridges, affirming that 'in place of jobs, there are part-time and temporary work situations' (1994: 48). He also spoke about the 'post-job organization', which beyond the neologism is no other than the new paradigm's postbureaucratic model. According to him, standardized work schedules were a social product of mass production and public bureaucracies and will go away with them.

The new image of the worker is in line with the rhetoric of the new paradigm and has been aptly synthesized by Bridges, who emphasized that 'everyone agrees that tomorrow's worker, untrammeled by old constraints of hierarchy and job boundaries, will be far more independent and self-directed than today's' (1994: 51). For Bridges, the knowledge worker, modeled after the expert or professional, constitutes undoubtedly the image of what will be the labor force of the future. Bridges interestingly observed a similarity between the post-job organization and the nineteenth-century organizations, in which there were owners and craft masters but not managers. In that situation, 'People were led, but whatever management existed was self-management'. Old self-management consisted in 'taking care of yourself while you followed the leader', whereas new self-management implies 'acting toward the business at hand as if you had an ownership stake in it' (1994: 51). Managers, however, will not disappear, although middle management will most likely be eliminated. Their new function will consist in training and supporting the employees, while also administering organizational processes. Bridges's conception about the new manager is not very illuminating, but what is indeed clear is that the employee of the future will have greater responsibilities and will have to act like today's manager, though lacking the prerogatives associated to that position.

In conclusion, the new image of the workers is that of people who do not need much control and discipline. They are self-managed by their own motivation about learning, continuous growth, and personal development, and their interests and expectations are in harmony with those of their employing organizations, in which they constitute the most vital asset. The worker of the future will be akin to a manager and will have to develop attitudes analogous to those of the latter.[9] In a comparison between the workers of the future and the craft masters, Bernard Avishai expressed a similar opinion, affirming that employees will have to be 'capable of taking on a task very nearly like that of the classical masters'. If not, he concluded, 'they will not work in businesses at all' (1994: 46).

Motivated, self-developer, self-managed (as well as quasi-manager), professional, and knowledge-friendly, the image of the worker under disorganized
capitalism is quite positive, contrasting notably with the image of the 'indolent
worker' typical of the nineteenth century. This new ideological representation may
serve the self-complacence of those who remain employed, or rather well
employed, as well as assuage the anxiety of those who expect to climb one more
step up a shortened managerial ladder. While the tedious and alienating job
allegedly disappears and leaves its place to a more enjoyable labor situation, an
increasing number of people are haunted by the spectre of unemployment because
of their lacking some particular trait or condition. Thus, some authors (Aronowitz
and DiFazio, 1994; Rifkin, 1995) have prophesied that even the end of work might
be approaching. This sounds awfully alarming, but the rationale explaining the
division between those who are privileged enough to hold a good organizational
position and those who are not has an undeniable social Darwinist flavor. I focus
my attention on this next.

The new social Darwinism

According to some advocates of the new paradigm, the selective pressures of a
highly competitive environment make the most efficient firms prevail, while those
that perform badly eventually cease to exist. Inefficient organizations do not
survive; they are eliminated by natural selection. In this regard, Gifford and
Elizabeth Pinchot, authors of the book *The End of Bureaucracy and the Rise of the
Intelligent Organization*, a true manifest of this new managerial ideology, wrote,
'The libertarians can appreciate this sometimes cruel discipline as the necessary
price of freedom from bureaucratic control by a government or corporate
hierarchy. Without the discipline of marketplace choices, freedom can lead to
confusion, chaos, selfishness, waste and despair' (1993: 54).[10]

However, in the popular business literature, the Darwinian conception of the
struggle for existence is not only used in reference to firms. The labor market is
perceived as more competitive than in previous decades, and most importantly,
there is a renewed impulse of the 'survival of the fittest' rhetoric. In the future,
Bridges (1994) prophesied, it is possible that half of the people will work 60 hours
per week while the rest will be unemployed. Stratford Sherman spoke about a
'brave new Darwinian workplace' in which the available job positions will
drastically outnumber the amount of people demanding them. Among the
tendencies that will characterize the new world of work, he mentioned some
already familiar to the reader: the disappearance of the managerial career and the
replacement of hierarchies by teamwork, emphasizing that 'workers will be
rewarded for knowledge and adaptability' (1993: 52). Those individuals with a
generalist mind-set who can work effectively switching functions that require
different abilities and disciplinary backgrounds as well as under diverse environments and situations will be the winners. Even though the Darwinian ferocity of
this situation is clear, Sherman maintained that the results are worth the trouble and
concluded with an extremely positive appraisal of all this, affirming that 'the

workplace will be healthier, saner, more creative, and yet more chaotic — like nature itself' (1993: 51).

It may appear as surprising that in the late twentieth century, a resurgence of social Darwinism occurred, but this is an undeniable fact. The rhetoric is the same, although the vehemence of some expressions has lessened. This phenomenon takes place in the context of the decline of the welfare state and the height of the neoconservative discourse. Michael Ruse (1998), a philosopher of biology, also noticed this renaissance of social Darwinism in the last decades of the twentieth century.[11] In the scientific discourse from the late 1970s onwards, a trend of positive reevaluation of Darwinism applied to the social sciences is easily discernible from the works of diverse authors.[12] The discipline of sociobiology, created by Edmund O. Wilson in 1975, is framed within this tendency. At present, this type of 'biologicist' theories has been applied to economics (Tullock and McKenzie, 1981), political science (White, 1981; Somit and Peterson, 1997), sociology (Maryanski and Turner 1993), and there has even been an attempt at reconciling sociobiology with a tradition apparently so opposite as Marxism (Paastela, 1991).[13]

Nineteenth-century social Darwinism provided a legitimating rhetoric but did not mean an important contribution to administrative thought, mainly because the discipline of management itself was in its infancy. This is not the case with this new wave of social Darwinism. In line with the attempts at basing the study of social behavior upon biological theories, some management scholars called for similar explanations to understand organizational outcomes. According to Pierce and White, the heritage from our hunter-gatherer ancestors, which we carry in our genetic blueprints, still influences our behavior today. They suggested that ethology and socioevolutionary theory should play a more prominent role to inform administrative practice. In particular, managers with a clear understanding of the relationship between evolutionary processes and human behavior 'can achieve desired organizational outcomes by cultivating a context consistent with the natural inclinations that influence human social action' (Pierce and White, 1999: 851). It appears that, insidiously, the search for the sociobiological basis of human behavior has already began to influence management thought. As the reader may imagine, a fertile theme for this kind of theories is leadership research. Actually, the new theories of leadership are turning away from situational concerns and focusing instead on the leader's traits, an emphasis that had been previously abandoned in the 1950s as a result of null findings. Robbins (1996), for example, affirmed that leadership might have a biological basis, and Nicholson (2000) has taken the issue one step further in his book about 'executive instinct'. The marriage between social Darwinism and management theory has never been so close to being consummated.

The world of the future, whose advent is imminent according to the recent management literature, is certainly a propitious place for a social Darwinist conception. George S. Odiorne, a disciple of McGregor and ardent defender of theory Y, expressed himself in his book *The Human Side of Management* with a tone quite compatible with that of neoconservative thinkers, criticizing amiability and 'niceness', and affirming that it was necessary to say farewell to 'Mr. Good-

Guy'. He described 'good-guyism' as a dominant cultural value in the United States, where 'the poor are "culturally disadvantaged", and midgets are "people of reduced stature"'. In this regard, he made the following observation:

> At a recent management conference I polled a group of executives on the question of whether it is now harder or easier to fire somebody than it used to be. About four out of five responded that it's now harder to fire people. This may be because of new laws and the limitations of new governmental controls, but I would suggest that it's also accounted for in part by the rising tide of 'niceness'. We let ourselves be patient when all of the evidence (and there's plenty of it, loud and continual) indicates that some action should be taken. Odiorne (1987: 145)

Not even William Graham Sumner would have put it in a cruder way, as this 'niceness', which should be eradicated, leads unquestionably to the survival of the 'unfittest'.

The massive layoffs of the 1980s may be explained on the basis of 'trimming the fat', streamlining organizations, and adjusting their structures to the new economic climate. In this new scenario, there is no room for good-guyism. The business firms are no longer secure resorts where the organization men and women exchanged loyalty in return for life-time employment, often regardless of their skills and productivity. At present, only the fittest are fortunate enough to remain employed. Sherman's article clearly exhibits a social Darwinist stance, and other authors who value positively this landscape also have certain affinities with a social Darwinist worldview. Beyond the 'moralizing ethics', which according to some management writers will guide the business world, the ideology of the new paradigm is clearly associated to a rebirth of social Darwinism that is part of the broader cultural realm.

The influence of sociobiology on the cultural climate of the 1980s and 1990s cannot be easily obviated. It is one more element demonstrating that this climate, within which the new paradigm of management is embedded, has a certain similarity with that of the managerial ideologies of the late nineteenth century, when social Darwinism was also a characteristic of the social thought of the time. Horowitz (1977), in his analysis of the dominant ideology in the United States, claimed that a revival of Malthusian and Darwinian conceptions was already clearly outlined in the early 1970s. The problem of unemployment was not so alarming then, but he noted an offensive of the bourgeoisie and the workers against the most unprotected social strata. This panorama did not alter, rather worsened in the 1980s and 1990s, as neoconservatism exhibited clear shades of social Darwinism in the work of intellectuals like George Gilder (1981). Furthermore, there is a consensus among social scientists that the sector of the underprivileged will increase considerably in the coming years, while in the American ideological realm there are no appreciable modifications: the presence of a social Darwinist stance remains firm.

This new social Darwinism provides a rationale for the dual or polarized society of disorganized capitalism. How are people sorted into the social structure? Is there any genetically inherited trait behind this process? The publication of

Richard Herschtein and Charles Murray's controversial book *The Bell Curve* offered a possible answer that must be understood as one more element within this broader ideological trend (Meyers, 1996). Herschtein and Murray asserted that intellectual ability is the most effective predictor of success, and the advocates of the new paradigm of management also raised similar claims. Their arguments, however, were not directly framed in terms of the struggle for existence or in a socioevolutionary theoretical framework. Rather, they pointed out at the emergence of a meritocratic society, which I discuss in the following section.

The ascent of meritocracy

The rhetoric of the emergence of talent and intelligence in the age of human capital, as shown in works like Crawford (1991) and Ridderstrale and Nordstrom (2000), suggests the idea of the establishment of a meritocratic basis for the new society. Saint-Simon's dream seems to become a reality. But to what extent is the new order 'meritocratic' and the social position of individuals determined by the knowledge they acquire? In a line of thinking that finds its antecedents in the Saint-Simonian utopia and in Bacon's New Atlantis, the defenders of the new paradigm assigned the role of central productive resource in the new society to knowledge.[14] In economics, the theory of 'human capital' endows this conception with academic rigor, establishing the importance of the knowledge acquired by people as a predictive element of their income and, therefore, of their social position. If it is true that greater intelligence leads to greater ability for learning and knowledge acquisition, then it is reasonable to think that the former will become an important competitive advantage for individuals. Robert Kelley (1985), for example, wrote about 'brainpower', the core strength of the 'gold-collar workers' who will be the stars of the workforce. Tom Peters underscored the importance of knowledge by saying 'it's skill-eat-skill' (1992: 758). In a similar vein, Thomas Clarke and Stewart Clegg (1998: 432) asserted, 'More than ever before management will be based on intelligence, creativity and the capacity to question and to learn'. For Charles Handy (1994), a renowned British guru, the new source of wealth in contemporary society is intelligence. In sum, the new paradigm indicates that the power and prestige, as well as the income level, of those with greater intelligence and knowledge will increase. However, in order to establish if this panorama is real or only a mere expression of desire, it is necessary to resort to the available empirical data.

Of course, the idea that our contemporary society is based on a totally opened system of social mobility predates the writings of the new paradigm theorists.[15] On this subject, William Goode wrote in the 1960s the following:

> we are assured that we live in an achievement oriented society, and the norm is to place individuals in their occupations by merit. Nevertheless, the inquiries of sociologists and psychologists demonstrate that as the child passes through the successive gateways to higher positions, the cumulative effect of class, race, sex, and other readily ascribed traits grows rather than lessens. (1967: 5)

The results of a very rigorous study carried out by Christopher Jencks et al. (1972) granted importance to the chance factor as a determinant of the individuals' social position and income. Yet, Arthur M. Okun, an Economics Nobel laureate, criticized this analysis by stating that the lack of an adequate explanation for the market's allocation of income to people did not imply that this allocation was the result of a chance game. The market, according to Okun, may reward a set of attributes that has yet not been identified or adequately operationalized. However, he points out that it is however possible to come to a negative conclusion: the intellectual quotient (IQ) might not be highly appreciated by the market, which values a multiplicity of individual characteristics of diverse nature (Okun, 1975).

Nevertheless, many people believe that IQ is the most important predictor of the income level. The publication of Herrnstein and Murray's (1994) book *The Bell Curve* is, perhaps, the latest and most popular version of this thesis.[16] Yet, available research does not support this belief. Samuel Bowles and Valerie Nelson (1974) found that the effect of intelligence (IQ), as a differentiated element with respect to the formal education level attained, is almost negligible in such a sense. More recently, Korenman and Winship (2000) concluded, using the same data of Herrnstein and Murray, that other variables, particularly parental family back-ground, might be more important than intelligence in determining economic success in American society.[17] John Cawley et al. (1997) also reported that observed cognitive ability is a poor predictor of an individual's wages, a finding that was confirmed in later studies (Cawley et al., 1999).[18] However, intelligence may be defined in an ampler sense, exceeding the mere IQ. This strategy is methodologically questionable inasmuch as a clear criterion of what exactly constitutes intelligence does not exist.[19] At this point, it is possible to fall in a peculiar circular argument. If one thinks that (1) 'success', which in our society is frequently identified with the income level, is determined by intelligence; but (2) intelligence, in turn, is measured on the basis of 'success', lacking a more elaborated indicator and responding to a tendency found in people's 'social imagery'; then the reasoning turns out to be self-referential and the prediction becomes trivial, since it only establishes an identity between two concepts. Obviously, this elementary reasoning error is in no way innocent, but has a deep legitimating effect.[20]

Perhaps the importance of intelligence has been overestimated. Therefore, I will consider the relevance of the individuals' education as predictor of their income level. Empirical analyses of factors determining the income level in Scandinavian countries revealed 'a decline of the role of education on income differentiation' (Therborn, 1992: 63). The result of these studies led Göran Therborn to think about the existence of 'a reason to doubt that the role of knowledge is the key to postindustrial societies' (1992: 65).[21] Naturally, it can be contended that the real impact of knowledge will only be observed in twenty years from now, since it would be premature to draw conclusions based on data from the 1970s and 1980s, or that the country sample was biased. However, Therborn's opinions are by no means isolated. More recently and with reference to the contemporary British society, Michelle Jackson et al. (2002) argued that, contrary to popular belief, there has been a decreasing trend in the importance of formal education as a determining factor of upward social mobility during the last decades. In any case, it is obvious that the knowledge-society meritocracy is quite far from what management theorists believe. The new paradigm's excessive emphasis in this aspect aims at legitimating an income distribution whose tendency is increasing inequality. To this end, this ideology stresses a meritocratic value that enjoys far-reaching respectability, as is the case of knowledge, while obscuring the role that ownership of the means of production and location within the existing structure of social privilege have in the perpetuation of social inequality.

Regarding this point and in consonance with previous research, Griffin and Kalleberg (1981) argued in their study of meritocracy in the United States that social class, operationalized through the criterion of ownership and control of the means of production, does influence economic and psychological rewards at work. They also indicated that 'at best, schooling serves to keep individuals out of the least advantaged classes, but its ability to place men in the most advantaged classes is weak indeed' (1981: 30). Their article tries to answer the question of the existence of a meritocracy in the United States. Although admitting that a direct relationship between occupational position and attained education exists, Griffin and Kalleberg wrote that, despite the popular acceptance that the idea of the meritocratic vision may possess 'and the uses to which it may be put, it does not appear to be the basis upon which men are sorted and selected into the American class structure' (1981: 31).

Moreover, it must be noted that the so-called structuralist models of individual earnings (i.e., those that privilege the individuals' positions in the structure of ownership and authority in capitalist firms as independent variables) have greater predictive power than those corresponding to human capital theory (Halaby and Weakliem, 1993). With this, I do not try to deny the relevance of knowledge and the role of education in the workforce formation; rather, I just intend to show the existence of a meritocratic fiction. Education is a valuable end by itself, given the personal development that people attain with this experience. Investment in education may also have a positive yield (Ashenfelter and Rouse, 2000), but what should not be lost sight of is that acquired knowledge is not the only, or even the most important, determinant of social position. As Tilly (1998) observed, there is ample evidence that some factors that can be characterized as categorical (e.g., race and gender) tend to offer a better explanation for the reproduction of social inequality and, in turn, account for much of the individual differences in human capital.

The analysis of the determinants of success on the basis of data from national surveys may prove a difficult task for identifying the various causal mechanisms at hand. Research with data from samples of individuals in particular work settings may be more apt to explain the processes that lead to career advancement and, therefore, economic inequality, since they may consider other types of variables that better represent the operating forces behind the process of reward allocation. Two theories are relevant in this regard. The first, contest-mobility systems, corresponds to the meritocratic ideal in which positions and salary raises are awarded based on ability and effort. The second, sponsored-mobility systems, suggests that the main determinant of the rewards obtained is the tenor of the relationship between employees and their supervisors. A recent study conducted by Sandy Wayne et al. (1999) in a large corporation located in the United Stated contrasted both types of mobility systems. The human capital and motivational variables of the contest-mobility theory were either not significantly or even negatively correlated to two dependent variables: assessment of promotability and salary progression, while the sponsored-mobility theory variables (quality of leader-subordinate exchange and mentoring relationship) had a positive and statistically significant relationship to both dependent variables. These findings clearly demonstrate that, contrary to the claim of the new paradigm pundits, the meritocratic ideal does not receive the expected support in organizational settings.

One of the most accurate answers to the question regarding a meritocracy based on intelligence, talent, and knowledge has been proposed by Jeffrey Pfeffer. According to him,

> In the so-called information age, a list of individual attributes providing power and influence is more likely to begin with great genius or intellect than with a physical characteristic such as strength, energy, and endurance. But such emphasis would be misplaced, for it is quite often the case that endurance triumphs over cleverness. (Pfeffer, 1992: 166)

For Pfeffer, the qualities that can give power to individuals are more related to those mentioned by C. Wright Mills when speaking about the 'market of personality'.[22] In fact, though it has been sustained that the individuals' contribution to a work team is basically a function of the pertinent knowledge brought to the task (Rockart and Short, 1991), other personal characteristics, in particular the ability for social interaction, are essential. This is recognized by several of the new paradigm theorists, and Goleman's (1995) providential 'discovery' of emotional intelligence is a proof of it.[23] Now, such social abilities are labeled as 'intelligent' in a legitimating attempt to preserve the banner.[24] The conclusion that must be learned is that knowledge, talent, and nonemotional intelligence are certainly not the sole determinants of success, but must be accompanied by other qualities. In fact, beyond a certain threshold, they may not even make a perceptible difference in the fate of individuals. In our contemporary society, the ability to establish satisfactory personal relationships, together with an acceptable level of knowledge, may well be the only 'meritocratic' factors determining success, social position, and income. Therefore, few grounds exist to trust in the imminent advent of a meritocracy based on knowledge and intelligence.

However, although meritocracy may be a fiction, the belief that it is real has real consequences. The legitimating effect this belief produces gives rise to what has been denominated the 'fairness trap' (Kaus, 1992). If the judgments of the market are perceived as supported on an authentic and socially accepted basis of merit and, therefore, as being 'fair', it is easier to equate economic success with 'personal worth'. This poses a great threat to social equality, as opportunities of advancement are limited to people not initially benefited with markets rewards. If, on the contrary, the judgments of the market are considered arbitrary, that is, based on chance or personal qualities considered irrelevant to the task in question, the risk of assimilating personal value with economic success or failure diminishes. So, the probability that later opportunities in life become governed by a vicious circle of path-dependence on previous failures decreases.

Unfortunately, the fairness trap is more real than hypothetical. As social psychologists have demonstrated, there is a generalized belief that we live in a just world (Lerner, 1998). People think that, in general, a fair correspondence is verified between each person's actions and the rewards and punishments obtained as a result of such actions. This notion serves to support the meritocratic fiction. Thus, although little evidence exists to believe that the imminent advent of a meritocracy based on knowledge and intelligence will occur, the new paradigm's advocates may probably gain some credibility in their fallacious proclamation of its present materialization or proximate rise. However, the attractive promises of this managerial ideology do not end there, since it also suggests more positive consequences for all workers: the psychological distress associated with the concept of 'alienation' will not be part of the future workplace.

The end of alienation

In many best-selling books and articles written by the most prominent thinkers of the new paradigm of management arises the implicit or explicit idea that the changes produced in administrative practices and theories follow a vector of progressive human liberation. The movement towards the postbureaucratic organization promises greater freedom for all, because work ceases to be a source of displeasure for employees, as it is presumed that the tedious, routine, or disagreeable tasks will be reserved to robots or computers. Such is, for example, the opinion of Avishai, who affirmed that 'for the first time in the history of industrial capitalism, the interests of the businesses are consistent with those of citizens, consistent with the yearning for intellectual cultivation, self-direction, uniqueness and zest in work' (1994: 46). In a time of epochal change, of the 'end of history', in which the revolutionary political ideologies of the past crumble like the Wall of Berlin, has it also arrived, in tight association with the advent of meritocracy, the end of alienation? To respond this question in an exhaustive manner is a task that exceeds the modest aims of this book. Nevertheless, the discussion of this issue deserves attention, as some of these ideas figure prominently in many writings dedicated to flexible structures, the end of hierarchy, employee 'empowerment', workplace 'democratization', organizational 'citizenship', and the overcoming of the labor-capital dichotomy in the new postindustrial order. Consequently, I will briefly contrast some claims of the advocates of this ideology against the available empirical evidence.

The term 'alienation' has been used with different scope and meaning by many authors. The great diffusion of the issue of alienation is rooted in Marxian thought, but the origin of the concept must be tracked back to German idealism. According to Bendix and Lipset (1966), Marx thought that the workers' alienation was inherent to the capitalist system and that the revolution of the proletariat would be precisely motivated by the psychological sense of deprivation produced by this situation.[25] Bendix and Lipset believed that the problem of alienation was associated to the dissatisfaction that people experience in their work. They considered that 'to Marx this psychological deprivation seemed more significant even than the economic pauperism to which capitalism subjected the masses of workers' (1966: 10). However, not only Marxists used the concept of alienation. Many scholars who do not respond to this tradition granted importance to this notion in order to understand social life. Robert Nisbet (1966), for example, affirmed that Marxian thought introduced the word into the social sciences of the twentieth century, but maintained that its contemporary usage also bears relation to some conceptions from Tocqueville, Weber, and Simmel. Similarly, Thompson (1980b) argued that non-Marxist theorists did not associate alienation with the capitalist system, but with bureaucracy. In this regard, the advent of the postbureaucratic, posthierarchic model of organization postulated by the new paradigm could be considered conducive to overcoming worker's alienation, since the organizacional cause that supposedly determines it tends to disappear.

Bernard Murchland observed that the alienation concept is multidimensional, being the object of diverse theoretical definitions. Among other aspects he emphasized that alienation 'is some form of nonparticipation' (1971: 14), in which the individual feels isolated while 'his needs (for identity, self-respect, and so forth) are frustrated by the contrary demands of the social structure in which lives' (1971: 15). This conception goes beyond the realm of the world of work, but it is illustrative to compare it with the discourse of the new paradigm, which very often highlights 'nonalienating' aspects like participation, identification with the organizational culture, and professional self-realization through the job performed. Michael Piore (1992) discussed the image of work under flexible production, and affirmed that the new organizational forms could be better understood as a return to what Hanna Arendt denominated 'action', which in Ancient Greece was a relationship between peers within a community of equals. This concept clearly differs from the idea of work (labor), characteristic of mass production and empirical referent of alienation in Marx. In a similar vein, Bridges's theory of the 'end of the job', portraying this as a 'much maligned' social institution (1994: 46), is suggestive of the same theme: if classic work (the 'job') is alienating, its disappearance may also imply that of alienation.[26] In sum, the recent management literature has depicted the changes happening in the world of organizations under an optimistic image of social progress, postulating the hypothesis of a progressive improvement in working conditions towards increasing autonomy, a diminution of oppressive and routine aspects, and greater possibility of self-realization.

A varied range of experiences is associated to the concept of alienation. Estrangement, lack of power, the sensation that the job performed does not cover one's expectations nor provides intrinsic satisfactions beyond mere monetary compensation; all of these can be considered indicators of alienation. It can be contended that a person who is not satisfied with his or her work undergoes a certain degree of alienation. Therefore, it is valid to use the notion of labor satisfaction as a proxy to the study of alienation, as Bendix and Lipset (1966) seem to suggest, though both concepts are not identical. It may be considered that someone who is not satisfied with the job does not perceive or experience it as a factor of self-realization. Such a sensation is undoubtedly included in the broader notion conveyed, from Marx onwards, by the term 'alienation'. This approach allows us to draw some provisional conclusions regarding the 'end of alienation' thesis.

Obviously, not all occupations or jobs produce the same degree of job satisfaction.[27] Those individuals who have greater control over their jobs, because they either are independent professionals or belong to higher managerial levels, tend to work longer hours than the rest. This led the economist Tibor Scitovsky (1976) to conclude that they might also experience more labor satisfaction. Thus, professionals and managers do not get the same psychological rewards from their occupations as the rest of the workers. So, if it is accepted that those jobs of a rather professional nature entail more satisfaction than other jobs, then the pretensions of the new paradigm of management could be well supported — at least, if it is also accepted that in the knowledge society the labor force will be mainly composed of professionals. At present, though, this perspective still resembles a futuristic utopia. Throughout the history of humankind, the more pleasant jobs or occupations were almost the exclusive patrimony of the ruling classes. Social privilege allowed individuals belonging to the upper social strata to choose the most pleasant occupations, in what Fernand Braudel (1983) deemed as a structural law. Will this law be reverted in the future? Will the knowledge society mean the generalization of some form of pleasant and nonalienating work?

Instead of developing a prophetic analysis, I will discuss whether work in contemporary society constitutes a motivating and satisfactory experience by itself. As I have already pointed out when referring to the human relations ideology, studies done at General Motors demonstrated that employees were content with their work, but at the moment of explaining the reasons for it, they talked about such aspects as pay, free time, and labor stability. This type of answer does not support the idea of the end of alienation, as work itself was not mentioned as being a self-realization experience. During the 1960s, several social researchers (e.g., Blauner, 1966) reported in their investigations a high index of job satisfaction, thus denying the significance of alienation in twentieth-century capitalism. These approaches were criticized by Daniel Bell in his article 'Work and its discontent', in which he argued that these studies, based on many cases in surveys conducted by management, ignored two fundamental points. In the first place, they failed to consider that what generated some level of satisfaction were not the intrinsic features of the task itself, but other aspects of the job situation — for example, the belonging group with its opportunities to socialize, to joke, etc. This, however, 'cannot be used to disprove the debilitating aspect of the organization of work and *its* failure to provide satisfactions [emphasis in original]' (1988 [1962]: 249).[28] In the second place, a positive answer in a questionnaire on labor satisfaction can be misinterpreted, since the worker is not often conscious about what other real options to his or her present job or occupation exist, and the mention of a state of satisfaction may actually be a disguised conformism. C. Wright Mills also adopted a similar position, raising a methodological caveat: 'we do not know what the questions mean to the people who answer them, or whether they mean the same thing to different strata'. Nevertheless, 'work satisfaction is related to income and, if we had measures, we might find that it is also related to status as well as to power', he concluded (1953: 229).

At the beginning of the 1970s, an ambitious study of the Work in America Institute indicated that a large number of American workers were dissatisfied with their jobs due to the tedious nature of their occupations (Moch and Bartunek, 1990).[29] The necessity to find a way out of this problem, which was clear at that time and could not be ignored, was a powerful determinant for the implementation of programs of job enrichment and quality of working life. In these programs, the idea of giving greater power of decision to the employees constitutes a central aspect.

Research performed by John Witte demonstrated that some elements of alienation could be reduced by means of participation. However, Witte (1980: 145) affirmed that 'increasing participation does not by itself guarantee a reduction in alienation'. In fact, the link between both aspects tends to be rather complex, as revealed by the findings of a recent study (Godard, 2001). Job satisfaction increases with low or moderate levels of implementation of the administrative practices associated to the new paradigm — those that involve participation and/or autonomous teamwork — but then decreases at higher levels, due perhaps to job stress. A similar nonmonotonic pattern was also observed with other variables like workers' self-esteem, sense of belongingness, etc.

Moreover, not only the organization of work can be oppressive, but also the boredom caused by an uninteresting or little challenging occupation constitutes in itself a potential source of alienation. 'Few tasks are more tedious and repetitive, for example, than stuffing computer circuit boards or devising routine coding for computer software programs', affirmed Robert Reich (1991: 175). In contrast to the 'prophets of the information era', whose prognostics spoke about the affluence of well remunerated positions for almost anyone possessing even minimal qualifications, Reich commented ironically that the dispassionate truth is that many jobs will fall within the category of 'routine production services'. In this regard, he wrote the following:

> The 'information revolution' may have rendered some of us more productive, but it has also produced huge piles of raw data which must be processed in much the same monotonous way that assembly-line workers and, before them, textile workers processed piles of other raw materials. (Reich, 1991: 175)

Although some current polls show that most workers declare to be satisfied with their jobs, a deeper analysis reveals, as discussed above, a different attitude. Robbins (1996), for instance, questioned the validity of such data given that in similar studies less than half of the workers responded affirmatively when asked whether they would choose the same job, and he also mentioned a survey of 600 employees at American corporations in which 34 per cent of them declared that they were considering quitting their current jobs because of stress. Furthermore, the available evidence demonstrates that there is a decline in reported job satisfaction in the United States (Sousa-Poza and Souza-Poza, 2000). This has even been recently admitted in the popular business press (Caudron, 2001). Not only is job satisfaction decreasing, but there is also evidence of a trend in rising job-related stress in many Western countries (Blanchflower and Oswald, 1999). All these facts suggest that for a large number of workers the job situation, instead of being a pleasant experience, has negative connotations.[30] This seriously undermines the belief in the coming of the end of alienation.

Notes

1   At that time, the denomination 'robber barons' was used in the United States to designate those industrials who amassed huge fortunes upon the sufferings of their workers and their unfortunate customers. Recent historical research from a neoconservative orientation has attempted to clean that image (Folsom, 1996).

2   See Parker (2002) for an interesting analysis of business ethics from a critical perspective.

3   For example, Goshal et al. (1999) suggested that corporations should demonstrate their true nature of 'value creators' by establishing a new 'moral contract' with employees and society.

4   Maynard and Mehrtens (1993) also emphasized the importance of ecological aspects in their book *The Fourth Wave: Business in the 21st. Century*. This concern is particularly evidenced in the literature on 'greening strategies' (Hart, 1997; Roome, 1998).

5   See also Sampson (1995) and Scarbrough and Burrell (1996).

6   These changes, however, are described in a positive light as being a turn towards interdependence. For Duck (1993: 115), 'employees are no longer dependent on the company in a hierarchical relationship. Now the company and its employees are interdependent.'

7   Heckscher (1995) also found this type of motivational drive in a qualitative study of the attitudes of middle managers, and referred to it as a 'professional ethic' in which there is a sense of loyalty to a task, mission, or project, but not to a company.

8   These same ideas were later presented in his best-selling book *Job Shift. How to Prosper in a Workplace without Jobs* (Bridges, 1995). For an even gloomier perspective on the disappearing world of work, see Rifkin (1995).

9   While this belief now seems commonplace, as suggested by Grey (1999), the idea is actually older. See, for example, M. Scott Myers's (1970) book *Every Employee a Manager*.

10 However, despite these opinions, which are particularly popular within the business community, more serious scholarly research has shown that Darwinian mechanisms do not necessarily sort out ineffective and inefficient organizations. The empirical evidence demonstrates that some witless and inefficient organizations may be profitable and grow, isolated in protective environmental niches (Hannan and Freeman, 1989; Carroll and Hannan, 2000).

11 A similar observation was made by Bannister (1988). For a detailed account on this revival, see Degler (1992).

12 See, for example, Dawkins (1976), Alexander (1979) and Barash (1986).

13 This work exemplifies the force of this approach, as even Wilson ironically condemned Marx saying that Marxism was 'sociobiology without biology' (1978: 191).

14 The novelty of a meritocratic system based on knowledge is not such. The Chinese social stratification system, whose mobility was based on rigorous examinations, is perhaps the oldest and best organized of all the known ones. However, the preparation for the examinations was long and expensive and those who came from wealthier

families had a clear advantage over the rest in these intellectual competitions. This suggests that meritocracy only existed in theory (Stewart and Glynn, 1971).

15 The term 'meritocracy' was coined by the British sociologist Michael Young, who published in 1961 *The Rise of Meritocracy*, a sociological fiction work.

16 See also Murray (1998).

17 See Fischer et al. (1996) for similar results and a sound methodological critique highlighting serious flaws in Herrnstein and Murray's book.

18 It has also been discussed the existence of a meritocracy in Great Britain. In this regard, Breen and Goldhthorpe (1999, 2002) appeared to close the debate, demonstrating that while 'merit', conceptualized in terms of cognitive ability and effort, may play a role in explaining mobility, its overall effect is quite minor in comparison to that of social class.

19 For more on the concept of intelligence, see Sternberg and Salter (1982). The existence of explicit and implicit theories of intelligence is explained in Sternberg and Powell (1982), whereas Carroll (1982) discusses some aspects of its measurement. At the moment, the identity between the denominated intellectual quotient (IQ) and the theoretical construct of 'intelligence' has frankly debilitated, since not only a theory of multiple intelligence appeared (Gardner, 1993) but also the concept of emotional intelligence (Goleman, 1995).

20 Interestingly, the association of social success to intelligence is not an idea that merely exists in the people's social imaginary. It has also been sustained by some intellectuals. For example, the father of sociobiology, Edward O. Wilson, even defined success as a form that intelligence adopts (Chorover, 1979), and. Robert Sternberg asserted that real intelligence should be translated into success. According to Sternberg (1996), a difference should be made between 'inert' intelligence (i.e., what IQ measures) and 'successful intelligence', which includes not only analytical ability (akin to IQ), but also the capability for creative thinking and practical intelligence to cope with and adapt to the demands of the environment.

21 Other authors would surely dispute such claim. Derber et al. (1990) argued that contemporary society could be characterized as a 'mandarin capitalism', in which there is a coexistence of the capitalist system of authority based on money with a new one commanded by the professionals who held the monopoly of credentialed expertise.

22 This type of criterion would seem to be applicable not only to income level but also to the access to labor positions within organizations. Jennifer Chatman concluded after a review of the available evidence that, instead of being based on 'job related criteria' (as could be attained knowledge and experience), 'selection appears to be based on such socially based criteria as "personal chemistry", values, personality traits and, possibly, on how closely recruits' preferences match organizational values' (1991: 461).

23 Not surprisingly, emotional intelligence has been applied to management. (Goleman, 1998; Goleman et al., 2002) in order to identify individuals with 'leadership potential'.

24 Similarly, the construct of 'leadership intelligence' (Murphy, 1996) is almost unrelated to the traditional concept of intelligence as cognitive ability.

25 According to Jonathan Wolff (1991), the problem of alienation in Marxist thought can be summarized in three aspects: first, that work under capitalism is meaningless for most of the workers; second, that they do not have control over their own job activities; and third, that they do not enjoy an effective participation in those aspects that concern them.

26 From a logical standpoint, this is not strictly so. The psychological malaise associated to the alienation experience may not necessarily be the result of a univocal cause, in this case 'classic work'.

27 It must also be noted that individual job satisfaction is contingent upon the fit between personality traits and job performed (Holland, 1985). Furthermore, it has also been

demonstrated that individuals who tend to be happier or experience things under a positive mood also tend to express higher levels of job satisfaction, independently of the type of job (Staw et al., 1986).

28 This type of reasoning is also present in Herzberg's two factor theory of job satisfaction.

29 In this case, the referent is the American society, but since management literature mostly refers to this country as an empirical exemplar, it may be considered significant. On the other hand, there are no powerful reasons to think that in other capitalist countries alienation does not exist.

30 See also Sennett (1998) for a grim portrait of the psychological consequences experienced by individuals in the 'flexible' workplace of the 1980s and 1990s. Moreover, in the United States, the adoption of innovative workplace practices (e.g., Total Quality, autonomous work teams, etc.) was associated not only to job stress, but also to a significant increase in occupational injuries and illnesses (Askenazy, 2001). Studies by Lewchuk and Robertson (1997), Yates et al. (2001), and Brenner et al. (2002) provide further evidence of the negative consequences that the adoption of supposedly empowering techniques has for workers.

Chapter 11

The Significance and Legitimating Contribution of the New Paradigm of Management

The significance of the new paradigm

Many of the recommendations made by the theorists and gurus of the new paradigm are based on lessons learned from the application of the latest administrative practices in real companies. Osterman (1994), using data from a survey of 694 American private establishments, reported that 35 per cent of those with more than 50 employees had developed some form of work reorganization (Total Quality, self-managed teams, and the like). Several variables appeared positively correlated with the adoption of these practices (e.g., the technological complexity of the productive process, a market highly exposed to international competitions, etc.). This demonstrates that the new paradigm had a repercussion in administrative practices, although it must also be indicated that a full-fledged adoption of the postbureaucratic model is not a reality. Advances in such direction exist, but there is no evidence affirming that even a small number of companies are presently managed according to this model (Thompson and O'Connell Davidson, 1995; Harley, 1999; Kärreman et al., 2002). On the matter, it suffices to remember Edward Lawler's comment, already mentioned, that he had been perhaps too optimistic in stating that all the conditions were set for a massive implementation of employee-involvement plans. An effective materialization of a posthierarchic model might be impossible. Such was, for example, the opinion of Edgar Schein (1989). For him, our deep assumptions about the organization of work might not favor such development. On the other hand, Elliot Jaques, another respected management guru, did not see the need for too radical organizational changes, affirming that 'the theorists' belief that our changing world requires an alternative to hierarchical organization is simply wrong, and all their proposals are based on an inadequate understanding of not only hierarchy but also human nature' (1990: 127).

Some opinions of the new paradigm theorists seem at first glance supported by empirical reality. One that seems quite credible is the pervading reference about an increase in the skills or knowledge level of the labor force. On this point, and in contrast to the deskilling literature led by Braverman in the 1970s, limited evidence would seem to exist (e.g. Howell and Wolff, 1992; Cappelli, 1993; Barley, 1994; Leigh and Gifford, 1999). However, the argument of some authors that suggests a competitive advantage for those individuals who possess a high level of knowledge is invalidated if a generalized upskilling trend really takes place. This occurs because a homogeneous increase of workers' skill in absolute terms tends to annul any previous relative increase, which is precisely what grants a real advantage to the individuals who have acquired greater skill than the rest. Therefore, the belief that the labor force is better educated and trained, as a whole, does not necessarily imply an improvement in the working conditions of the most educated. This improvement could take place solely if the upskilling movement is selective. In any case, what we are witnessing is not a general upskilling, as suggested by some theorists of the new paradigm, but rather skill polarization (Bradley et. al., 2000).[1]

It is also postulated that technology will lead to greater productivity, but the evidence at present is not so convincing. For James Krohe, the investment in computer technology has had a limited or null impact in this regard: 'Either the presumed productivity gains made possible by computers were illusory, or they were being offset by inefficiencies elsewhere' (1993: 16). In this regard, he cited, among other sources, a study made by Gary Loveman, who ironically remarked that the companies he analyzed 'would have been better off investing their money in worker training or more efficient boilers or bigger coffee cups — almost anything but computers' (Krohe, 1993: 16). On the other hand, Lee Sproull and Sara Kiesler considered that, in comparison with other technological advances like the telephone, the railroad, and certain office paperwork technologies, 'structural changes associated with computing up to now have been puny indeed' (1991: 144-145). However, they foresaw that new developments in communications technology could make possible more substantive structural changes. These transformations were ultimately triggered by the Internet and other related developments.

Nevertheless, the productivity paradox is still here: beyond the sophistication of the new technology, the great changes did not have the revolutionary impact anticipated by some. This issue has spurred much debate. Several researches argued that the so-called productivity paradox was a mere methodological artifact, resulting from either measurement error (Diewert and Fox, 1999) or an inadequate level of analysis (Brynjolfsson and Hitt, 1999). However, an important number of IT projects do not reap the expected benefits. In this regard, and in sharp contrast with the discourse exalting technological advances, Donald Marchand et al (2000: 10) recognized that 'many senior executives have a decidedly negative opinion of the relationship between IT and business performance. They are dissatisfied with the investments and practices related to IT and information use in their companies.' This does not imply that the promise of productivity will not materialize in the future. In fact, it cannot be predicted with any certainty what modifications technology will introduce in the dynamics of the world of the work. According to Soshana Zuboff (1988), the future is not predetermined and two possibilities exist: automatization and informatization. While the former will not affect substantially the organization of work, except through the suppression of a great number of jobs, the latter could potentially entail a true democratization of the workplace. These avenues to the future use of information technology are not conceptual opposites. Rather, automatization is a prerequisite for informatization. However, the business elite might decide not to advance further once the automatization stage has been reached. For Zuboff, technology allows to decentralize efficiently, but it also has a powerful centralizing effect, which she aptly denominated the 'information panopticon', that could enormously, and in previously unthinkable ways, favor the possibilities of managerial control. Therefore, its liberatory force, if any, is minimal.

Technology may not have produced a leap in productivity, but what about the benefits of one of the new paradigm's core features: teamwork? Again, the answer is negative. Decisive support to the hypothesis that teamwork necessarily favors productivity does not exist. In a review of the subject, Richard Hackman indicated that groups can be effective in promoting innovation, in making better decisions than individuals in certain circumstances and tasks, in better controlling the behavior of their members than by means of formal rules and procedures, and in mitigating the consequences of organizational size by facilitating internal communications and allowing flatter hierarchies. Nevertheless, he did not hesitate in emphasizing that 'given possible benefits such as these, one can view work groups as a panacea for organizational problems, which assuredly they are not' (1978: 62).[2] The dynamics they can generate may be negative, he argued, as a number of studies revealed that groups can support norms of low, instead of high, effectiveness, make remarkably deficient decisions, engage in conflict with other groups, and even disturb some of their members' well-being. In fact, groups may produce what has been called 'social loafing', which means that the group's productivity is less than the sum of the individual productivity of the group members (Kravitz and Martin, 1986; Harkins and Szymanski, 1989). Moreover, as Michael Brooke observed, 'Small can be very ugly indeed if all the individual's discretion is absorbed in that of the unit — like some tribes and communities and other groups with fierce procedures to safeguard conformity and ensure obedience'. When the position of the dissident within the group is evaluated, it is possible to notice that this later can also 'easily become the enemy of innovation' (1984: 339).[3]

Perhaps these critics are extreme, but even considering self-managed groups with sympathy, it must be acknowledged that it is not yet adequately known what causes some groups to work successfully, while 'others turn out to be a source of continual difficulty and dismay for both group members and organizational management' (Hackman, 1978: 62). Katzenbach and Smith indicated that a remarkable difference of performance exists between an effective team and the 'amorphous groups that we call teams because we think that the label is motivating and energizing' (1993: 111). For them, to develop a team in an organization is not an easy task. Actually, their claim that productivity 'requires preserving direction and guidance through hierarchy while drawing on energy and flexibility through self-managing teams' (1993: 119), reaffirms the idea that the reforms advocated by the new paradigm are, at present, very far from being widely implemented and might even be not very effective.

James Barker (1993, 1999), after an analysis of a specific case of application of self-managed teams, introduced the notion of 'concertive control' as a form of overcoming bureaucratic control that may be subtler and more oppressive than the

Weberian 'iron cage' for the employees. Paradoxically, the own group dynamics give origin to a set of rules that, in turn, 'creates a new iron cage whose bars are almost invisible to the workers it incarcerates' (Barker, 1993: 435). Employees under this type of system 'must invest a part of themselves in the team: they must identify strongly with their team's values, goals, its norms and rules' (1993: 436). Individual autonomy is severely limited and the members who have opposite ideas or directions to those declared by the group undergo laborious psychological costs, since they might be considered undeserving as mates by the other group members. The behavior of individuals within the group does not differ much from what could be expected under a bureaucratic system, as the 'concertive system' also establishes 'its own powerful set of rational rules' (1993: 435). However, authority is transferred from the formal hierarchic system to the work team. This form of control results in a 'communal-rational' system, according to Barker's expression, that is in no way liberating. Furthermore, it must also be pointed out that instrumental rationality does not disappear from the scene, since management adopts this strategy with the intention of increasing its control over the workers' production through the manipulation of their values and feelings. These do not arise from the group spontaneously, for the own genesis of the self-managed team is governed by the adhesion to organizational values imposed by management.

Participation and empowerment have produced some disappointing results. The evidence about the effect of participation on productivity is mixed, casting some doubts on the usefulness of the new paradigm's recipe in this regard. John Wagner's (1994) meta-analysis of research on the participation-performance link revealed that the connection between both variables, although statistically significant, is so small to become of practical relevance. Even the current application of employee empowerment in business firms appears to be unrelated to the desired improvements in productivity, as recently indicated by Chris Argyris (2000). This, however, is not surprising since workers cannot easily behave like owners, even if told so, because precisely they are not owners (Argyris, 1998). It is also pertinent to mention the research conducted by David Storey (1998), under the auspices of Deloitte and Touche, one of the largest auditing and consulting firms, with the objective of identifying the common characteristics of fast growing small and medium enterprises in the United Kingdom. His findings showed that the majority of a representative sample of these firms had an autocratic organizational culture and not the democratic and team based features attributed by the gurus to the successful and innovative firms.

The anomalies between the new paradigm's prescriptions and the empirical world are even more surprising in the case of large enterprises, which tend to be precisely the first to adopt the newest management theories. A recent study by Staw and Epstein (2000) reported no relationship between organizational performance and the implementation of several 'popular management techniques' (quality, empowerment, and teams) in a sample of 100 of the largest U.S. corporations. Their longitudinal analysis tested the possibilities of a lagged effect of these three independent variables, even after a five-year time period, but the researchers found no significant relationship with performance. Interestingly, what this study did demonstrate is that the adoption of these popular fads produced a positive and significant short-term effect on CEO compensation. The results of these and other studies (Wood and de Menezes, 1998; Salas et al., 1999; Freeman and Kleimer, 2000; Cappelli and Neumark, 2001) seriously undermine the credibility of the new paradigm.[4] Nevertheless, the theorists of this discourse are still reputed as being the ultimate authoritative source of management knowledge, and their influence is unharmed by the more scholarly work rebutting many of their prescriptions.

The rhetoric of this ideology is not only deceiving in terms of its ability to achieve its promise of liberating effects on the workforce and of improvements in productivity. It is also deceptive in a very particular aspect: the importance assigned to the interests of a set of stakeholders as opposed to the exclusive prerogatives of the proprietors or shareholders. The new paradigm theorists do not question the privilege of the owners, but neither do they consider it as unique. Some management pundits are very explicit about this. According to Handy (1997: 26), for example, 'the language of property and ownership is an insult to democracy.' However, recent changes in the control of organizations indicate a recovery of the shareholders' power in relation to that of managers (Useem, 1993), which had a subsequent impact on organizational behavior. Linda Brewster Stearns wrote that the objectives of the organizations undergoing changes of ownership reflect 'more attention on shareholders, less on other stakeholders (creditors, customers, suppliers, employees, and local communities)' (1994: 174). Given that this tendency is not limited but generalized and includes many important companies in the United States and Europe, the divorce between the literature discourse and the real business world becomes extremely noteworthy.

Another interesting issue regarding this gap is the image of the top managers' behavior as being increasingly sensitive to ethical concerns. The recent scandal related to the abuses of 'creative accounting' at Enron and other well-known firms has shown that this picture is quite inaccurate. Although the media may offer a legitimating account of this case as an example of capitalism depurating itself, it is more likely the tip of an iceberg whose actual magnitude is yet unknown. This is just another illustration of the mystifying nature of the dominant managerial ideology in which appreciations loaded with positive values appear prominently. None of them is perhaps more popular than the idea that the work force must be considered the most valuable resource for organizations. No other ideology has gone so far in this respect. Nevertheless, even some advocates of this ideology (e.g., Gratton et. al., 1999) admit that, in actual practice, these prescriptions are mere rhetorical declarations of principles for corporations.

The ideological character of the new paradigm is unequivocal, as I have tried to illustrate in this section. According to Barley and Kunda (1992), this ideology, to which they refer as 'organizational culture and quality', is a new phase of normative control over the workers.[5] The strategy of indoctrination by means of organizational culture and the utilization of elements destined to create cohesive groups operating under the logic dictated by management are inspired by the objective of increasing control in order to obtain performance improvements in organizations (Barley et al., 1988; Willmott, 1993). Although this is basically a correct interpretation, it should not be forgotten that many practices of the new paradigm combine elements of normative control with those of rational control, as Drucker indicated for the case of Total Quality and Just-in-Time. This is something that Barley and Kunda completely disregarded. Business Process Reengeniering is eminently rational as well, though it has a space for self-managed teams and responds to a more 'flexible' and horizontal organizational model. In fact, rational and normative control are actually combined in the new paradigm, whose discourse implies a rupture with the bureaucratic model, very visible at the ideological, but much less perceptible at the realm of the real organizational world.

Several scholars have criticized particular aspects or strands of this emergent consensus shared by the most respected management theorists and gurus. Armstrong (2000) discussed the ideological character of the concept of the 'learning organization'. Silver (1987) identified the neoconservative ideological influence in Peters and Waterman's best selling book *In Search of Excellence*, and Du Gay (1991) linked the neoliberal agenda to the emergence of what he called the 'enterprise culture'.[6] Other authors stressed that the managerial appeals to organizational culture, empowerment, and self-managed teams, instead of involving liberating experiences, represent new but equally oppressive forms of domination that ultimately attempt at regulating the workers' identity (Casey, 1996; Ezzamel and Willmott, 1998; Alvesson and Willmott, 2002) or at constituting a relationship of vassalage between them and their employers (Hancock, 1997). However, these critical approaches have not paid due attention to one of the most noteworthy facts about the new paradigm: the failure to fulfill its very ultimate goal in terms of instrumental rationality, that is, the enhancement of organizational productivity, a point that I particularly want to emphasize. Moreover, at the empirical level and except for a selected group of organizations, the new paradigm's so publicized model has not yet overthrown the reign of bureaucracy. In sum, the contrast between discourse and reality is evident. And nevertheless, divulged by a myriad of best-selling books, the new paradigm enjoys an enviable popularity when compared to previous ideologies.

The legitimation of disorganized capitalism

Two aspects are particularly important when analyzing the relationship between managerial ideologies and disorganized capitalism: the new cultural climate, the so-called postmodernism, and the changes in the patterns of social stratification in core Western countries. Postmodernism is, according to Fredic Jameson (1991), the cultural logic of late capitalism. For him, postmodernism is a form of consciousness, or even a 'life style', of a social stratum composed by managers, artists, intellectuals, and professionals, which can be assimilated to the so-called yuppies. He did not claim that the yuppies were the new ruling class, but rather that their distinctive set of beliefs and values became an ideology functional to this stage of capitalism (Jameson, 1989). This new style has been aptly captured by Gilles Lipovetsky, who spoke about the enthronement of narcissism, the 'end of *homo politicus* and the birth of *homo psicologicus*, in search of his Self and well-being' (1990 [1983]: 51). The retirement of individuals from the public life to the private sphere, the permanent search for satisfaction by means of consumption, and the 'pure indifference', in Lipovetsky's terms, act as tendencies functional to the strengthening of capitalism.

   This phase of capitalism clearly constitutes an exacerbation of certain tendencies of the system. Jameson (1991: 36) affirmed that late capitalism is 'the purest form of capital yet to have emerged'. In this new stage, the emphasis is displaced from production to consumption (Bauman, 1992). Individuals do not obtain satisfaction through their participation in the world of work, but in that of consumption. This is not new; as I have already argued, this tendency dates back to the consolidation of the consumer society. But during disorganized or postmodern capitalism, consumerism has intensified. However, if this is correct, how can the 'new individualism' of the postmodern stage, about which Lipovetsky spoke, be compatibilized with Riesman's groupism and Marcuse's death of traditional individualism? They are different aspects. When Lipovetsky referred to a new Narcissistic individualism, he developed a keen interpretation of the contemporary social reality, but what he really meant was that an expansion of the sphere of individual consumption has taken place. The body itself, for example, increasingly becomes an object of consumption and pleasure (Lipovetsky, 1990 [1983]). The postmodern individuals do not live their individuality as something opposed to their life as members of groups. In fact, the business world proclaims, much more than at the time of the human relations ideology, the necessity and importance of teamwork. The new individualism and groupism are far from being incompatible. A connection would seem to exist between the exacerbation of consumption under disorganized capitalism and elements of the new paradigm of management that put the accent on teamwork and groups more emphatically than the human relations ideology. This suggests the hypothesis that there is a direct relationship between progroup ideologies and consumerism. Nevertheless, such conjecture might be falsified by the new paradigm's belief in the necessity of individuals to achieve self-realization through their jobs. This reasoning seems to indicate the existence of a tension between both progroup and proindividualism stances within this new managerial ideology. This terminological tension, or alleged conflict, however, is more apparent then real. Groupism as well as possessive and consumeristic individualism are both functional to the development of capitalism. The cohesive group does not stifle the identity of the individual as a consumer of goods and services. On the contrary, group norms exacerbate it, while the 'individualistic' side of the new paradigm's rhetoric perfectly corresponds to the cultural construct of the postmodern man, Lipovestky's *homo psicologicus*. In this latter sense, it can be affirmed that an optimum fit exists between the cultural climate of postmodernity and the ideology of the new paradigm.

   The second relevant point regarding disorganized capitalism is the structure of social privilege and social stratification in core capitalist countries. John Kenneth Galbraith (1992) developed an interesting argument, suggesting that in developed countries there is a contented majority that cohabits with an underclass of individuals who constitute a stratum severely deprived from material well-being. The effects of automatization and the technological revolution can generate an extension of this underclass due to an increase in the unemployment rate. This poses the threat of creating a dual society. José Felix Tezanos pointed out that the social structure corresponding to technologically advanced societies would be a dual or polarized structure, composed by two separated subsystems with minimum communication between them. The superior subsystem is compatible with Galbraith's description of the contented majority. The inferior subsystem will be integrated by the members of the underclass, the unemployed, and other marginal sectors whose situation will be harmed by the crisis of the welfare state, which will limit its role as a social services provider (Tezanos, 1992).

The upper part of this structure will concentrate the privileged people of the new social order. It will continue to exist an elite composed by the owners of the means of production to which a stratum of business managers is associated. Waiting for their possibilities of ascending mobility will be the knowledge workers, the elite employees of the companies of the future. To some extent, the contemporary transformations of capitalism have already generated a structure of social privilege responding to the characteristics of this stratification subsystem. Such a privileged set of social and occupational groups is compatible with what Leslie Sklair (2001) denominated the 'transnational capitalist class', which is composed of entrepreneurs, managers, professionals, and high government officials — all actively engaged in furthering the cause of the free enterprise system to which their own social privilege is tied.[7]

The new paradigm of management, whose basic features are summarized in Table 11.1, is aimed at legitimizing this new social structure through its emphasis on the meritocracy of the knowledge society. Those who, in this context, obtain an adequate professional formation and possess the other personal traits allowing them to get a job (aptitude for teamwork, fluency in communication, and the like) will belong to the upper subsystem. There, according to the new paradigm theorists, upward social mobility will be governed by meritocratic criteria. The marginalized minorities will populate the remaining subsystem, whose dimension will not be small. The acceptance that, contemporaneously with the emergence of disorganized capitalism and the height of the neoconservative discourse, has gained the new social Darwinism also contributes to legitimize this polarized social structure. Individuals who are relegated to the subsystem of the underprivileged are depicted as surely lacking the necessary qualities for social advancement, intelligence in particular. While people in the diverse strata that constitute the contented majority subsystem will presumably be gifted with the required aptitudes to be located in the higher social place that corresponds to them.

It may be contended that these are speculative remarks, but there is ample evidence documenting a trend of growing inequality in both income and wealth distribution not only in the United States, but in other Western countries as well.[8] As noted by Manuel Castells, some countries have nevertheless improved their inequality record (e.g., Spain), but polarization, which occurs when the upper and lower societal levels grow at a faster rate than the middle one, 'is on the rise everywhere. At a global level, the ratio of income for the top 20 per cent of the population to the income of the bottom 20 per cent jumped from 30 to 1 in 1960 to 78 to 1 in 1994' (1998: 5). Therefore, unless this tendency reverses in the future, which seems rather unlikely, a polarized or dual social structure, with the features

Table 11.1 Main aspects of the new paradigm of management

Basic tenets	Science and technology as driving forces of change, both at the organizational and at the societal level
	The rise of the 'knowledge society' determines the apparition of new organizational forms involving a postbureaucratic management model with flattened structures and increased workers' involvement and participation
	The generalization of the postbureaucratic model is a decisive step towards the end of alienation
	Organizations and, consequently, society at large will be governed by a meritocracy of talent, knowledge, and intelligence
	Influence from a new social Darwinism
Image of the manager	Managers give up control and become leaders focused on encouraging participation and trust; like everyone in the new society, they also need to have a strong aptitude to acquire knowledge
Image of the worker	The difference between workers and managers becomes blurred: 'every worker is a manager'
	Workers are portrayed in a very positive light, epitomized by the image of the 'knowledge-worker'; they are presented as motivated, pursuing self-development, and capable of self-management
Legitimated interests	Capitalist class
	Upper-level managers
	Management Consultants
Areas of application	All areas of the organization from production to general management
Main exponents	Peters
	Handy
	Drucker
	Senge
	Lawler

Table 11.1 *(continued)*

Period of predominance	1985 to the present
Impact on practices	Many of the practices associated to the new paradigm (e.g., TQM, self-managing teams, etc.) have been selectively adopted worldwide
Misrepresentations detected	Although this ideology did have an impact on administrative practices, there has not been a full-blown adoption of the postbureaucratic model
	The thesis of the emerging meritocracy of talent and the thesis of the end of alienation are not empirically supported so far
	The impact of new work practices upon organizational performance and labor productivity is, in many cases, negligible

outlined above, will be a prominent characteristic of disorganized capitalism. In fact, the flexible organizational forms endorsed by the new paradigm may contribute to this outcome, since they generate a dualism in the internal labor markets as workers are categorized as being 'core' or 'peripheric' to the firm, which results in growing wage polarization (Harrison, 1994).

The new paradigm of management includes conspicuous elements of legitimation of a social order of increasing inequality through the coming of a supposed knowledge meritocracy. Its discourse proclaims a postbureaucratic and posthierarchic model in which organizations are great spaces of horizontal and, to a lesser extent, vertical mobility. Under this model, organizational members have a similar hierarchy of equals and peers. This clearly differs from the old and 'dysfunctional' bureaucratic model of management, characteristic of a previous stage in the development of capitalism. It is expected that the members of the contented majority will feel comfortable and find self-realization in their work within the new, flatter and more democratic organizations. The rhetoric emphasizing the importance of knowledge, talent, and intelligence in postcapitalist society is an attempt to introduce a mythical meritocratic base to legitimize the emerging structure of social privilege. What André Gorz described as a glorification of 'work and the dedication to the own job position', central element of the rhetoric of the new paradigm, fosters in a context of job scarcity 'the corporative egoism of a stratum of elite workers'. For him, it is a 'form of demanding the belonging to an elite of "winners", who own their position privileged to their superior ability and ambition . . . the "losers" cannot blame anyone but themselves' (1992: 28).

To sum up, there is a suggestive correspondence between these two central features of this stage of the development of capitalism — the increased social polarization and the exacerbation of the consumer society — and certain equally important characteristics of the dominant managerial ideology. In the first place, the emergence of flatter organizations and flexible workplaces is not precisely a neutral process, but one that contributes to the growth of social inequality, which generates a need for legitimation. The reference to a talent meritocracy in several best-selling management books of the period, as evidenced by the writings of Peters, Handy, and other respected gurus, fulfills that goal of legitimation. The rise of a new social Darwinism, which is part of the broader cultural climate that also permeates the writings of some management theorists, operates in the same manner. In the second place, the exacerbation of the consumer society explains the conspicuous progroup stance of the new paradigm of management (i.e., self-managed teams and the appeal to adopt the norms and values of the organizational culture). Finally, other important elements of the new paradigm's discourse legitimate the social order through mystifying conceptions like the end of alienating work and the growing importance of ethics, empowerment, and participation in the management of organizations. The legitimating force of these elements is strengthened by their consistency with a significant political value in the Western world: formal democracy.

While the role performed by the new paradigm in type 1 legitimation has been clearly shown, it is more difficult to isolate the social groups whose interests are served under type 2 legitimation. The most obvious candidate is the amorphous group of the knowledge workers, whatever that label means.[9] However, as the figure of the knowledge worker is largely modeled after the image of the management consultant, one might conclude that type 2 legitimation favors this latter group of professionals. This legitimation also extends to the firms where they work, which allegedly embody the management expertise whose virtues are so vividly extolled by the new paradigm. Moreover, in the past, other administrative ideologies justified claims to prominence in organizations for different professional groups, but also legitimated management consultants. Taylor, for instance, was a management consultant; but this was not the case with Mayo, Barnard, Simon, and other theorists who were, first and foremost, academics. While their discourse also favored the interest of the consultants, a sector that was not so powerful at that time, it was basically aimed at the figure of the professional employed in private and public organizations. At present, upper-level managers, particularly CEOs of multinational corporations, are also legitimated, since the popular business literature often depicts them as 'heroes' or simply as very smart people. Nevertheless, the new paradigm seems mostly concerned with the interests of the consultants, rather than with those of the line managers. In fact, this is also consistent with a new business world in which job stability ceased to exist and the knowledge worker became a temporary consultant. In this context, the best way to legitimize professionals is to depict them as consultants, either external or internal to organizations. It seems as if the independent experts, the consultants rather than the managers, are the group that is the privileged object of legitimation by this discourse.

The emergence of the new paradigm coincides with a boom in the consulting industry that happened from the 1980s onwards (Nohria and Berkley, 1994;

Ramsay, 1996). The number of both management gurus and consulting firms also grew. The consulting industry has undisputedly 'become one of the most successful businesses in history' (O'Shea and Madigan, 1998: 10). This growth was fueled by the new fads that followed one another: TQM, Reengineering, Knowledge Management, and the like. A burst of managerial publications also occurred from 1980 onwards. This landscape is perceived as a commodification of management knowledge (Fincham, 1995; Carter and Crowther, 2000) and, according to some authors (Hilmer and Donaldson, 1996) as a trivialization of the discipline. If management knowledge can now be considered a product, then someone must benefit from its sale. Although the yield accrues not only to management consultants but also to other actors dealing with the production and diffusion of this particular product, such as business schools, those who profit the most from the legitimation endowed by the managerial literature are ultimately these consultants (Berglund and Werr, 2000; Carter and Crowther, 2000). The new ideas about organizational culture, teamwork, high-involvement, and the like are exposed in management books only at a very cursory level. The firms that want a more detailed advice should directly contract consultants, who will implement the desired changes and charge the corresponding fees for their services. The management pundits who generate the wisdom of the new managerial thinking are, in most cases, consultants, and they legitimate the particular interests of their colleagues and certainly their own.[10] The logic here is straightforward: if management knowledge is a product on the market, the act of promoting it clearly serves the interest of those who produce and sell this product.

In synthesis, the new paradigm of management performs both type 1 and type 2 legitimation functions. According to Hood and Jackson, the most convincing argumentations in management theory are those based on metaphor and fiction. 'Reality is complex and diffuse, seldom yielding a single clear meaning', they explain, 'Metaphor, on the other hand, simplifies, while fiction persuades' (1991: 158). In this sense, the power of the new paradigm's rhetoric resides in the impressionistic use of technology and knowledge — which both enjoy an admirable reputation in our society — coupled with ideals of freedom and democracy. The postulated fictions, in particular the emergent meritocracy and the human liberation resulting from the overcoming of the bureaucratic model, provide in this context a clear legitimating effect. However, if the deceiving character of these discursive constructions is so obvious, one may ask to what extent their target audiences believe in them. Judging by the burgeoning nature of the industry of the production and diffusion of popular business knowledge (publishers, consultants, trainers, business schools, etc.), it may be affirmed that the new paradigm has certainly generated wide interest and, also, certain credibility.

Some managers and employees may have doubts about the virtues and the factual scope of many claims of the dominant management thinking.[11] Yet this postmodern fairy tale about democratic, flat, agile, innovative, creative, and efficient organizations inhabiting a brave new world of justice and merit is repeated *ad nauseum* in thousands of books and articles, closely following the lines of the basic model discussed in this chapter. This constitutes an indirect indicator of success in terms of achieving legitimation objectives. Otherwise, if nobody agrees with these beliefs, why would they get published and sell so widely? Furthermore, although comments about the potentially negative features of the new organizational forms and practices (e.g., Grenier, 1988; Heydebrand, 1989; Sewell and Wilkinson, 1992) appeared as soon as these administrative techniques were first described, even progressive critics of the bureaucratic model seem vulnerable to the seductive siren's song of the new paradigm. David Boje and Robert Dennehy (1994) presented some of these discursive developments as a 'postmodern alternative', which is portrayed from the very subtitle of their book as '*America's revolution against exploitation*'.[12] So, for all practical purposes, the solutions offered by some 'progressive' management scholars are absolutely similar to those of the 'conservative' management gurus.[13]

The unprecedented success of popular management discourse, turned into a true cultural industry, has been explained by its function as common language of the business elite (Micklethwait and Wooldridge, 1997). Nevertheless, the contents of this language and its very nature are in need of explanation. In this regard, it can be argued that the sense of meritocratic superiority that the new paradigm of management gives to those who belong to the elite of the business world is what makes it so appealing. But this is not the only element. In addition, the current dominant discourse emphasizes the liberating character of the domination exerted by the entrepreneurial and managerial elite in organizations through a democratic, participative, and posthierarchical model. This is a characterization of power that, besides being founded in criteria of efficiency and scientificity in the same way as previous administrative ideologies, exhibits an ethical and generous face since it is presented as entailing benefits for the workers and for society at large. If the discipline of management is considered as a product that also performs an ideological function of legitimation, then it comes as no surprise that a discourse with the aforementioned characteristics has such a great demand on the part of its target audience.

Notes

1 In fact, the very notion of skill, in terms of its definition and operationalization is what may be at issue here. For an interesting analysis of the 'myth of the skills revolution', see Bradley et al. (2000).

2 See also Sinclair (1992) for a discussion of what she called the 'tyranny' of the team ideology.

3 In this regard, see also Janis (1972) on the phenomenon of 'group think'.

4 For results supporting the new paradigm, see Huselid (1995).

5 Barley and Kunda's (1992) approach is too limited in this respect since, as I have shown, the emphasis on culture and the issue of Total Quality Management are only two aspects of a more encompassing ideology. In a latter work (Barley and Kunda, 2001), however, they acknowledged all the features of the postbureaucratic model.

6 It must be noted that there is no need for a deep hermeneutical analysis to prove such connections, as Tom Peters (1994) himself told his readers that Hayek's book *The Fatal Conceit* is the only volume required to fully understand how the economy functions in the real world.

7   See also Parker (2002: 56), who nevertheless recognized the speculative character of the thesis about the existence of a 'self-conscious and coherent' global business elite.

8   See, for example, Krugman (1994), Bluestone (1995), Wolff (1995) and Keister (2000) on inequality in the United States and Birdsall et al. (2000) in relation to other Western countries. For a report on the United Kingdom, see Bennett (2001).

9   Following the line of legitimation of professionals presented in the analysis of organized capitalism, it may be contended that the figure of the knowledge worker acts as a legitimating icon for diverse types of experts. However, the case of information technology experts, to whom the new paradigm contributes a welcome quota of ideological support, deserves special mention in this regard.

10 The discourse of the new paradigm explicitly recognizes that those who have more wits to generate meaningful organizational transformations are the management consultants, whatever their area of expertise. Most of the authors quoted in this chapter are, or were, management consultants (e.g., Peters, Waterman, Pinchot, Hammer, Champy, Drucker). Others are academics, but nevertheless some of them occasionally engage in consulting assignments.

11 The rhetorical excesses of the management gurus and the techniques they recommend (e.g., reengineering, TQM, etc.) have been sometimes ludicrously satirized in the popular press as well as in best-selling books. The best example in this respect is the enormous success achieved by the Dilbert character, created by Scott Adams, some of whose books like *The Dilbert Principle* and *The Joy of Work* achieved top ten places in Business Week's list of management best sellers. However, this amusing character has been rapidly metabolized by the pop management knowledge industry, whose stupidity the cartoon has attempted to denunciate. In fact, several corporations like Xerox now use Dilbert in their training materials (Solomon, 1997).

12 But see Boje and Winsor (1993), in which the authors concluded that TQM entailed a new form of Taylorism.

13 See Parker (2002) for a reflection about the difference between the postbureaucratic management discourse and the more scholarly work of critical management studies.

Chapter 12

Managerial Ideologies in Historical Perspective

Up to this point, I have offered the reader an overview of the evolution of managerial ideologies. In this chapter, I analyze these ideologies in a comparative historical framework. In the first section, I briefly discuss how the two theoretical perspectives dealing with this subject, the theory of the subtilization of control and Barley and Kunda's pendulum thesis, stand in the light of the historical reconstruction outlined throughout this book. In the next section, I review the key findings obtained by relating stages of capitalism's development to managerial ideologies, discussing three propositions about possible links between these two categories. Finally, I argue that a tendency of increasing fictional content can be observed in the discourse of management thought.

Two views on the evolution of administrative thought

The approach emphasizing an increasing subtilization of management discourse on labor force control does not receive total support. While it is certain that, if we compare the postbureaucratic model of the new paradigm of management with Taylorism, such subtilization does exist, this process must be subject to some qualifications. In the nineteenth century, the discourse of authors like Owen and Montgomery presented clear elements of normative control, something that does not seem to be in consonance with the hypothesis of coercive control as the dominant form of the period. Besides, the managerial ideologies that did not legitimize the social order of the time advocated the creation of exemplary communities to increase economic productivity. The fact that these were socialist attempts does not invalidate their relevance from the standpoint of administrative experimentation. The ideology of industrial betterment, which enjoyed wide diffusion at its time, also displayed a normative and subtle view of workforce control. Moreover, when we compare the discourse of the human relations ideology with systemic rationalism, its successor as a dominant ideology, it is difficult to ascertain whether the ineluctable tendency towards a refinement of control methods existed or if, in reality, a return to an earlier form of control (rational control) actually occurred. These reservations notwithstanding, this approach does not lack plausibility.

According to Michael Burawoy and Eric Olin Wright (1990), administrative practices of control in business enterprises are increasingly based not in exerting coercion over the workers, but in trying to elicit their consent. Burawoy and Wright asserted that this latter form of control is the most adequate for highly skilled or managerial personnel. If the number of workers at expert or managerial positions increased throughout the twentieth century, as they suggested, then their thesis could explain the subtilization process at the level of both administrative practices and managerial ideologies. However, the search for consent began in the nineteenth century at a time when organizations exhibited simpler structures and managerial positions were less numerous. Therefore, Burawoy and Wright's account seems valid mainly for recent changes in administrative ideologies, and it must be subject to further elaboration in order to make sense of the evolution of management thought since the period of liberal capitalism.

Regarding the theory of cycles of normative and rational control, I must point out that both forms of control were present since the first managerial ideologies I have examined. Although this distinction is useful for certain analytical purposes, the succession of cycles can, to a great extent, be a construct of the researcher. For instance, profit sharing, one of the practices most recommended by the industrial betterment theorists, is more related to rational than to normative control, as it appeals to the workers' economic interests and not to their values and feelings. Moreover, although the posthierarchic model of the new paradigm clearly exhibits elements of normative control, some theorists also include elements of rational control in their arguments in favor of this model.[1] Even Barley and Kunda (1992: 393) admitted that 'there is considerable evidence that rational ideologies have always "dominated" the managerial community, in the sense that they are more prevalent and more tightly linked to managerial practice'. But if the basic distinction between dominant forms of normative and rational control is proven problematic when confronting the empirical material (the actual ideological discourses), the theory looses much of its appeal.

While there is still much to explore in relation to these two perspectives, they do not focus on some aspects that deserve a closer analysis. In particular, how some concerns and themes emerge as 'problem issues' or 'distinctive emphasis' in certain specific periods, and how managerial ideologies serve their basic legitimating function. The analysis of the evolution of managerial ideologies vis-à-vis their relationship with the three stages of capitalism addresses precisely these issues.

Managerial ideologies and stages of capitalism

Before discussing the theoretical implications of this approach, it is convenient to briefly recapitulate some of the main points developed in the previous chapters. As I have pointed out, it is possible to identify three differentiated stages in the evolution of administrative ideologies: (1) the ideologies associated to the authoritarian paternalism model, (2) the ideologies supporting the bureaucratic model (Taylorism, human relations, and systemic rationalism), and (3) the new paradigm of management. Two important discontinuities can be clearly observed. The first is the emergence of management as discipline with Taylorism,[2] and the second is the new paradigm's rupture with the bureaucratic and hierarchic model of management. The three stages in which the evolution of administrative ideologies can be divided correspond with three differentiated moments of the evolution of capitalism: (1) liberal capitalism, which lasted until the late nineteenth century; (2) organized capitalism, which was displaced by a new form in the 1980s; and (3) disorganized capitalism.

During liberal capitalism, the enterprises were of small dimension, some activities or processes were decentralized, and their administration, mainly in the hands of the owners, did not pose major problems. The management model of the period was authoritarian paternalism, which consisted in the predominance of direct control over the labor force by the employer combined, in some cases, with a mild form of benevolence towards the workers. It was a society with a polarized social structure, and the prosystem managerial ideologies aimed at legitimizing the ruling class on the basis of the superior personal traits of its members. Thus, the workers were considered as deserving their subordinate position.

As capitalism evolved from the stage of free competition towards organized capitalism, the organizational landscape also altered, and with it, the managerial ideologies. The emergence of the bureaucratic organization and the discipline of management were almost simultaneous. The bureaucratic enterprise became the epitome of rationality; and administrative knowledge, the basis upon which this rationality was built. Managerial ideologies fulfilled a legitimating role for the access to the social privilege structure of a stratum of professionals from disciplines akin to those of the main proponents of each ideology. First, it was a group of engineers and accountants with Taylorism. Then came the social scientists with the rise of the human relations ideology; and finally the experts in management, when systemic rationalism emerged as an integrative stage of the discipline. Each layer of experts contributed its quota of rationality and knowledge. Taylor endowed the discipline with 'scientificity', and other theorists soon followed. The human relations ideology, which began in the 1930s but achieved greater influence in the 1940s and 1950s, was associated to the consolidation of the consumer society and the birth of the 'organization man'. The climate of Riesman's 'groupism' and Whyte's 'new social ethics' are closely linked to this ideology, which aimed at generating social cohesion and conformism, turning individuals into consumers, on the one hand, and docile agents of production, on the other. Once the consumer society was firmly established, in a time when technology was on the rise and the first speculations about the postindustrial society were conceived, systemic rationalism emerged as a dominant managerial ideology. Its discourse dealt with the construction of the manager's image as being a rational decision-maker and left aside the concern for the labor force, which was merely considered a set of individuals amenable to social manipulation.

The appearance of disorganized capitalism meant important changes in the social and economic order. The state diminished its role in the economy, and the market returned to be considered as the more efficient mechanism for resource allocation. The economy went global as barriers to capital mobility were progressively reduced, and international competition turned ferocious in a changing world where everything appeared to move faster. The cultural climate was dominated by the so-called postmodernity, which is just another name for the exacerbation of certain tendencies of capitalism, especially consumerism. Moreover, the social structure is currently undergoing major transformations. Under organized capitalism, a numerous middle class existed, whereas this new stage is characterized by an increasingly dual structure with two differentiated subsystems that have little social mobility between them. The position in the social structure is fundamentally determined by the place individuals occupy in the world of work, which runs through some transformations as well. All these changes have altered the realm of managerial ideologies. In this aspect, the old bureaucratic and hierarchic model of management began to be perceived as an endangered specie. The alternative offered by the new paradigm of management is one of smaller, more flexible, and flatter organizations that will provide a more significant and motivating work for their members: the knowledge workers. Thus, hierarchy yields place to the self-managed work team. It is further expected that alienation, a remnant of an industrial world, will disappear in the knowledge society, which carries the promise of a meritocratic world where inequalities persist, but are justified on the basis of the ability and the talent of each person. By the hand of the new paradigm emerges a 'new individualism', narcissistic and consumeristic, while social Darwinism reappears.

The new paradigm of management tries to legitimate a new stage of capitalism that shows a polarized social structure with a progressive increase in inequality. The rich get richer while the poor become poorer; and everything indicates that the 'knowledge society' will maintain this tendency or, at least, will not revert it. By depicting this social order as desirable, the new paradigm does legitimate it. On the other hand, it also legitimates particular social interests by portraying a totally favorable image of the knowledge worker, largely modeled after that of the management consultant.

The idea that there is a certain degree of association between managerial ideologies and phases of capitalism suggests that certain aspects of the evolution of the former are a result of changes in the latter. I will present three propositions about potential trajectories of causality and change, which were supported in the historical reconstruction developed in this book. Of course, the discourse of each managerial ideology contemplates the consideration of many issues, each with its own different explanatory factors, so the total causal picture is actually quite complex. However, in illustrating these propositions, I only deal with what I consider to be the highlights of my historical analysis. In propositions 2 and 3, an obvious ceteris paribus clause is implicit.

Proposition 1: If new developments in capitalism occur, they must be accompanied by new issues, themes, or concerns in managerial ideologies.

This is what happened as capitalism evolved from the liberal to the organized stage. The bureaucratic model entailed new ideologies designed to legitimate both the social order (type 1) and the access of certain professional groups to privileged positions within the organizational world (type 2). This proposition is valid not only for changes that occur between different stages of capitalism, but also for those happening within these stages as well. For example, the period of consolidation of the consumer society, an important development within organized capitalism, is associated to the human relations ideology.

Proposition 2: If certain characteristics of one stage of capitalism persist or are exacerbated at the following stage, then those aspects of the managerial ideologies that supported or legitimated such particular characteristics will persist or be accentuated in the managerial ideologies of this new stage.

An interesting illustration of this proposition is the progroup stance of the new paradigm, which is akin to an exacerbation of certain aspects of the human relations ideology. If disorganized capitalism involves an exacerbation of the consumer society, then the managerial ideology corresponding to it would have to include a progroupism component. This indeed occurs: the new paradigm exalts teamwork, as it recommends that the control of the labor force be transferred from hierarchy to self-managed teams. However, within the ideology of the new paradigm there is also an individualistic strand, which is focused on the self-realization of the individual and the search for singularity. This rhetoric is also closely associated with Lipovetsky's new individualism. Does it conflict with groupism? Does it invalidate the hypothesis associating consumerism with managerial ideologies fostering groupism? In my opinion, the answer is no: the tension is more apparent than real. Furthermore, in the human relations ideology there were already humanist manifestations in favor of individual self-realization, particularly in Maslow, and that did not imply any contradiction with groupism.

At present, consumerism is more individualistic than ever, since tastes do not need to be homogenized, nor manipulated because a true 'menu à la carte' exists (Lipovetsky 1990 [1983]). Consumerism and 'new individualism' go hand in hand. The 'postmodern individual' maintains an individuality that is largely based in his or her identity as a consumer. In 1958, the French conservative thinker Jean François Revel stated that the essence of individualism in mass society was conditional freedom. The same can be said today: the post-modern individual is 'totally determined at the precise moment in which he affirms with more conviction his own personality' (1969 [1966]: 161).

Completely dominated by the arbitrariness of fashion, the *Homo Psychologicus* identity is that of an eager consumer, whose tastes and choices are to a large extent programmed by the 'forces of the market'. Though pretending to be different, unique, and the absolute master of his/her own fate, *Homo Psychologicus* is actually the epitome of the Riesmanian other-directed personality. New individualism and groupism are present in the discourse of the new paradigm. They are not contradictory, but perfectly functional to the exacerbation of the consumer society.

Proposition 3: If certain characteristics of one stage of capitalism reappear at a later stage, then the managerial ideologies of this later stage will exhibit some aspect(s) similar to the ideologies associated to such particular characteristics in the former stage.

This proposition considers the reappearance of features of capitalism, which can also be interpreted as a regress to characteristics of earlier periods. To illustrate this point, I will examine the similarities existing between liberal and disorganized capitalism, for although they are clearly differentiated stages, they share some common features. Two basic parallelisms exist:

1. Liberal capitalism had a dual and antagonistic class structure. The social structure of disorganized capitalism, not yet totally crystallized, is also polarized, although it does not present the same class antagonisms. In fact, the proletarian class seems to have disappeared from the scene (Gorz, 1982), whereas the capitalist class is not the sole privileged one. Around this class exists an associated stratum whose members obtain their social privilege through their holding of managerial positions.

2. Under disorganized capitalism, the state changes its role, much resembling its equivalent during liberal capitalism. The economic discourse of liberalism receives a renewed positive appraisal, and on the ideological plane, the state intervention in the economy is perceived as harmful and inefficient. In contrast, private enterprise gains greater legitimation, while the market is deemed as a much more efficient resource allocator than the distributive state. However, this does not mean that the state ceases to intervene in the economy. Rather, the type of intervention is qualitatively different.[3] The predominance of neoconservative discourse and the crisis of the welfare state tend to support the prospects of a dual social structure as inherent characteristic of disorganized capitalism.

Regarding managerial ideologies, another central similarity is noteworthy: the existence of social Darwinism as a legitimating ideology during the last decades of liberal capitalism and the emergence of a new social Darwinism that fulfills the same role in the period of disorganized capitalism. In sum, a revival of several elements seems to exist: (a) social Darwinism; (b) a political and economic ideology of a liberal conservative orientation that prescribes a restrictive role for the state, contemplating its retrenchment as social welfare provider; and (c) the existence of a polarized social structure under both historical stages: in the older one, the dual structure is manifestly antagonistic and conflicting, while in the contemporary one, the duality arises from the existence of two subsystems with little social mobility between them and a remarkable difference in the social privilege enjoyed by their members.

In order to explain the similarities mentioned in items (a) and (c), it can be argued that in stages of capitalism characterized by polarized societies, the ruling class appeals to an ideology that legitimizes its social privilege on the basis of the alleged superiority of its members. Thus, high social unfairness appears to be associated to a rhetoric of justification whose preferred argument is the existence of marked differences in the individuals' traits and in their ability to accede to privileged social positions. In the case of disorganized capitalism, the legitimation is twofold: on the one hand, the new social Darwinism teaches that some people are better prepared than others to compete for scarce resources, and on the other one, the new paradigm adds that this conforms a strict meritocracy based on talent.

There are, of course, other similarities between both periods that are worth mentioning. Under liberal capitalism, the owner-managers largely monopolized power in organizations. With the coming of organized capitalism, they were forced to share it with nonowning managers; however, this tendency would seem to revert itself in American Capitalism beginning in the 1980s. As Useem (1992: 55) indicated, 'the 1980s were marked by a slowing or even a reversing of this quiet revolution'. This process of reaffirmation of ownership control aimed at increasing profits. Regardless of whether 'the intensification of ownership interests' really achieved that objective, Useem concluded, 'available research suggests it has had organizational impact' (1992: 56).

Another similitude is related to the characteristics of productive organizations. During liberal capitalism, these had typically a simple hierarchic structure and, sometimes, certain functions were decentralized to contractors. In disorganized capitalism, the organizations described by the new paradigm thinkers are highly decentralized (virtual corporations, networked organizations, or whatever one wants to denominate them) and their hierarchic structure is predominantly flat. This coincidence, however, is not strictly true, because we compare an organizational model, in the case of the new paradigm, to the real organizations of the liberal capitalism stage. Of course, for those who believe that the model prescribed by the theorists is indeed on its way to generalization, the similarity acquires an authentic character.[4]

It is also interesting to observe the existence of a parallelism between the antisystem managerial ideologies of the nineteenth century and the ideology of the new paradigm. Both perceived the utility of cohesive collectives as ways to increase organizational productivity or just to control organization members. The difference lies in the fact that the new paradigm uses this weapon of normative control to legitimate the social order, while this recommendation was initially formulated in the context of ideologies that sought some changes to the existing order. Moreover, the rhetoric of the new paradigm about the importance of a meritocracy of knowledge finds a precedent, and perhaps its purest form, in Saint-Simonian discourse. Nevertheless, Saint-Simon pleaded for a meritocratic order to counter the irrationality of the social order of his time, but never suggested that meritocracy was a reality, as does the new paradigm. In any case, what must be noted is that the new paradigm resembles some sort of utopic socialism transformed, subverted, and adapted to the effect of legitimating the very capitalist order.

In synthesis, following the three propositions stated above and independently of accidental similarities, it can be concluded that several relationships (summarized in figure 12.1) become evident. One of the constitutive features of liberal capitalism was the high level of social polarization. This aspect is reflected in the prosystem managerial ideologies of the period (employers' superiority, social Darwinism, and industrial betterment). They all legitimated the social privilege enjoyed by the owner-managers by arguing that these individuals were gifted with superior personal traits. On the other hand, all the managerial ideologies of the nineteenth century, regardless of their stance towards the capitalist system, made an issue of the situation of conspicuous social unfairness. Industrial betterment, although aligned with the interests of the capitalist class, sought to alleviate the workers' miseries in a variety of ways, while utopic socialism attempted to

LIBERAL CAPITALISM

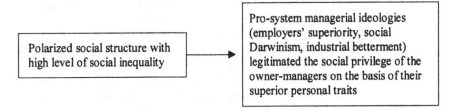

ORGANIZED CAPITALISM

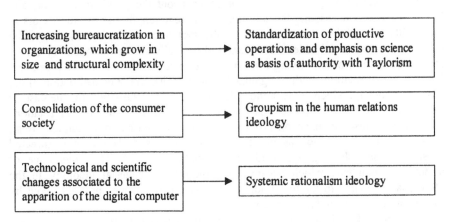

DISORGANIZED CAPITALISM

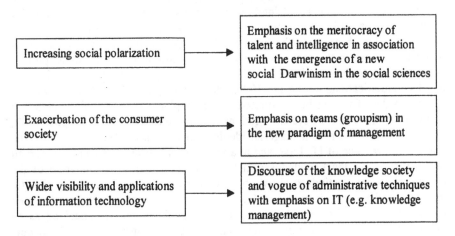

Figure 12.1 Main changes in the phases of capitalism and managerial ideologies

gradually extinguish social unfairness by creating organizations that did not reproduce such manifest inequality through their reward structure.

The rise of organized capitalism meant the generalization of the bureaucratic model of management. This process was reflected in the scientific management ideology with its emphasis on standardization of productive activities and science as basis of authority. From Taylorism onwards, the legitimating force of the members of the upper strata in organizations was not their mere personal superiority, but their possession of scientific knowledge. During this phase of capitalism, there was a gradual reversion in social inequality, something that was made possible, among other factors, by a more active role of the state as welfare services provider. Consequently, the concern of administrative ideologies for social problems decayed progressively. Taylor spoke about the problem of labor, and Mayo discussed the existing 'social malaise' at some length, but his successors in the 1950s paid little attention to it. In the systemic rationalism ideology, the references to the social order were scant and basically showed a laudatory stance stressing that the workers' living conditions improved during the twentieth century. Internal transformations within organized capitalism led to the consolidation of the consumer society, which some authors date to the years 1930-1960 for the case of the United States. This process is related to the birth of the human relations movement, whose emphasis on groupism was considered by some authors (e.g., Riesman, Guerreiro Ramos) as an element favoring individuals with other-directed personality and shaping this kind of personality as well. The emergence of systemic rationalism, which became the dominant managerial ideology in the 1960s, is associated to the technological and scientific changes brought about by the invention of the digital computer.

In the period of disorganized capitalism, social polarization began to increase. Not surprisingly, the rhetoric of the new paradigm of management insidiously legitimated the existence of social inequality, by particularly underscoring the idea of a meritocracy of talent and intelligence. Its discourse claimed that in the flat organizations of a highly competitive, almost 'Darwinian' business environment those who triumph are only the best and the brightest. The emergence of a new social Darwinism in the social sciences was somehow instrumental in supporting this notion. With the introduction of the personal computer and the new advances in telecommunications during the 1980s, the visibility of information technology became wider. This can be interpreted as a new phase of the developments that allowed the apparition of systemic rationalism. In consonance with proposition 2, the discourse of the new managerial ideology clearly shows the influence of the ubiquitous presence of IT. First, and at a more general level, this can be observed in the rhetoric of the knowledge society, which is a logical continuation of the debates about the postindustrial society of earlier decades, and second, in specific techniques like reengineering and knowledge management and their associated philosophies. Most importantly, disorganized capitalism can be conceived as an exacerbation of the consumer society, and the progroupism stance of the new paradigm can be interpreted as functional to such exacerbation, in the same way as the human relations' groupism was functional to the consolidation of this type of society.

In conclusion, the issues and shifting emphasis of managerial ideologies reflect relevant changes in the development of capitalism (e.g., its level of social inequality, the transformation of the productive forces due to technological advances, and the very way in which the system works as a consumer society). But in addition, the reconstruction of the history of administrative thought that I have offered in this book lends itself to another interesting hypothesis about its overall direction. Beyond the somewhat controversial thesis of the subtilization of control over the labor force, what can be perceived is a trend of increasing fictionalization in the evolution of managerial ideologies, a topic that I consider next.

Increasing fictionalization in management thought

The idea that the fictional character of administrative thought has increased with time, instead of diminishing, may seem indeed strange, especially more than a hundred years after the birth of 'scientific management' with Taylor, and having already gone through the processes of professionalization and institutionalization of the discipline. Those who consider management as a science may contend that, far from degenerating epistemically, it has progressed throughout its history.[5] Even if it could be concluded that management is a science, it is not possible to affirm that, as such, it has progressed. Philosophers of science do not agree about what constitutes scientific progress, and the very hypothesis of the existence of scientific progress has been falsified in various opportunities.[6] What can indeed be affirmed is that management knowledge has grown in complexity since its apparition. At present, there can be identified two distinctive strands or ideal types of management knowledge, which differ in their discursive style, data generation procedures, methodological rigor, and diffusion channels. The first is the academic-oriented strand, whose developments are diffused through scholarly refereed journals, thus being subject to the same canons of rigor as other social sciences. The second is the practitioner-oriented strand, which is basically targeted at managers and professionals and a quite profitable industry for the actors who are concerned with its creation and diffusion. Of course, these two camps are not so neatly divided, and their separation was almost irrelevant until the late 1950s and early 1960s.

It is widely acknowledged that the academic strand receives low or no interest on the part of management practitioners, who deem it as being irrelevant for their practical purposes (Nohria and Eccles, 1998). This, however, was not always so. Arthur Brief (2000) pointed out that the discipline's first behavioral scientists were useful at least up to the 1950s as 'servants of power', to use Loren Baritz's expression, while present-day scholars are mainly concerned with issues that seem relevant only to other members of their academic community. Thus, they are no more useful to power, Brief concluded. Yet he perceived the positive and even liberating side of this situation.[7] Speaking in the name of the community of management scholars, he made this position quite clear: 'We need not worry about the ethics of how our research findings are applied if our intended audience is not listening to what we have to say' (2000: 349). For my part, and far from considering 'fictional' the outcomes of this scientific strand, I largely base my argumentation on the research that is produced by this strand.

My basic referent when speaking about a trend of increasing fictionalization is the practitioner-oriented or popular management knowledge, which is constructed by journalist, consultants, and in some cases scholars as well. The actual usefulness of the models and techniques that this strand of knowledge successfully promulgates as panaceas for improving organizational effectiveness has been questioned in diverse occasions by some academics in the discipline –and by several outsiders as well.[8] For them, these recipes, many of which came from the consulting realm, should be seriously analyzed in order to find out if, to whom, and under which conditions are they beneficial for the firms that adopt them. William Barnett and Glenn Carroll went so far as to think that it would be convenient to create 'an authoritative body to regulate the sale and promotion of organizational regimes much like the Food and Drug Administration (FDA) does pharmaceutical drugs'. According to them, this would reduce the costs for both organizations and individuals of 'ill-designed programs' (1995: 232). However, managers do not rely much on the scholars' advice, unless it comes from the organizational structures (i.e., consulting firms) and diffusion channels (i.e., business press, etc.) of the practitioner-oriented strand of the discipline. In the real world of organizational praxis, academics are no competence to management consultants (Ernst and Kieser, 2000). Therefore, in terms of administrative thought as an ideology, it is this popular strand of management knowledge that counts.

The central concept that I use to make sense of the evolution of managerial ideologies is that of 'fictionalization', which I define as the lack of correspondence between the statements of the ideologies and factual reality. A weakness of this approach might be the difficulty of operationalizing and measuring the level of fictionalization; nevertheless, it can be done. Each managerial ideology is composed of many fundamental statements or claims that conform a more or less systematic set of beliefs. In order to analyze the degree of fictionalization, I identify categories or dimensions under which selected thematic statements of these ideologies can be classified. Then, I establish whether the available research supports these statements; that is to say, ideologies are evaluated in terms of a fundamental epistemic value: empirical adequacy. The larger the number of categories in which an ideology has fictional content, the more fictional that ideology is. However, not all ideologies refer to the same things, nor do their statements necessarily have the same empirical domain. Moreover, they are not totally incommensurable, but some common ground exists, which makes a comparison possible.

To this end, I refer to the following categories:

1. Statements about the social order. It must be evaluated whether the existence of social inequality and the miseries endured by the workers and other unprivileged social strata are recognized by the managerial ideologies, regardless of their legitimating stance towards such situations.

2. Statements about the organizational world. Managerial ideologies are basically concerned with both descriptive models (how the organizational world functions) and prescriptive ones (how organizations should be conducted in order to achieve

desired effects on selected dependent variables like efficiency, productivity, etc.). So, it must be analyzed if there is correspondence between the ideologies' claims in these two domains and the empirical evidence, as well as the existence of deliberate misrepresentation of evidences in order to favor such claims.

3. Statements about the dominant management model. Every period has a dominant management model, and it must be established whether an ideology contends that its own management model is actually replacing the dominant one.

These three categories try to capture the essential elements of managerial ideologies: the basic claims of their descriptive and prescriptive frameworks, their characterization of the broader social order in which organizations are embedded, and their own evaluation about the impact of their prescriptions in the organizational world. Next, I examine the fictional content of each ideology in terms of these three aspects. Table 12.1 summarizes the conclusions of the analysis.

The reader may point out that I have started my historical reconstruction with the ideas of some utopic socialists, and what could be more fictional than that? To this, I must respond that utopian socialists were in general accurate critics of the capitalist order of their time. Therefore, in terms of how this order was depicted, I do not find much fictional content. They devised curious schemes of work organization, but it is not correct to call them fictions because their creators did not state that these arrangements were easily applicable in practice. The discourse of Owen, Saint-Simon, and Fourier was a call for action, reform, and experimentation. They did not describe these projects as something that was invariably generating positive outcomes in the real world, as usually do the theorists of the new paradigm. There were more examples of failure than of success, but as I have argued in chapter 2, many of these authors (e.g., Kropotkin, Noyes, Owen, etc.) reflected on this in their writings, making insightful analysis about the reasons why the communitarian projects failed. Furthermore, some of the most audacious projects were initially conceived and written as fictional works, and they were carried out in practice later. A particular case in this respect is that of Ettiene Cabet. His work *Voyage to Icaria*, published in 1840, was a fiction about a utopian society. The book had such a success that many persons inspired by this vision made a real experiment out of it. The management gurus of the new paradigm usually proceed the other way round, that is, their books pretend to describe organizations in the real world, but portray the image of idyllic enterprises that do not exist. Some ideas of utopian socialists like the importance of workers' feelings and values for the organization's success, albeit simple, are surprising anticipations of what would come later. Few thinkers wrote about the dominant management model of the times, except perhaps Owen, who recognized it aptly and, of course, did not risk the hypothesis that this model was utopian socialism. It must also be taken into account that even utopian communities did share some features of authoritarian paternalism (e.g., the strong authority of the community leader). Therefore, there is no fictionalization regarding the statements about the dominant management model of the period.

The procapitalist system ideologies of the nineteenth century did not ignore social problems. Although perhaps Ure downplayed certain aspects in this respect, that was not the attitude of others thinkers like Sumner, Gladden, and Carnegie.

Table 12.1 Fictional character of managerial ideologies compared

Ideologies	Statements about the social order	Statements about the dominant management model	Statements about the organizational world
Utopian socialism	Realistic appraisal of the social unfairness of the period	No fictional content; it does not affirm that the proposed model was actually replacing the capitalist firm	No fictional content; some of the main authors wrote about the failure of their communitarian projects
Prosystem ideologies of liberal capitalism	Realistic; acknowledges the existence of social problems	No fictional content; there is adherence to the authoritarian paternalist model	No fictional content is evident; not enough empirical evidence to judge the benefits of the full-blown industrial betterment model
Scientific management	Realistic; deals with workers' turmoil	No fictional content; adheres to the bureaucratic model	Only a minor misrepresentation: Taylor's use of inaccurate standards
Human relations	Realistic; deals with social malaise	No fictional content; adheres to bureaucratic model	Fictional content: myth of the 'happy worker'
Systemic rationalism	Not an issue, although Drucker tended to downplay the existing social problems	No fictional content; adheres to bureaucratic model	Fictional content: myth of the rational manager
New paradigm of management	Fictional content: myth of the end of alienation; increasing social unfairness is not of much concern	Fictional content: the postbureaucratic management model is still not dominant in the real world	Fictional content: growing concern for all stakeholders, alleged importance of ethics; some of its practices did not have the expected positive effect on productivity

This latter author, a well-known social Darwinist, explicitly observed that the new industrial system led to greater social inequality. The advocates of industrial betterment theorized about different ways by which entrepreneurs could help to mitigate the miseries of the working classes. The existence of a polarized society was legitimated through moral arguments (e.g., Smiles's doctrine of personal effort) or scientific systems (e.g., the Darwinian 'survival of the fittest'), but its nature as such was not denied. So, I do not consider that this set of ideologies has fictional content with relation to the social order. These managerial ideologies were not much concerned with understanding how organizations function. Ure made some reflections on the importance of machinism, which certainly contributed to increase industrial efficiency and to reduce the cost of many products. The proponents of industrial betterment presented diverse schemes to increase efficiency while simultaneously benefiting the workers. Unfortunately, the practical implementation of the full-blown model was limited to quite a few isolated examples. Although there are records documenting the positive results of some of these experiences (e.g., Godin Palace, NCR, Pullman), this does not constitute conclusive evidence supporting the claims of this ideology. But neither can it be concluded that this approach to management has fictional character with respect to the statements about the organizational world. Besides, it must be pointed out that many of the practices inspired by welfare capitalism continued in the first decades of the twentieth century, even after this ideology lost its preeminence (Jacoby, 1997; 2001). The dominant management model of the period was not questioned by these ideologies. For social Darwinism and the ideology of employers' superiority, any measure taken by entrepreneurs in their factories was considered legitimate, and the recommendations advanced by the industrial betterment thinkers were consistent with an authoritarian paternalist management model.

Taylorism, the first dominant ideology during organized capitalism, does not exhibit a high degree of fictionalization. The writings of some theorists of scientific management demonstrated a realistic reading of the social problems of the period. Taylor himself spoke largely about the 'problem of labor'. This ideology adhered to the bureaucratic model of management, to whose dominance it also contributed. Its impact on practices showed, in general, positive effects on productivity. Undoubtedly, the scientific management techniques were correlated with greater efficiency and yield. The only misrepresentation detected, quite minor though, is Taylor's use of inaccurate or distorted standards in some of his examples, contradicting the rigorous methodology that he should have actually employed (Wrege and Stotka, 1978).

The human relations school has a greater degree of fictionalization in comparison to Taylorism, since one of its central claims, the association of greater productivity with greater labor satisfaction (myth of the 'happy worker'), was falsified in diverse opportunities. Nevertheless, the existence of social problems in the period under analysis was not denied. Mayo himself wrote extensively about the causes of the 'social malaise' of the times, although his successors were more strictly focused on organizational concerns. Another aspect in which this approach does not have a fictional character is its stance towards the dominant management model. It basically adhered to the bureaucratic model. It is true that some authors (e.g., Likert, Argyris) pleaded for greater levels of autonomy and participation for the employees, especially in the early 1960s, but clearly within the essentially rigid patterns of the vertical authority structure of the organizations of the time. Most importantly, even the few authors who went further in their criticism of bureaucracy acknowledged that it was still the ruling model (e.g., Slater and Bennis, 1990 [1964]).

Systemic rationalism exhibits a degree of fictionalization similar to the human relations ideology. The problems of the social order were not an issue for this ideology, although Drucker portrayed the economic order in extremely laudatory terms, anticipating his contributions to the new paradigm of management. However, Drucker's appreciations were, to some extent, realistic because they were made in a period of decreasing social inequality, when the growth of the middle classes, to which he repeatedly referred, was a real fact. The adherence to the bureaucratic model of management is evident in the writings of the main exponents of this ideology. With respect to the statements about the organizational world, one important misrepresentation is detected: the myth of the rational manager. In fact, the construction of the image of managers as rational decision makers immersed in a complex game of chess against competitors and environmental forces does not have an empirical counterpart in the real activities of these actors within organizations. Regarding the contributions of this approach to increase organizational productivity, the evidence is mixed. Although there are successful real examples of the application of techniques like operations research (OR) or strategic planning, some of the leading contributors in these areas showed their disappointment with them. For example, Mintzberg (1994) criticized some strands of strategic management, and Ackoff (1979, 1987) referred to what he considered the excesses of OR models, although this is a minor point.

The authentic and undeniable qualitative leap takes place with the appearance of the new paradigm. Its discourse does not contain many references to the social order, other than those made to a new type of meritocratic society governed by knowledge. The issue of growing social unfairness, despite being a central characteristic of our contemporary stage of capitalism, is not of much concern for this ideology's proponents. The principal management gurus rarely commented on this problem, although their works exceeded mere technical subjects, contemplating broader philosophical, political, and economic issues. There are, of course, some gloomy prophecies, those that anticipate the end of the job (e.g. Bridges, 1994). But these were not empirically supported either: at the time of this writing (2003), unemployment rates have not increased dramatically in the US, the reference country for this discourse. A more important misrepresentation is the myth of the 'end of alienation' in a world where, as I have already discussed, far from living richer and more significant lives, workers worldwide tend to face increased job stress and related inconveniences, as well as longer working hours (Basso, 2003). In short, in the main writings of the new paradigm of management there is a slightly distorted vision of the social order, which exaggerates positive characteristics, proclaims some nonexistent ones, and obscures problematic aspects.[9]

But the fictionalization is even greater. Regarding the statements about the world of work, there are many claims that can be considered misrepresentations. The alleged importance that stakeholders receive at the discursive level is contradicted by Useem's (1992, 1993) findings about the reaffirmation of the shareholders' interests. The high priority supposedly assigned by corporations to the ethical aspects of their business has proven to be a myth, especially in the light of the empirical evidence of the Enron fiasco and other related scandals of 'creative accounting'. The assertion, so popular in best-selling management books, that employees are the organizations' main assets is a myth that is more rhetoric than reality. All are clear indicators of fictional content. Moreover, it must also be taken into account that there is no convincing evidence that the utilization of the administrative techniques associated to this ideology are necessarily correlated with economic benefits for the organizations that adopt them. This is not a case of insufficient evidence, as in the case of industrial betterment. There are concrete examples that falsify the claim that certain practices of the new paradigm improve productivity and/or profitability. However, while not universally proven effective yet, some elements in the prescriptive model of the new paradigm might be useful in particular circumstances. In any case, regardless of whether the postbureaucratic and participative model is more efficient than the traditional one, it must be recognized that its generalization in the realm of business firms has not taken place yet. Therefore, it can be concluded that the postbureaucratic model resides more in the theorists' minds than in the real world of corporations. In this regard, and unlike the preceding managerial ideologies whose statements about the dominant management model cannot be considered fictional ones, the new paradigm has a claim that clearly does not correspond with factual reality. It considers that the dominant management model has been replaced, or is currently being outmoded, by postbureaucratic organizational forms. But this is not correct, since the reign of bureaucracy has not ended yet.

Once the three categories combined are analyzed, it becomes evident that the fictional content of the new paradigm of management surpasses that of any previous administrative ideology. The foregoing analysis shows that the increasing fictionalization thesis receives empirical support. It can be contended that the categories considered were not appropriate or that the claims of the different ideologies should be chosen on a more homogeneous basis or somehow weighed.[10] Also, particular points of the trajectory of fictionalization can be debated. For example, whether Taylorism had more fictional content than the nineteenth-century managerial ideologies, given that Taylor's use of inflated standards is too minor a misrepresentation, and it might not be fair to exaggerate the importance of a methodological negligence on the part of Taylor. In turn, critics of scientific management may dispute my claim that it has less fictional content than the human relations ideology. Nevertheless, what is more difficult to deny categorically is the fact that the new paradigm, an authentic fairy tale for managers, has more fictional content than the administrative ideologies that preceded it.

Notes

1 Similarly, Guillén (1994) criticized Barley and Kunda's cycles theory by pointing out that contemporary management discourse blends normative and rational elements in such approaches as TQM and lean production. See also Ramsay (1996).
2 The first formulations of administrative principles appeared contemporaneously with Taylorism, being those elaborated by Fayol the most important ones.
3 Regarding the desirable role of the state in disorganized capitalism, see for example Lind's (1992) characterization of the 'Catalytic State' and Hilpert (1990), who emphasized the role of the state as enabler of technological innovation.
4 See Lazerson (1995), who considered that flexible production involves a return to the putting-out system characteristic of many industries during the eighteenth and nineteenth centuries. Similarly, Piore and Sabel (1984) presented the model of flexible specialization as an alternative industrial paradigm to mass production, assimilating it to the production techniques previous to Fordism and even to a return of craft production.
5 The thesis that management knowledge has progressed steadily is not without criticism. For an approach challenging this view, see Jacques (1996).
6 For example, Popper (1976) developed one of the most interesting theories of scientific progress introducing the notion of 'degree of verisimilitude', but he later admitted, given the severe criticism against the logical structure of his formulation, that science does not progress, just changes.
7 Other scholars, in contrast, perceive this state of affairs as a matter of growing concern. Richard Mowday (1997: 337), for example, conceded in his presidential address to the Academy of Management that the criticisms about 'the irrelevance of our research' had solid grounds and should be taken seriously by the academic community.
8 See, for example, Thomas Frank's (2000) trenchant critique of contemporary management discourse.
9 Christopher Grey made a similar appreciation about management education. For him, although 'there is well-documented evidence' about some dark realities on the treatment received by workers at some subsidiaries of multinational corporations in developing countries, 'these experiences rarely figure in management textbooks', which portray a 'more sanitized, if not sentimentalized' version of reality (2002: 497).
10 As the number of testable implications of each managerial ideology differs, it can be argued that not only should the empirical inadequacies of such discourses be considered, but also the cases in which the available evidence supported the ideologies' claims. In this regard, the notion of fictionalization could be interpreted as the opposite concept of verisimilitude or truthlikeness of scientific theories. However, while some philosophers of science still hold that truthlikeness can be measured (Niiniluoto, 1999), it remains a very controversial issue.

Chapter 13

Conclusion: Management Today

Throughout this book, I have tried to demonstrate how management discourse has fulfilled a legitimating function. In this regard, not only capitalism has been supported by diverse dominant managerial ideologies, but they have also been instrumental in legitimating the social privilege of an elite of professionals upon the possession of a particular expert knowledge. The central ideological operation that allowed this was the effective characterization of management as a discipline involving a complex knowledge of wide social relevance, whose mastery requires an intense theoretical and practical education. This successful construction of the social importance of management made possible a remarkable expansion of the institutional apparatus upon which rests the industry of production and diffusion of administrative knowledge, in particular business schools. But despite this formidable institutional presence, many of the problems that organizations faced in the past resonate today with inexplicable familiarity. For example, in his study of Pullman, the model industrial community, Richard Ely (1885: 463) observed, 'Favoritism and nepotism, out of place as they are in an ideal society, are oft-repeated and apparently well-substantiated charges'. Similar complaints, as well as many others, are still heard about many organizations. More than a century later, the alleged progress of administrative knowledge has been unable to eliminate this, although it should be one of its central goals. Given this state of affairs, I believe it is pertinent to conclude this work with some reflections on the current state of the discipline and with some speculative remarks about what management scholars could do to generate changes that favor interests broader than those currently legitimated by the dominant thought in the field.[1]

At present, the discipline of management appears to navigate a dangerous sea, threatened by the menace of both the Scylla of academic irrelevance and the Charybdis of the fictionalization of its popular strand. In this latter aspect, the new paradigm of management receives more support and adherence than any other preceding managerial ideology, a phenomenon that deserves closer attention. What is more striking about this ideology is that it is proclaimed as desirable even by theorists who came from a radical tradition. Its rhetoric is so appealing in its image of an idyllically fairer, democratic, and challenging workplace, governed by an equitable meritocracy and eliminating bureaucracy and the alienation associated to routine tasks, that even former critics of management theory become its adherents or, at least, timid advocates.

Some authors associated to the Marxian tradition view this administrative ideology sympathetically. For instance, echoing the supporters of the new paradigm, Benjamin Coriat (1991) argued, in reference to the practices of Japanese companies and to the fact that workers regain somewhat the control over the productive process that was lost with Taylorism, that a libertarian step in the world of work occurred. It is also the case of Stewart Clegg, once a tenacious critic of the legitimating role of management discourse. He and Thomas Clarke offered in their book *Changing Paradigms: The Transformation of Management Knowledge for the 21st Century* an interesting presentation of this new management catechism. They contrasted the old, negatively connoted features of the bureaucratic model, which shows a Taylorist emphasis on control, direction, and hierarchy, with the new model, mostly loaded with positive values like autonomy, participation, creativity, and empowerment (Clarke and Clegg, 1998). This supporting attitude is comparable to the embrace of the human relations theory despite the methodologically feeble, and theoretically misguided perspective of the Hawthorne studies.[2] Perhaps some progressive scholars feel identified with the utopian discourse of the new paradigm, and certainly, many of them perceive the critic appeal of Marxism as outmoded in the light of factual reality.[3]

In any case, the point is that the new paradigm enjoys ideological hegemony. The domination of disorganized capitalism is also a fact, despite the talk about national variants and more and less 'humane' versions of this economic system (e.g., Albert, 1993).[4] Interestingly, there was never existed before such an overt contradiction between a managerial ideology and the reality of the social world.[5] In fact, we have seen that current managerial discourse presents a more favorable picture of life in organizations than all previous ideologies did, raising the idea of the emergence of an organizational utopia, as observed by Collins (1988). However, this marks a striking contrast with the contemporary social order that exhibits a tendency towards higher social inequality both between and within countries. There is a disturbing cognitive dissonance between the new paradigm's organizational utopia and the social reality of the dystopian world in which these ideal organizations are embedded. How can we account for this contradiction? Although we have entered an era with a strong parallel with liberal capitalism, social unfairness being the most noteworthy, our contemporary capitalist society appears to have progressed morally. Concomitantly, the new dominant managerial ideology also reflects an image of improved morality; it has a distinctive utopian flavor, highly charged with democratic and egalitarian connotations.

Management knowledge offers today the promise of an organizational utopia with flat organizations inhabited by polite organizational citizens, who are motivated individuals, knowledgeable workers, and masters of their own fate within a meritocratic world. Moral capitalism has been equated with moral managerial thinking. Ideological mystification has reached new heights in order to be in harmony with a 'formally' democratized world. Yet, behind the surface of the discursive level, the contradiction remains. The gap between fact and fiction, legitimating discourse and bitter reality, broadens. When we observe factual reality, it is clear that not all organizations obey to the utopian model advocated in best-selling management books. Furthermore, the growing stress of employees and the falling levels of work satisfaction blatantly contradict the seductive sirens' chant of the new paradigm. Clarke and Clegg (1998) wrote that the business world will not be the same from the end of the millennium onwards, but there are evidences that changes in the world of work have been cosmetic, at best, and more exploitative, at worst. Immersion techniques of indoctrination that seek to conflate the private sphere of the individual with the work sphere and heavy workloads that require a full-life, not a full-time, job are manifest examples of how some organizations, far from being utopian communities, demand complete loyalty on the part of their members.

In this context, the emergence of a critical perspective to the current management orthodoxy becomes of paramount importance. Fortunately, acknowledging the formidable hegemony of the new paradigm and its remarkable power of co-optation (i.e., its ability to incorporate into its own discourse arguments that were central points of doctrines opposing management and even hostile to capitalism), it can be observed that pockets of intellectual resistance to popular management discourse (PMD) exist within the discipline and may even grow in the future. Among them, I can mention Critical Management Studies, the literature on the faddish nature of PMD,[6] and some nonradical approaches to organization theory that falsify some of the characteristic tenets of PMD.[7] This allows one to harbor hopes for renewal in the face of the new paradigm of management.

To improve organizations is one of the basic functions of administration. However, the idea of greater well-being for all the members of organizations — and for society in general — is something that has only advanced at the level of discourse and at the expense of the divorce from the realities of the business world. This being so, the management scholar faces two main options. Which one to choose will depend on his or her stance towards the social order. The first option is to celebrate the achievements of PMD and join the choir of those who sing praises to the system. The second one is to adopt a critical attitude, which in turn involves a set of possibilities that goes from expressing disapprobation from the safe vantage point of the ivory tower to an active involvement in the design of alternatives to the dominant management model. This latter, more positive form of engagement, would demand the articulation of a discourse that could draw more attention than the mere internalist dialogue of the academic community, limited to refereed journals and ad-hoc conferences and symposia (Parker, 2002). To this end, a change of language and strategy will certainly be required. While voicing disagreement with what is in existence will still be part of the rhetoric, the formulation of viable alternatives should be the main topic.

For this kind of scholarly work to make a difference in the real world, it is necessary, in addition to reaching a wider audience, to demonstrate in practice how this form of critical consciousness relates to actual organizational practice. Alternative forms of organizing are not only desirable, but also possible,[8] and this invites to reflect on models born in the past. The nineteenth century was a time of ferment for social experimentation, perhaps because the social order of the period was perceived as 'susceptible of change'. Although that sense of 'changeableness' is now almost null, it would be interesting to recreate such a spirit of 'institutional entrepreneurship' in order to make possible significant transformations of organizations and society. It is not my purpose in this book to discuss new forms of organizing and, in consequence, I will not extend myself on this issue. I will just say that I am not thinking in a 'progressive' version of the postbureaucratic paradigm, but in distinctive forms of organizing in which the system of rewards and punishments as well as the structure of authority are fundamentally attentive and subordinated to 'organizational justice'. It can be argued that business schools might not be the best place to look for those who will save us from the iniquities of the contemporary social order. But it is logical to hope that management scholars, at least those with a critical bent, could contribute to improve the functioning of organizations.

This book has been one more attempt at exhibiting the emperor's new clothes of management thinking, As buyers of management texts and audience for the ideas transmitted by them, we should become more educated consumers. Nonetheless, we must also try to see how the ideological mirage of the new paradigm can be overcome in practice and how an alternative paradigm can be designed. This should contemplate not only the management discipline, but also how the organizational world is articulated within the broader political and economic order. This is an enormous task, since the prospects for the emergence of a counterparadigm of management seem, at present, as utopian as the contemporary dominant ideology in the field. Yet, if Western countries manage to transcend the current phase of disorganized capitalism, diluting its perverse features and transforming the current structure of social privilege, it is certain that another managerial ideology will emerge. Perhaps, it is now time to start envisaging its defining features and supporting rationale. It will certainly be a particularly difficult mission, but one that is indeed worthy.

Notes

1 Of course, I do not think that management scholars are the only actors able to produce a renovation of administrative thinking.
2 I do not affirm that this support for the new paradigm is without qualification. For example, Coriat (1994) warned that post-Fordism might involve some form of neo-Taylorism.
3 Several academics who belong to the so-called critical management school prefer to embrace a post-structuralist approach, which draws mainly on the work of Foucault and, to some extent, is inspired by Habermas as well.
4 The notion of 'globalization', omnipresent in contemporary social science discourse, refers to this fact. What is being globalized is capitalism, not any other thing. Actually, attempts at defining globalization in terms of increasing share of foreign commerce or foreign direct investment do not succeed in documenting abrupt changes (Sutcliffe and Glyn, 1999). Moreover, in relation to the distinctive variants of capitalism, it has been recently demonstrated that the East Asian road is not free from disturbances (Bello et al., 2000), and even the Japanese model, authentic landmark for most management gurus, has revealed its weaknesses (Cowling and Tomlinson, 2000).
5 A similar opinion is held by Le Goff (1995).
6 See, for example, Kieser (1997), Furusten (1999), and Newell et al. (2001).
7 One example is organizational ecology, which has, as recognized by Hannan and Freeman (1989: 40), inescapable 'antiheroic implications' for the figure of the manager. According to this perspective, organizational evolution does not follow a Lamarckian adaptation path under the rational guidance of the top managers, but a Darwinian

process in which the external environment 'selects' organizations. Not surprisingly, this approach was considered by Lex Donaldson (1995) as one of the 'antimanagement' theories of organization.

8 For a preliminary but extremely interesting discussion about these possibilities, see Parker (2002).

References

Abercrombie, N. and Turner, B.S. (1978), 'The Dominant Ideology Thesis', *British Journal of Sociology*, 29: 149-170.

Abrahamson, E. (1997), 'The Emergence and Prevalence of Employee-Management Rhetorics: The Effect of Long Waves, Labor Unions and Turnover, 1875 to 1992', *Academy of Management Journal*, 40: 491–533.

Abrahamson, E. and Eisenman, M. (2001), 'Why Management Scholars Must Intervene Strategically in the Management Knowledge Market', *Human Relations*, 54: 67-75.

Ackoff, R.L. (1979), 'The Future of Operational Research is Past', *Journal of the Operational Research Society*, 30: 93-104.

Ackoff, R.L. (1987), 'Presidents' Symposium: OR, A Post Mortem', *Operations Research*, 35: 471-474.

Adler, P. (1993), 'Time-and-Motion Regained', *Harvard Business Review*, 71, (1): 97-108.

Aharoni, Y. (1986), *The Evolution and Management of State-Owned Enterprises*, Cambridge, MA: Ballinger.

Albert, M. (1993), *Capitalism vs. Capitalism: How America's Obsession with Individual Achievement and Short-term Profit Has Led It to the Brink of Collapse*, New York: Four Walls Eight Windows.

Alexander, R. (1979), *Darwinism and Human Affairs*, Seattle, WA: University of Washington Press.

Alvarez, J.L., Enrione, A. and Mazza, C. (1997), 'Legitimation and Integration Through Dependency: Graduate Business Education in Latin America', *Organization*, 4: 564-581.

Alvesson, M. and Willmott, H. (1996), *Making Sense of Management. A Critical Introduction*, London: Sage.

Alvesson, M. and Willmott, H. (2002), 'Identity Regulation as Organizational Control: Producing the Appropriate Individual', *Journal of Management Studies*, 39: 619-644.

Andrle, V. (2001), 'The Buoyant Class: Bourgeois Family Lineage in the Life Stories of Czech Business Elite Persons', *Sociology*, 35: 815-833.

Ansoff, H.I. (1979), *Strategic Management*, New York: John Wiley.

Anthony, P.D. (1977), *The Ideology of Work*, London: Tavistock Publications.

Apel, K.O. (1979), 'Types of Rationality Today: The Continuum of Reason between Science and Ethics', in T. Geraets (ed.), *Rationality Today*, Ottawa: The University of Ottawa Press.

Argyris, C. (1998), 'Empowerment: The Emperor's New Clothes', *Harvard Business Review*, 76 (3): 98-105.

Argyris, C. (2000), *Flawed Advice and the Management Trap*, Oxford: Oxford University Press.

Arias, M.E. and Guillén, M. (1998), 'The Transfer of Organizational Techniques across Borders: Combining Neo-Institutional and Comparative Perspectives', in J.L. Alvarez (ed.), *The Diffusion and Consumption of Business Knowledge*, New York: St. Martin's Press.

Armstrong, H. (2000), 'The Learning Organization: Changed Means to an Unchanged End', *Organization*, 7: 355-61.

Aronowitz, S. and DiFazio, W. (1994), *The Jobless Future: Sci-Tech and the Dogma of Work*, Minneapolis, MN: University of Minnesota Press.

Ashenfelter, O. and Rouse, C. (2000), 'Schooling, Intelligence, and Income in America' in K. Arrow, S. Bowles, and S. Durlauf (eds.), *Meritocracy and Economic Inequality*, Princeton, NJ: Princeton University Press.

Ashford, D.E. (1986), *The Emergence of the Welfare States*, Oxford: Blackwell.

Askenazy, P. (2001), 'Innovative Workplace Practices and Occupational Injuries and Illnesses in the United States', *Economic and Industrial Democracy*, 22: 485-516.

Avishai, B. (1994), 'What is Business's Social Compact?', *Harvard Business Review*, 72 (1): 38-48.

Badaracco, J.L. (1997), *Defining Moments: When Managers Must Choose between Right and Right*, Boston, MA: Harvard Business School Publishing.

Bailyn, L. (1992), 'Changing the Conditions of Work: Responding to Increasing Work Force Diversity and New Family Patterns', in T. Kochan and M. Useem (eds.), *Transforming Organizations*, New York: Oxford University Press.

Bannister, R. (1988), *Social Darwinism: Science and Myth in Anglo-American Social Thought*, Philadelphia, PA: Temple University Press.

Barash, D.P. (1986), *The Hare and the Tortoise: Culture, Biology, and Human Nature*, New York: Viking Press.

Baritz, L. (1960), *The Servants of Power: A History of the Use of Social Science in American Industry*, New York: John Wiley.

Barker, J. (1993), 'Tightening the Iron Cage: Concertive Control in Self-Managing Teams', *Administrative Science Quarterly*, 38: 408-437.

Barker, J. (1999), *The Discipline of Teamwork: Participation and Concertive Control*, Thousand Oaks, CA: Sage.

Barley, S. R (1994), '[book review of] Paul S. Adler (ed.), *Technology and the Future of Work*', *Administrative Science Quarterly*, 39: 183-186.

Barley, S.R. and Kunda, G. (1992), 'Design and Devotion: Surges of Rational and Normative Control in Managerial Discourse', *Administrative Science Quarterly*, 37: 363-399.

Barley, S.R. and Kunda, G. (2001), 'Bringing Work back in', *Organization Science*, 12: 76-95.

Barley, S.R., Meyer, G. and Gash, D. (1988), 'Cultures of Culture: Academics, Practitioners and the Pragmatics of Normative Control', *Administrative Science Quarterly*, 33: 24-60.

Barnard, C. (1976 [1938]), *The Functions of the Executive*, Cambridge, MA: Harvard University Press.

Barnett, W.P. and Carroll, G.R. (1995), 'Modeling Internal Organizational Change' *Annual Review of Sociology*, 21: 217-236.

Basil, D.C. (1971), *Leadership Skills for Executive Action*, New York: American Management Association.

Basso, P. (2003), *Modern Times, Ancient Hours: Working Lives in the Twenty-First Century*, London: Verso.

Bauman, Z. (1992), *Intimations of Postmodernity*, London: Routledge.

Beder, S. (2000), *Selling the Work Ethic: From Puritan Pulpit to Corporate PR*, London: Zed Books.

Beer, S. (1972), *Brain of the Firm: A Development in Management Cybernetics*, New York: Herder and Herder.

Bell, D. (1973), *The Coming of Post-Industrial Society: A Venture in Social Forecasting*, New York: Basic Books.

Bell, D. (1988 [1962]), *The End of Ideology: On the Exhaustion of Political Ideas in the Fifties*, Cambridge, MA: Harvard University Press.

Bello, W., Bullard, N. and Malhotra, K. (eds.) (2000), *Global Finance: New Thinking on Regulating Speculative Capital Markets*, London: Zed Books.

Bendix, R. (1956), *Work and Authority in Industry: Ideologies of Management in the Course of Industrialization*, New York: John Wiley.

Bendix, R. and Lipset, S.M. (1966), 'Karl Marx's Theory of Social Classes', in R. Bendix, and S.M. Lipset (eds.) *Class, Status and Power: Social Stratification in Comparative Perspective*, 2nd ed., New York: The Free Press.

Bennet, A. (1990), *The Death of the Organization Man*, New York: William Morrow.

Bennett, F. (2001), 'Seeking Equality in an Unequal Society', *Social Watch*, 5: 164-165.

Bennis, W. and Slater, P. (1968), *The Temporary Society*, New York: Harper & Row.

Berglund, J. and Werr, A. (2000), 'The Invincible Character of Management Consulting Rhetoric: How One Blends Incommensurates While Keeping Them Apart', *Organization*, 7: 633-655.

Bergquist, W.H. (1993), *The Postmodern Organization: Mastering the Art of Irreversible Change*, San Francisco, CA: Jossey Bass.

Berle, A. and Means, G. (1968 [1932]), *The Modern Corporation and Private Property*, rev. ed., New York: Harcourt, Brace and World.

Bierstedt, R. (1981), *American Sociological Theory: A Critical History*, New York: Academic Press.

Birdsall, N., Graham, C. and Pettinato, S. (2000), 'Stuck in the Tunnel: Is Globalization Muddling the Middle Class?', Carnegie Endowment for International Peace, Discussion Paper No. 1.

Blanchflower, D. and Oswald, A. (1999), 'Well-being, Insecurity and the Decline of American Job Satisfaction', Working Paper, Dartmouth College.

Blau, P. (1968), 'The Study of Formal Organizations', in T. Parsons (ed.) *American Sociology: Perspectives, Problems, Methods*, New York: Basic Books.

Blauner, R. (1966), 'Work Satisfaction and Industrial Trends in Modern Society', in R. Bendix and S.M. Lipset (eds.) *Class, Status and Power: Social Stratification in Comparative Perspective*, 2nd ed., New York: The Free Press.

Block, P. (1987), *The Empowered Manager: Positive Political Skills at Work*, San Francisco, CA: Jossey Bass.

Bluestone, B. (1995), *The Polarization of American Society: Victims, Suspects, and Mysteries to Unravel*, New York: Twentieth Century Fund Press.

Boje, D. and Dennehy, R. (1994), *Managing in the Postmodern World: America's Revolution against Exploitation*, Dubuque, IA: Kendall Hunt.

Boje, D. and Winsor, R. (1993), 'The Resurrection of Taylorism: Total Quality Management's Hidden Agenda', *Journal of Organizational Change Management*, 6 (4): 57-70.

Boltanski, L. and Chiapello, E. (1999), *Le nouvel esprit du capitalisme*, París: Gallimard.

Borgmann, A. (1992), *Crossing the Postmodern Divide*, Chicago, IL: University of Chicago Press.

Bottomore, T. (1992), 'Breves notas críticas sobre el trabajo y el desempleo', *El Socialismo del Futuro*, 6: 119-121.

Bowles, S. and Nelson, V. (1974), 'The "Inheritance of IQ" and the Intergenerational Reproduction of Economic Inequality', *Review of Economics and Statistics*, 56: 39-51.

Boyett, J. and Conn, H. (1991), *Workplace 2000: The Revolution Reshaping American Business*, New York: Dutton.

Boyns, T. (1998), 'Budgets and Budgetary Control in British Businesses to c.1945', *Accounting, Business and Financial History*, 3: 261-301.

Bradley, H., Erickson, M., Stephenson, C. and Williams, S. (2000), *Myths at Work*, Cambridge: Polity Press.

Braudel, F. (1983), *The Wheels of Commerce: Civilization and Capitalism 15th.-18th. Century*, vol. 2, New York: Harper & Row.

Braverman, H. (1974), *Labor and Monopoly Capital: The Degradation of Work in the Twentieth Century*, New York: Monthly Review Press.

Breen, R. and Goldthorpe, J.H. (1999), 'Class Inequality and Meritocracy: A Critique of Saunders and an Alternative Analysis', *British Journal of Sociology*, 50: 1-27.

Breen, R. and Goldthorpe, J.H. (2002), 'Merit, Mobility and Method: Another Reply to Saunders', *British Journal of Sociology*, 53: 575-582.

Brenner, M., Fairris, D. and Ruser, J. (2002), '"Flexible" Work Practices and Occupational Safety and Health: Exploring the Relationship Between Cumulative Trauma Disorders and Workplace Transformation', Political Economy Research Institute, University of Massachussets at Amherst, Working Paper No. 30.

Brevoort, K. and Marvel, H. (2001), 'Successful Monopolization Through Predation: The National Cash Register Company', Working Paper, Ohio State University, Department of Economics.

Bridges, W. (1994), 'The End of the Job', *Fortune*, September 19: 46-51.

Bridges, W. (1995), *Job Shift: How to Prosper in Workplace without Jobs*, Reading, MA: Perseus Books.

Brief, A.P. (2000), 'Still Servants of Power', *Journal of Management Inquiry*, 9: 342-351.

Brody, D. (1980), 'Labor and Small-Scale Enterprise During Industrialization' in S.W. Bruchey (ed.) *Small Business in American Life*, New York, Columbia University Press, quoted in E.J. Englander, 'The Inside Contract System of Production and Organization: A Neglected Aspect of the History of the Firm', *Labor History* 28 (1987): 429-446.

Brooke, M.Z. (1984), *Centralization and Autonomy: A Study in Organization Behaviour*, London: Holt, Rinehart and Winston.

Brown, H. (1980), 'Work Groups', in G. Salaman and K. Thompson (eds.) *Control and Ideology in Organizations*, Cambridge, MA: The MIT Press.

Brynjolfsson, E. and Hitt, L. (1999), 'Paradox Lost? Firm-Level Evidence on the Returns to Information Systems Spending', in L.P. Willcocks and S. Lester (eds.), *Beyond the IT Productivity Paradox*, San Francisco, CA: Jossey Bass.

Buber, M. (1987 [1949]), *Caminos de Utopía*, México: F.C.E.

Buckingham, W. (1961), *Automation: Its Impact on Business and People*, New York: Harper & Row.

Bunge, M. (1981), 'Status epistemológico de la administración', *Administración de Empresas*, 11: 1145-1149.

Burawoy, M. (1978), 'Toward a Marxist Theory of the Labor Process: Braverman and Beyond', *Politics and Society*, 8: 247-312.

Burawoy, M. (1985), *The Politics of Production: Factory Regimes under Capitalism and Socialism*, London: Verso.

Burawoy, M. and Wright, E.O. (1990), 'Coercion and Consent in Contested Exchange', *Politics and Society*, 18: 251-266.

Burnham, J. (1941), *The Managerial Revolution*, New York: John Day Company.

Burns, T. (1969), 'On the Plurality of Social Systems', in T. Burns (ed.) *Industrial Man*, Harmondsworth: Penguin.

Burns, T. and Stalker, G.M. (1961), *The Management of Innovation*, London: Tavistock Publications.

Business Week (1993), 'The Virtual Corporation', February 8: 36-40.

Cage, J. (1992), *From the Ground Up: The Resurgence of American Entrepreneurship*, New York: Simon and Schuster.

Cameron, K. and Quinn, R.E. (1999), *Diagnosing and Changing Organizational Culture: Based on the Competing Values Framework*, Reading, MA: Addison Wesley.

Capon, N., Farley, J. and Hulbert, J. (1994), 'Strategic Planning and Financial Performance: More Evidence', *Journal of Management Studies*, 31: 105-110.

Cappelli, P. (1993), 'Are Skill Requirements Rising? Evidence from Production and Clerical Jobs', *Industrial and Labor Relations Review*, 46: 515-530.

Cappelli, P. and Neumark, D. (2001), 'Do 'High Performance' Work Practices Improve Establishment-Level Outcomes?' *Industrial and Labor Relations Review*, 54: 737-775.

Carew, A. (1987), *Labour under the Marshall Plan: The Politics of Productivity and the Marketing of Management Science*, Detroit, MI: Wayne State University Press.

Carey, A. (1967), 'The Hawthorne Studies: A Radical Criticism', *American Sociological Review*, 32: 403-416.

Carnegie, A. (1889), 'Wealth,' *North American Review*, 148 (391): 653-664.

Carroll, G. and Hannan, M. (2000), *The Demography of Corporations and Industries*, Princeton, NJ: Princeton University Press.

Carroll, J.B. (1982), 'The Measurement of Intelligence', in R.J. Sternberg (ed.), *Handbook of Human Intelligence*, Cambridge: Cambridge University Press.

Carter, C. and Crowther, D. (2000), 'Organizational Consumerism: The Appropriation of Packaged Managerial Knowledge', *Management Decision*, 38: 626-637.

Casey, C. (1996), 'Corporate Transformations: Designer Culture, Designer Employees and "Post-occupational" Solidarity', *Organization*, 3: 317-339.

Castells, M. (1998), 'Information Technology, Globalization and Social Development', Paper prepared for the UNRISD Conference on Information Technologies and Social Development, Palais des Nations, Geneva, 22-24 June.

Caudron, S. (2001), 'The Myth of Job Happiness', *Workforce*, 80 (4): 32-36.

Cawley, J., Conneelly, K., Heckman, J. and Vytlacil, E. (1997), 'Cognitive Ability, Wages, and Meritocracy', in B. Devlin, S. Fienberg, D. Resnick, and K. Roeder (eds.), *Intelligence, Genes, and Success: Scientists Respond to the 'The Bell Curve'*, New York: Springer Verlag.

Cawley, J., Heckman, J. and Vytlacil, E. (1999), 'Meritocracy in America: An Examination of Wages Within and Across Occupations', *Industrial Relations*, 38: 250-296.

Chandler, A.D. (1977), *The Visible Hand: The Management Revolution in American Business*, Cambridge, MA: The Belknap Press of Harvard University Press.

Chandler, A.D. (1992), 'Organizational Capabilities and the Economic History of the Industrial Enterprise', *Journal of Economic Perspectives*, 6: 79-100.

Chatman, J.A. (1991), 'Matching People and Organizations: Selection and Socialization in Public Accounting Firms', *Administrative Science Quarterly*, 36: 459-484.

Chiapello, E. and Fairclough, N. (2002), 'Understanding the New Management Ideology: A Transdisciplinary Contribution from Critical Discourse Analysis and New Sociology of Capitalism', *Discourse and Society*, 13: 185-508.

Child, J. (1969), *The Business Enterprise in Modern Industrial Society*, London: Collier Macmillan.

Chinoy, E. (1955), *Automobile Workers and the American Dream*, New York: Random House, quoted in A. Raucher (1987), 'Employee Relations at General Motors: The 'My Job Contest' (1947), *Labor History*, 28: 221-232.

Chorover, S.L. (1979), *From Genesis to Genocide: The Meaning of Human Nature and the Power of Behavior Control*, Cambridge, MA: The MIT Press.

Cilliers, P. (1998), *Complexity and Postmodernism: Understanding Complex Systems*, London: Routledge.

Clarke, T. and Clegg, S. (1998), *Changing Paradigms: The Transformation of Management Knowledge for the 21st Century*, London: Harper Collins.

Clawson, D. (1980), *Bureaucracy and the Labor Process: The Transformation of U.S. Industry, 1860-1920*, New York: Monthly Review Press.

Clegg, S. (1981), 'Organization and Control', *Administrative Science Quarterly*, 26: 545-562.

Clegg, S. and Palmer, G. (1996), 'Introduction: Producing Management Knowledge', in S. Clegg and G. Palmer (eds.), *The Politics of Management Knowledge*, London: Sage.

Clevelan, H. (1989), 'Control: The Twilight of Hierarchy', in G. Morgan, *Creative Organization Theory*, Newbury Park, CA: Sage.

Collins, R. (1988), *Theoretical Sociology*, New York: Harcourt Brace Jovanovich.

Cooley, C.H. (1922 [1902]), *Human Nature and the Social Order,* New York: Charles Scribner's Sons.

Coombs, R. (1984), 'Long Waves and Labour-Process Change' *Review*, 7: 675-701.

Coriat, B. (1979), *L'atelier et le chronomètre. Essai sur le taylorisme, le fordisme et la production de masse*, París: Christian Bourgois.

Coriat, B. (1991), *Penser à l'envers. Travail et organisation dans l'entreprise japonaise*, París: Christian Bourgois.

Coriat, B. (1994), 'Los desafíos de la competitividad', *Realidad Económica*, 125: 61-91.

Cornaton, M. (1969), *Groupes et société,* Toulouse: Edouard Privat.

Cowling, K. and Tomlinson, P. (2000), 'The Japanese Crisis: A Case of Strategic Failure?', *The Economic Journal*, 110 (464): F358-F381.

Crawford, R. (1991), *In the Era of Human Capital: The Emergence of Talent, Intelligence and Knowledge as the Worldwide Economic Force and What It Means to Managers and Investors*, New York: Harper Business.

Cross, G. (2002), *An All-Consuming Century: Why Commercialism Won in Modern America*, New York: Columbia University Press.

Cyert, R.M. and March, J.G. (1963), *A Behavioral Theory of the Firm*, Englewood Cliffs, NJ: Prentice-Hall.

Dahrendorf, R. (1959), *Class and Class Conflict in Industrial Society*, Stanford, CA: Stanford University Press.

Dalla Costa, J. (1998), *The Ethical Imperative: Why Moral Leadership is Good Business*, New York: Addison Wesley.

Dannel, R. (2000), 'Stratification among Journals in Management Research: A Bibliometric Study of Interaction between European and American Journals', *Scientometrics*, 49: 23-38.

Davidow, W. and Malone, M. (1992), *The Virtual Corporation: Structuring and Revitalizing the Corporation for the 21st Century*, New York: Harper Collins.

Dawkins, R. (1976), *The Selfish Gene*, New York: Oxford University Press.

de Gaudemar, J.-P. (1982), *L'ordre et la production. Naissance et formes de la discipline d'usine, París:* Dunod.

Deal, T. and Kennedy, A. (1982), *Corporate Cultures: The Rites and Rituals of Corporate Life*, Reading, MA: Addison-Wesley.

Degler, C. (1992), *In Search of Human Nature: The Decline and Revival of Darwinism in American Social Thought*, New York: Oxford University Press.

den Hertog, F. (1998), '[book review of] Matts Alvesson, *Management of Knowledge-Intensive Companies* and Georg von Krogh and Johan Roos (eds.), *Managing Knowledge: Perspectives on Cooperation and Competition'*, *Organization Studies*, 19: 1053-1058.

Derber, C., Schwartz, W. and Magrass, Y. (1990), *Power in the Highest Degree: Professionals and the Rise of a New Mandarin Order*, New York: Oxford University Press.

Despres, C. and Chauvel, D. (1999), 'Knowledge Management(s)', *Journal of Knowledge Management*, 3 (2): 110-120.

Diewert, W.E. and Fox, K. (1999), 'Can Measurement Error Explain the Productivity Paradox?', *Canadian Journal of Economics*, 32 (2): 251-280.

Donaldson, L. (1995), *American Anti-management Theories of Organization: A Critique of Paradigm Proliferation*, Cambridge: Cambridge University Press.

Donaldson, L. (1996a), *For Positivist Organization Theory: Proving the Hard Core*, London: Sage.

Donaldson, L. (1996b), 'The Normal Science of Structural Contingency Theory', in S. Clegg, C. Hardy, and W. Nord (eds.), *Handbook of Organization Studies*, Newbury Park, CA: Sage.

Drucker, P.F. (1954), *The Practice of Management*, New York: Harper & Row.

Drucker, P.F. (1969), *The Age of Discontinuity*, New York: Harper & Row.

Drucker, P.F. (1990), 'The Emerging Theory of Manufacturing', *Harvard Business Review*, 68 (3): 94-102.

Drucker, P.F. (1992a), *Managing for the Future: The 1990s and Beyond*, New York: Truman Talley Books / Dutton.

Drucker, P.F. (1992b), 'The Post-capitalist World', *The Public Interest*, 109 :89-101.

Drucker, P.F. (1992c), 'The New Society of Organizations', *Harvard Business Review*, 70 (5): 95-104.

Drucker, P.F. (1993 [1974]), *Management: Tasks, Responsibilities, Practices*, New York: Harper Business.

Drucker, P.F. (1993a), *Post-capitalist Society*, New York: Harper Business.

Drucker, P.F. (1993b), 'The Post-capitalist Executive', interview by George T. Harris, *Harvard Business Review*, 71 (3): 115-122.

du Gay, P. (1991), 'Enterprise Culture and the Ideology of Excellence', *New Formations*, 13: 45–61.

Duck, J.D. (1993), 'Managing Change: the Art of Balancing', *Harvard Business Review*, 71 (6): 108-118.

Duménil, G. and Lévy, D. (1993), 'The Emergence and Functions of Managerial and Clerical Personnel in Marx's Capital', in N. Garston (ed.), *Bureaucracy: Three Paradigms*, Boston, MA: Kluwer Academic Publishers.

Dupin, C. (1832), 'Rapport à l'Académie des sciences, sur un mémoire de M. Emile Béres', in M. E. Béres, *Causes du malaise industriel et commerciel de la France et moyens d'y remédier*, París: Paulin.

Eagleton, T. (1991), *Ideology: An Introduction*, London: Verso.

Eccles, R. and Nohria, N. (1992), *Beyond the Hype: Rediscovering the Essence of Management*, Boston, MA: Harvard Business School Press.

Edwards, R. (1979), *Contested Terrain: The Transformation of the Workplace in the Twentieth Century*, New York: Basic Books.

Edwards, S. (2001), 'Factory and Fantasy in Andrew Ure', *Journal of Design History*, 14: 17-34.

Ely, R.T. (1885), 'Pullman: A Social Study', *Harper's New Monthly Magazine*, 70: 452-466.

Emmet, B. (1917), 'Extent of Profit-Sharing in the United States: Its Bearing on Industrial Unrest', *Journal of Political Economy*, 25: 1019-1033.

Emshoff, J.R. (1971), *Analysis of Behavioral Systems*, New York: Macmillan.

Englander, E.J. (1987), 'The Inside Contract System of Production and Organization: A Neglected Aspect of the History of the Firm', *Labor History*, 28: 429-446.

Engwall, L. (1996), 'The Vikings versus the World: An Examination of Nordic Business Research', *Scandinavian Journal of Management*, 12: 425-436.

Engwall, L. (2000), 'Foreign Role Models and Standardisation in Nordic Business Education', *Scandinavian Journal of Management*, 16: 1-24.

Ernst, B. and Kieser, A. (2000), 'How Consultants Outcompete Management Scientists on the Market of Management Knowledge', Paper prepared for presentation at the Workshop of the Kommission für Organisation, Zurich.

Ezzamel, M. and Willmott, H.C. (1998), 'Accounting for Teamwork: A Critical Study of Group-Based Systems of Organizational Control', *Administrative Science Quarterly*, 43: 358-396.

Farson, R. (1996), 'Managing: The Art of the Absurd', *Psychology Today*, 30 (3): 44-46.

Fierman, J. (1994), 'The Contingency Work Force', *Fortune*, January 24: 20-25.

Fincham, R. (1995), 'Business Process Re-engineering and the Commodification of Management Knowledge', *Journal of Marketing Management*, 11: 707-720.

Fischer, C.S., Hout, M., Sánchez M., Lucas, S., Swidler A. and Voss K. (1996), *Inequality by Design: Cracking the Bell Curve Myth*, Princeton, NJ: Princeton University Press.

Fleischman, R.K. (2000), 'Completing the Triangle: Taylorism and the Paradigms', *Accounting Auditing & Accountability Journal*, 13: 597-623.

Folsom, B.W. (1996), *The Myth of the Robber Barons: A New Look at the Rise of Big Business in America*, Herndon, VA: Young America's Foundation.

Fontaine, P. and Marco, L. (1993), 'La gestion d'entreprise dans la pensée économique française aux XVIIIe et XIXe siècles', *Revue d'economie politique*, 103: 483-612.

Fourier, C. (1831), *Pièges et charlatanisme des deux sectes Saint-Simon et Owen qui promettent l'association et le progrès*, París: Bossange.

Fourier, C. (1971 [1829]), *Le nouveau monde industriel et sociétaire ou Invention du procédé d'industrie attrayante et naturelle distribuée en séries passionnées*, París: Anthropos.

Frank, T. (2000), *One Market under God: Extreme Capitalism, Market Populism, and the End of Economic Democracy*, New York: Doubleday.

Franke, R.H. and Kaul, J.D. (1978), 'The Hawthorne Experiments: First Statistical Interpretation', *American Sociological Review*, 43: 623-643.

Frankel, L. and Fleisher, A. (1920), *The Human Factor in Industry*, New York: The Macmillan Company.

Freedman, D.H. (1992), 'Is Management Still a Science?', *Harvard Business Review*, 70 (6): 26-38.

Freeman, R.B. and Kleimer, M. (2000), 'Who Benefits Most from Employee Involvement: Firms or Workers?', *American Economic Review*, 90 (2): 219-223.

Fromm, E. (1963), 'Man is not a Thing', in H.M. Ruitenbeek (ed.), *The Dilemma of Organizational Society*, New York: Dutton.

Frost, C., Wakeley, J.H. and Ruh, R.A. (1974), *The Scanlon Plan for Organizational Development: Identity, Participation and Equity*, East Lansing, MI: Michigan State University Press.

Fry, B.R. and Thomas, L.L. (1996), 'Mary Parker Follett: Assessing the Contribution and Impact of Her Writings', *Journal of Management History*, 2 (2): 11-19.

Furusten, S. (1998), 'The Creation of Popular Management Texts', in J.L. Alvarez (ed.), *The Diffusion and Consumption of Business Knowledge*, New York: St. Martin's Press

Furusten, S. (1999), *Popular Management Books: How They Are Made and What They Mean for Organizations*, London: Routledge.

Gabor, A. (2000), *The Capitalist Philosophers. The Geniuses of Modern Business: Their Lives, Times and Ideas*, New York. Times Books.

Galbraith, J. K. (1992), *The Culture of Contentment*, Boston, MA: Houghton Mifflin.

Gamache, R.D. and Kuhn, R.L. (1989), *The Creative Infusion: How Managers Can Start and Sustain Creativity and Innovation*, New York: Harper & Row.

Gantman, E.R. (1994), 'Reflexiones desde el podio', *Desarrollo Económico*, 33: 612-615.

Gantt, H. (1970 [1919]), 'The Parting of the Ways', in H.F. Merrill (ed.), *Classics in Management*, New York: American Management Association.

Gardner, H. (1993), *Frames of Mind: The Theory of Multiple Intelligence*, New York: Basic Books.

Garvin, D. (1988), *Managing Quality: The Strategic and Competitive Edge*, New York: The Free Press.

George, C.S. (1968), *The History of Management Thought*, Englewood Cliffs, NJ: Prentice Hall.

Gilbreth, F. (1970 [1923]), 'Science in Management for the One Best Way', in H.F. Merrill (ed.), *Classics in Management*, New York: American Management Association.

Gilder, G. (1981), *Wealth and Poverty*, New York: Basic Books.

Gillespie, R. (1991), *Manufacturing Knowledge: A History of the Hawthorne Experiments*, Cambridge: Cambridge University Press.

Gilman, N. (1892), 'Profit Sharing in the United States', *The New England Magazine*, 13 (1): 120-128.

Gladden, W. (1876), *Working People and Their Employers*, Boston, MA: Lockwood, Brooks.

Gladden, W. (1886), *Applied Christianity: Moral Aspects of Social Questions*, Boston, MA: Houghton Mifflin.

Godard, John (2001), 'High Performance and the Transformation of Work? The Implications of Alternative Work Practices for the Experience and Outcomes of Work', *Industrial and Labor Relations Review*, 54: 776-805.

Goleman, D. (1995), *Emotional Intelligence*, New York: Bantam Books.

Goleman, D. (1998), *Working with Emotional Intelligence*, New York: Bantam Books.

Goleman, D., Boyatzis, R. and McKee, A. (2002), *Primal Leadership: Realizing the Power of Emotional Intelligence*, Boston, MA: Harvard Business School Press.

Goode, W.J. (1967), 'The Protection of the Inept', *American Sociological Review*, 32: 5-19.

Gordon, D., Edwards, R. and Reich, M. (1982), *Segmented Work, Divided Workers: The Historical Transformation of Labor in the United States*, Cambridge: Cambridge University Press.

Gorz, A. (1982), *Farewell to the Working Class*, London: Pluto Press.

Gorz, A. (1992), 'La declinante relevancia del trabajo y el auge de los valores post-económicos', *El Socialismo del Futuro*, 6: 25-31.

Goshal, S., Bartlett, C. and Moran, P. (1999), 'A New Manifesto for Management', *Sloan Management Review*, 40 (3): 9-20.

Gouldner, A.W. (1976), *The Dialectic of Ideology and Technology: The Origins, Grammar, and Future of Ideology*, New York: Seabury Press.

Gratton, L., Hope-Hailey, V., Stiles, P. and Truss, C. (1999), *Strategic Human Resource Management: Corporate Rhetoric and Human Reality*, Oxford: Oxford University Press.

Grenier, G. (1988), *Inhuman Relations: Quality Circles and Anti-Unionism in American Industry*, Philadelphia, PA: Temple University Press.

Grey, C. (1999), ' "We Are All Managers Now"; "We Always Were": On the Development and Demise of Management', *Journal of Management Studies*, 36: 561-585.

Grey, C. (2002), 'What Are Business Schools For? On Silence and Voice in Management Education', *Journal of Management Education*, 26: 496-511.

Griffin, L.J. and Kalleberg, A.L. (1981), 'Stratification and Meritocracy in the United States: Class and Occupational Recruitment Patterns', *British Journal of Sociology*, 32: 1-35.

Guerreiro Ramos, A. (1981), *The New Science of Organizations: A Reconceptualization of The Wealth of Nations*, Toronto: University of Toronto Press.

Guillén, M. (1994), *Models of Management: Work, Authority and Organization in a Comparative Perspective*, Chicago, IL: University of Chicago Press.

Guiot, J.M. (1980), *Organisations sociales et comportements*, París: Editions Hommes et Techniques.

Habermas, J. (1972), *Knowledge and Human Interests*, London: Heinemann.

Hackman, R. (1978), 'The Design of Self-Managing Groups', in B. King, F. Fiedler and S. Streufert (eds.), *Managerial Control and Organizational Democracy*, Washington, DC: W.H. Winston.

Halaby, C.N. and Weakliem, D. (1993), 'Ownership and Authority in the Earnings Function: Nonnested Test of Alternative Specifications', *American Sociological Review*, 58: 16-30.

Halal, W. (1986), *The New Capitalism*, New York: John Wiley.

Hammer, M. (1993), 'The Age of Reengineering [Interview with Michael Hammer and James Champy]', *Across the Board*, 30 (6): 26-33.

Hammer, M. and Champy, J. (1993), *Reengineering the Corporation: A Manifesto for Business Revolution*, New York: Harper Collins.

Hancock, P.G. (1997), 'Citizenship or Vassalage? Organizational Membership in the Age of Unreason', *Organization*, 4: 93-112.

Handy, C. (1994), *The Age of Paradox*, Boston, MA: Harvard Business School Press.

Handy, C. (1997), 'The Citizen Corporation', *Harvard Business Review*, 75 (5): 26-28.

Hannan, M. and Freeman, J. (1977), 'The Population Ecology of Organizations', *American Journal of Sociology*, 82: 929-964.

Hannan, M. and Freeman, J. (1989), *Organizational Ecology*, Cambridge, MA: Harvard University Press.

Harkins, S.G. and Szymanski, K. (1989), 'Social Loafing and Group Evaluation', *Journal of Personality and Social Psychology*, 56: 934-941.

Harley, B. (1999), 'The Myth of Empowerment: Work Organisation, Hierarchy and Employee Autonomy in Contemporary Australian Workplaces', *Work, Employment & Society*, 13: 41-66.

Harmon, F.G. (1996), *Playing for Keeps: How the World's Most Aggressive and Admired Companies Use Core Values to Manage, Energize, and Organize Their People and Promote, Advance, and Achieve their Corporate Missions*, New York: John Wiley.

Harrington, M. (1972), *Socialism*, New York: Saturday Review Press.

Harris, P. (1985), *Management in Transition: Transforming Managerial Practices and Organizational Strategies for a New Work Culture*, San Francisco, CA: Jossey Bass.

Harrison, B. (1994), *Lean and Mean: The Changing Landscape of Corporate Power in the Age of Flexibility*, New York: Basic Books.

Hart, S.L. (1997), 'Beyond Greening: Strategies for a Sustainable World', *Harvard Business Review*, 75 (1): 66-76.

Harvey, D. (1989), *The Condition of Postmodernity*, Oxford: Basil Blackwell.

Hayek, F.A. (1944), *The Road to Serfdom*, London: Routledge.

Hayek, F.A. (1973), *Law, Legislation and Liberty*, vol. 1, *Rules and Order*, Chicago, IL: The University of Chicago Press.

Hayes, R. and Watts, R. (1986), *Corporate Revolution: New Strategies for Executive Leadership*, London: Heinemann.

Hayes, R.H. (1975), 'Qualitative Insights from Quantitative Methods' in *Harvard Business Review, On Management*, New York: Harper & Row.

Heckscher, C. (1995), *White-Collar Blues: Management Loyalties in an Age of Corporate Restructuring*, New York: Basic Books.

Heizer, J.H. (1998), 'Determining Responsibility for Development of the Moving Assembly Line', *Journal of Management History*, 4 (2): 94-103.

Herman, E. (1981), *Corporate Control, Corporate Power*, Cambridge: Cambridge University Press.
Herrnstein, R. and Murray, C. (1994), *The Bell Curve: Intelligence and Class Structure in American Life*, New York: Free Press.
Heydebrand, W. (1989), 'New Organizational Forms', *Work and Occupations*, 16: 323-357.
Hilmer, F. and Donaldson, L. (1996), 'The Trivialization of Management', *The McKinsey Quarterly*, no. 4: 26-37.
Hilpert, U. (1990), 'Techno-Industrial Innovation, Social Development, and State Policies', *International Political Science Review*, 11: 75-86.
Hirschhorn, L. and Gilmore, T. (1992), 'The New Boundaries of the "Boundaryless" Company', *Harvard Business Review*, 70 (3): 104-115.
Hofstadter, R. (1992 [1944]), *Social Darwinism in American Thought*, Boston, MA: Beacon Press.
Holland, J.L. (1985), *Making Vocational Choices. A Theory of Vocational Personalities and Work Environments*, Englewood Cliffs, NJ: Prentice Hall.
Hood, C. and Jackson, M. (1991), *Administrative Argument*, Aldershot: Dartmouth.
Horowitz, I.L. (1977), *Ideology and Utopia in the United States, 1956-1976*, New York: Oxford University Press.
Howell, D.R. and Wolff, E.N. (1992), 'Technical Change and the Demand for Skills by US Industries', *Cambridge Journal of Economics*, 16: 127-146.
Howland, E. (1872), 'An Industrial Experiment at South Manchester', *Harper's New Monthly Magazine*, 45: 836-844.
Hoxie, R. (1915), *Scientific Management and Labor*, New York: D. Appleton.
Hoxie, R. (1916), 'Scientific Management and Labor Welfare', *Journal of Political Economy*, 24: 833-854.
Huber, G.P (1996), 'Organization Learning: The Contributing Processes and the Literatures', in M.D. Cohen and L.S. Sproull (eds.), *Organizational Learning*, Thousand Oaks, CA: Sage.
Huczynski, A. (1993), *The Management Gurus: What Makes Them and How to Become One*, London: Routledge.
Huggins, L.P. (1998), 'Total Quality Management and the Contributions of A.V. Feigenbaum', *Journal of Management History*, 4 (1): 60-67.
Hunt, F. (1856), *Worth and Wealth: A Collection of Maxims, Morals and Miscellanies for Merchants and Men of Business*, New York: Stringer & Townsend.
Huselid, M.A. (1995), 'The Impact of Human Resource Management Practices on Turnover, Productivity, and Corporate Financial Performance', *Academy of Management Journal*, 38: 635-672.
Jackson, M., Goldthorpe, J. and Mills, C. (2002), 'Education, Employers and Class Mobility', Paper prepared for the meeting of the International Sociological Association, Research Committee 28, Social Stratification and Mobility, Nuffield College, University of Oxford, April 10-13.
Jacoby, S. (1997), *Modern Manors: Welfare Capitalism since the New Deal*, Princeton, NJ: Princeton University Press.
Jacoby, S. (2001), 'A Century of Human Resource Management', Paper presented at the 75th Anniversary Conference of Industrial Relations Counselors, Princeton University, September 11.
Jacques, R. (1996), *Manufacturing the Employee: Management Knowledge from the 19th to 21st Centuries*, London: Sage.
Jameson, F. (1989), 'Marxism and Postmodernism', *New Left Review*, no. 176: 31-45.
Jameson, F. (1991), *Postmodernism, or, The Cultural Logic of Late Capitalism*. Durham, NC: Duke University Press.

Jamieson, D. and O'Mara, J. (1991), *Managing Workforce 2000: Gaining the Diversity Advantage*, San Francisco, CA: Jossey Bass.

Janet, P. (1915), *Les néuroses*, París: Flammarion, quoted in E. Mayo, *The Social Problems of an Industrial Civilization*, (1945), Boston, MA: Division of Research, Harvard University, Graduate School of Business Administration/The Andover Press.

Janis, I.L. (1972), *Victims of Groupthink: A Psychological Study of Foreign-Policy Decisions and Fiascoes*, Boston, MA: Houghton Mifflin.

Jaques, E. (1990), 'In Praise of Hierarchy', *Harvard Business Review*, 68 (1): 127-133.

Jencks, C., Smith M., Acland H., Bane M., Cohen D., Ginits H., Heyns B. and Michelson S. (1972), *Inequality: A Reassessment of the Effect of Family and Schooling in America*, New York: Basic Books.

Johnson, R., Kast, F. and Rosenzweig, J. (1963), *The Theory and Management of Systems*, New York: McGraw-Hill.

Johnson, T. and Kaplan, R.S. (1987), *Relevance Lost: The Rise and Fall of Management Accounting*, Boston, MA: Harvard Business School Press.

Kakar, S. (1970), *Frederick W. Taylor: A Study in Personality and Innovation*, Cambridge, MA: The MIT Press.

Kanter, R.M. (1972), *Commitment and Community: Communes and Utopias in Sociological Perspective*, Cambridge, MA: Harvard University Press, quoted in R. Russell, *Sharing Ownership at the Workplace*, (1985), Albany, NY: State University of New York Press.

Kanter, R.M. (1989a), 'The New Managerial Work', *Harvard Business Review*, 67 (6): 85-92.

Kanter, R.M. (1989b), *When Giants Learn to Dance*, New York: Simon and Schuster.

Kärreman, D., Sveningsson S. and Alvesson M. (2002), 'The Return of the Machine Bureaucracy? Management Control in the Work Settings of Professionals', *International Studies of Organization and Management*, 32: 70-92.

Katzell, R., Yankelovich, D. et al. (1975), *Work, Productivity and Job Satisfaction: An Evaluation of Policy-Related Research*, New York: The Psychological Corporation, quoted in I. Berg, M. Freedman and M. Freeman, (1978), *Managers and Work Reform. A Limited Engagement*, New York: The Free Press.

Katzenbach, J. and Smith, D.K. (1993), 'The Discipline of Teams', *Harvard Business Review*, 71 (2): 111-120.

Kaus, M. (1992), *The End of Equality*, New York: Basic Books.

Keister, L.A. (2000), *Wealth in America: Trends in Wealth Inequality*, Cambridge. Cambridge University Press.

Keller, R.T. (1984), 'The Harvard 'Pareto Circle' and the Historical Development of Organization Theory', *Journal of Management*, 10: 193-203.

Kelley, R.E. (1985), *The Gold-Collar Worker: Harnessing the Brainpower of the New Workforce*, Reading, MA: Addison-Wesley.

Kidwell, R.E. (1995), 'Social Darwinism and the Taylor System: A Missing Link in the Evolution of Management?', *International Journal of Public Administration*, 18: 767-791.

Kiechel, W. (1993), 'How We Will Work in the Year 2000', *Fortune*, May 17: 38-52.

Kieser, A. (1997), 'Rhetoric and Myth in Management Fashion', *Organization*, 4: 49–74.

Kilmann, R., Saxton, M., Serpa, R. and associates (1985), *Gaining Control of the Corporate Culture*, San Francisco: CA, Jossey Bass.

Kipping, M. (1996), 'The U.S. Influence on the Evolution of Management Consultancies in Britain, France, and Germany since 1945', *Business and Economic History*, 25: 112-123.

Kipping, M. (1997), 'Consultancies, Institutions and the Diffusion of Taylorism in Britain, Germany and France, 1920s to 1950s', *Business History*, 39 (4): 67-83.

Kipping, M. (1999), 'American Management Consulting Companies in Western Europe, 1920 to 1990: Products, Reputation, and Relationships', *Business History Review* 73: 190-220.

Klant, J.J. (1990), 'The Natural Order' in N. de Marchi (ed.), *The Popperian Legacy in Economics*, Cambridge: Cambridge University Press.

Kohler, P., Zacher, H. and Partington, M. (eds.) (1982), *The Evolution of Social Insurance 1881-1981*, New York: St. Martin's Press.

Koontz, H. and O'Donnell, C. J. (1976), *Management: A Systems and Contingency Analysis of Managerial Functions*, 6th ed., New York: McGraw-Hill.

Korenman, S. and Winship, C. (2000), 'A Reanalysis of The Bell Curve: Intelligence, Family, Background, and Schooling', in K. Arrow, S. Bowles and S. Durlauf (eds.). *Meritocracy and Economic Inequality*, Princeton, NJ: Princeton University Press.

Kotter, J.P. (1982), 'What Effective General Managers Really Do?', *Harvard Business Review*, 60 (6): 156-167.

Kotter, J.P. (1990), 'What Leaders Really Do?', *Harvard Business Review*, 68 (3): 103-111.

Kravitz, D.A. and Martin, B. (1986), 'Ringelmann Rediscovered: The Original Article', *Journal of Personality and Social Psychology*, 50: 936-941.

Krohe, J. (1993), 'The Productivity Pit', *Across the Board*, 30 (10): 16-21.

Kropotkin, P. (1892), *La conquète du pain*, París: Tresse & Stock.

Krugman, P. (1994), *The Age of Diminished Expectations*, Cambridge, MA: The MIT Press.

Lafargue, P. (1900), *Le socialisme et les intellectuels*, Paris: V. Giard & E. Brière.

Langley, A. (1989), 'In Search of Rationality: The Purposes Behind the Use of Formal Analysis in Organizations', *Administrative Science Quarterly*, 34: 598-631.

Larsen, B. (2003), 'German Organization and Leadership Theory — Stable Trends and Flexible Adaptation', *Scandinavian Journal of Management*, 19: 103–133.

Lash, S. and Urry, J. (1987), *The End of Organized Capitalism*, Madison, WI: University of Wisconsin Press.

Lash, S. and Urry, J. (1994), *Economies of Signs and Space*, London: Sage.

Laumann, E., Nadler, G. and O'Farrell, B. (1991), 'Designing for Technological Change: People in the Process', in National Academy of Engineering, National Research Council, *People and Technology in the Workplace*, Washington, DC: National Academy Press.

Laurie, B. (1989), *Artisans into Workers: Labor in Nineteenth Century America*, New York: The Noonday Press.

Lawler, E.E. (1986), *High-Involvement Management: Participative Strategies for Improving Organizational Performance*, San Francisco, CA: Jossey Bass.

Lawler, E.E. (1993), 'Bureaucracy Busting: Interview', *Across the Board*, 30 (3): 23-27.

Lawrence, P. and Lorsch, J. (1967), *Organization and Environment*, Boston, MA: Harvard Business School Press.

Lazerson, M. (1995), 'A New Phoenix? Modern Putting-Out in the Modena Knitwear Industry', *Administrative Science Quarterly*, 40: 34-59.

Leborgne, D. and Lipietz, A. (1994), 'Ideas falsas y cuestiones abiertas sobre el posfordismo', *Doxa*, no. 11/12: 32-40.

Le Goff, J.-P. (1995), *Le mythe de l'entreprise. Critique de l'idéologie managériale*, París: La Découverte.

Leigh, D.E. and Gifford, K.D. (1999), 'Workplace Transformation and Worker Upskilling: The Perspective of Individual Workers', *Industrial Relations*, 38: 174-191.

Lenin, V.I. (1965 [1918]), 'The Immediate Task of the Soviet Government', in V.I. Lenin, *Collected Works*, vol. 27, 1965, Moscow: Progress Publishers, quoted in S. Kakar, *Frederick W. Taylor: A Study in Personality and Innovation*, (1970), Cambridge, MA: The MIT Press.

Lenski, G. (1966), *Power and Privilege: A Theory of Social Stratification*, New York: McGraw-Hill.

Lerner, M.J. (1998), 'The Two Forms of Belief in a Just World: Some Thoughts on Why and How People Care about Justice', in L. Montada and M.J. Lerner (eds.), *Responses to Victimizations and Belief in a Just World*, New York: Plenum.

Levinson, H. (1975), 'Management by Whose Objectives?' in *Harvard Business Review, On Management*, New York: Harper & Row.

Lewchuk, W. and Robertson, D. (1997), 'Production Without Empowerment: Work-Reorganization from the Perspective of Motor Vehicle Workers', *Capital and Class*, 63: 37-63.

Liebowitz, J. and Suen, C.Y. (2000), 'Developing Knowledge Management Metrics for Measuring Intellectual Capital', *Journal of Intellectual Capital*, 1: 54-67.

Likert, R. (1961), *New Patterns of Management*, New York: McGraw-Hill.

Lind, M. (1992), 'The Catalytic State', *The National Interest*, 27: 3-12.

Lindert, P.H. (2000a), 'Three Centuries of Inequality in Britain and America', in A.B. Atkinson and F. Bourguignon (eds.), *Handbook of Income Distribution*, vol. 1, Amsterdam: Elsevier.

Lindert, P.H. (2000b), 'When Did Inequality Rise in Britain and America?', *Journal of Income Distribution*, 9: 11-25.

Lipietz, A. (2001), 'The Fortunes and Misfortunes of Post-Fordism', in R. Albritton, M. Itoh, R. Westra and A. Zuege (eds.), *Phases of Capitalist Development: Booms, Crises and Globalizations*, London: Palgrave.

Lipovetsky, G. (1990 [1983]), *La era del vacío*, Barcelona: Ed. Anagrama.

Litterer, J.A. (1986), *The Emergence of Systematic Management as Shown by the Literature of Management from 1870-1900*, New York: Garland.

Locke, E.R. (1968), 'Toward a Theory of Task Motivation and Incentives', *Organizational Behavior and Human Performance*, 3: 157-189.

Locke, R.R. (1989), *Management and Higher Education since 1940: The Influence of America and Japan on West Germany, Great Britain, and France*, Cambridge: Cambridge University Press.

Lorsh, J.W. and Morse, J. (1975), 'Beyond Theory Y', in *Harvard Business Review, On Management*, New York: Harper & Row.

Luthans, F. (1988), 'Successful vs. Effective Real Managers', *Academy of Management Executive*, 2 (2): 127-132.

Luthans, F., Hodgetts, R.M. and Rosenkrantz, S. (1988), *Real Managers*, Cambridge, MA: Ballinger.

Lyotard, J.-F. (1992 [1986]), *La posmodernidad explicada a los niños*, Barcelona: Gedisa.

Maccoby, M. (1988), *Why Work: Leading the New Generation*, New York: Simon and Schuster.

Mandell, N. (2002), *The Corporation as Family: The Gendering of Corporate Welfare, 1890-1930*, Chapel Hill, NC: University of North Carolina Press.

Manz, C.C. and Sims, H.P. (1993), *Business Without Bosses: How Self-Managing Teams Are Building High-Performing Companies*, New York: John Wiley.

March, J.G. (1976), 'The Technology of Foolishness', in J.G. March and J.P. Olsen (eds.), *Ambiguity and Choice in Organizations*, Bergen: Universitetsforlaget.

March, J.G. and Simon, H.A. (1958), *Organizations*, New York: John Wiley.

Marchand, D., Kettinger, W. and Rollins, J. (2000), 'Company Performance and IM: The View from the Top', in D.A. Marchand, T.H. Davenport and T. Dickson (eds.), *Mastering Information Management*, London: Financial Times / Prentice Hall.

Marcuse, H. (2001 [1966]), 'The Individual in the Great Society' in H. Marcuse, D. Kellner (ed.), *Towards a Critical Theory of Society*, London: Routledge.

172   *Capitalism, Social Privilege and Managerial Ideologies*

Marglin, S.A. (1984), *Growth, Distribution and Prices*, Cambridge, MA: Harvard University Press.

Markland, R.M. (1983), *Topics in Management Science*, New York: John Wiley.

Marshall, L.C. (1920), 'Incentive and Output: A Statement of the Place of the Personnel Manager in Modern Industry', *Journal of Political Economy*, 28: 713-734.

Marx, K. (1972 [1864]), 'Inaugural Address of the Working Men's International Association', in R.C. Tucker (ed.), *The Marx-Engels Reader*, New York: W.W. Norton.

Maryanski, A. and Turner, J. (1993), *The Social Cage: Human Nature and the Evolution of Society*, Stanford, CA: Stanford University Press.

Mayhew, I. (1866), *Mayhew's Practical Book-Keeping Embracing Single and Double Entry, Commercial Calculations, and the Philosophy and Morals of Business*, Boston, MA: S. F. Nichols.

Maynard, H. and Mehrtens, S. (1993), *The Fourth Wave: Business in the 21st. Century*, San Francisco, CA: Berrett-Koehler.

Mayo, E. (1945), *The Social Problems of an Industrial Civilization*, Boston, MA: Division of Research, Harvard University, Graduate School of Business Administration.

Mayo, E. (1946 [1933]), *The Human Problems of an Industrial Civilization*, 2nd ed., Boston, MA: Division of Research, Harvard University, Graduate School of Business Administration.

McGill, M. (1988), *American Business and the Quick Fix*, New York: Henry Holt.

McGregor, D. (1960), *The Human Side of Enterprise*, New York: McGraw-Hill.

McKenna, C. (2001), 'The World's Newest Profession: Management Consulting in the Twentieth Century', *Enterprise & Society*, 2: 673-679.

McKersie, R.B. and Walton, R. (1991), 'Organizational Change', in M.S. Scott Morton (ed.), *The Corporation of the 1990s: Information Technology and Organizational Transformation*, New York: Oxford University Press.

McKinsey, A. and Starkey, K. (eds.) (1998), *Foucault, Management and Organization Theory: From Panopticon to Technologies of Self*, London: Sage.

Merkle, J.A. (1980), *Management and Ideology: The Legacy of the International Scientific Management Movement*, Berkeley, CA: University of California Press.

Meyers, B. (1996), 'The Bell Curve and the New Social Darwinism', *Science and Society*, 60: 195-204.

Michels, R. (1949 [1927]), *First Lectures in Political Sociology*, Minneapolis, MI: University of Minnesota Press.

Micklethwait, J. and Wooldridge, A. (1997), *The Witch Doctors: Making Sense of the Management Gurus*, New York: Times Books.

Mills, C.W. (1953), *White Collar: The American Middle Classes*, New York: Oxford University Press.

Mintzberg, H. (1973), *The Nature of Managerial Work*, New York: Harper & Row.

Mintzberg, H. (1990), 'Strategy Formation: Schools of Thought', in J.W. Frederickson (ed.), *Perspectives on Strategic Management*, New York: Harper Business.

Mintzberg, H. (1994), 'The Fall and Rise of Strategic Planning', *Harvard Business Review*, 72 (1): 107-114.

Moch, M.K. and Bartunek, J.M. (1990), *Creating Alternative Realities at Work: The Quality of Work Life Experience at Food Com*, New York: Harper Business.

Monroe, P. (1898), 'Possibilities of the Present Industrial System', *American Journal of Sociology*, 3: 729-753.

Montgomery, D. (1981), *Beyond Equality: Labor and the Radical Republicans, 1862-1872*, Urbana, IL: University of Illinois Press.

Montgomery, D. (1983), 'Labor in the Industrial Era' in R.B. Morris (ed.), *A History of the American Worker*, Princeton, NJ: Princeton University Press.

Montgomery, J. (1832), 'Remarks on the Management and Governance of Spinning Factories', in *The Carding and Spinning Masters Account; or the Theory and Practice of Cotton Spinning*, Glasgow, quoted in A.D. Chandler (1977), *The Visible Hand. The Management Revolution in American Business*, Cambridge, MA: The Belknap Press of Harvard University Press.

Morgan, G. (1986), *Images of Organization*, Newbury Park, CA: Sage.

Morrisson, C. (2000), 'Historical Perspectives on Income Distribution: The Case of Europe', in A. B. Atkinson and F. Bourguignon (eds.), *Handbook of Income Distribution*, vol. 1, Amsterdam: Elsevier.

Mowday, R.T. (1997), 'Reaffirming Our Scholarly Values', *Academy of Management Review*, 22: 335-346.

Münsterberg, H. (1913), *Psychology and Industrial Efficiency*, Boston, MA: Mifflin.

Murchland, B. (1971), *The Age of Alienation*, New York: Random House.

Murphy, E.C. (1996), *Leadership IQ: A Personal Development Process Based On A Scientific Study of A New Generation of Leaders*, San Francisco, CA: Jossey Bass.

Myers, M.S. (1970), *Every Employee a Manager: More Meaningful Work through Job Enrichment*, New York: McGraw-Hill.

Murray, C. (1998), *Income Inequality and IQ*, Washington, DC: AEI Press.

Nanus, B. (1992), *Visionary Leadership: Creating a Compelling Sense of Direction for Your Organization*, San Francisco, CA: Jossey Bass.

Neff, W. (1968), *Work and Human Behavior*, New York: Atherton Press.

Nelson, D. (1980), *Frederick W. Taylor and the Rise of Scientific Management*, Madison, WI: The University of Wisconsin Press.

Nelson, D. (1991), 'Scientific Management and the Workplace, 1920-1935', in S. Jacoby (ed.), *Masters to Managers: Historical and Comparative Perspectives on American Employers*, New York: Columbia University Press.

Nelson, N.O. (1887), 'Profit-Sharing', *The North American Review*, 144 (365): 388-394.

Newell, A. and Simon, H.A. (1972), *Human Problem Solving*. Englewood Cliffs, NJ: Prentice-Hall.

Newell, S., Robertson, M. and Swan, J. (2001), 'Management Fads and Fashions', *Organization*, 8: 5-15.

Nichols, M. (1994), 'Does New Age Business Have a Message for Managers?', *Harvard Business Review* 72 (2): 52-60.

Nicholson, N. (2000), *Executive Instinct: Managing the Human Animal in the Information Age*, New York: Crown Business.

Niiniluoto, I. (1999), *Critical Scientific Realism*, Oxford: Oxford University Press.

Nisbet, R. (1966), *The Sociological Tradition*, New York. Basic Books.

Nohria, N. and Berkley, J. (1994), 'Whatever Happened to the Take-Charge Manager?', *Harvard Business Review*, 72 (1): 128-137.

Nohria, N. and Eccles, R. (1998), 'Where Does Management Knowledge Come From?', in J.L. Alvarez (ed.), *The Diffusion and Consumption of Business Knowledge*, New York: St. Martin's Press.

Nordhoff, C. (1875), *The Communistic Societies of the United States: from Personal Visit and Observation, Including Detailed Accounts of the Economists, Zoarites, Shakers, the Amana, Oneida, Bethel, Aurora, Icarian and Other Existing Societies, Their Religious Creeds, Social Practices, Numbers, Industries, and Present Condition*, New York: Harper.

Noyes, J.H. (1870), *History of American Socialisms*, Philadelphia, PA: J.B. Lippincott.

O'Connor, E.S. (1999a), 'The Politics of Management Thought: A Case Study of the Harvard Business School and the Human Relations School', *Academy of Management Review*, 24: 117–131.

O'Connor, E.S. (1999b), 'Minding the Workers: The Meaning of "Human" and "Human Relations" in Elton Mayo', *Organization*, 6: 223-246.

O'Shea, J. and Madigan, C. (1998), *Dangerous Company: The Consulting Powerhouses and the Businesses They Save and Ruin*, London: Nicholas Brealey.

Odiorne, G.S. (1987), *The Human Side of Management: Management by Integration and Self-Control*, Lexington, MA: Lexington Books.

Okun, A.M. (1975), *Equality and Efficiency: The Big Tradeoff*, Washington, DC: The Brookings Institution.

Osborne, D. and Gaebler, T. (1992), *Reinventing Government: How the Entrepreneurial Spirit is Transforming the Public Sector*, Reading, MA: Addison Wesley.

Osterman, P. (1994), 'How Common is Workplace Transformation and Who Adopts It?', *Industrial and Labor Relations Review*, 47: 173-188.

Ouchi, W.G. (1981), *Theory Z: How American Business Can Meet the Japanese Challenge*, Reading, MA: Addison-Wesley.

Owen, R. (1970 [1813]), 'An Address To the Superintendants of Manufactories, and to Those Individuals Generally, Who, by Giving Employment to an Aggregated Population, May Easily Adopt the Means to Form the Sentiments and Manners of Such a Population', in H.F. Merrill (ed.), *Classics in Management*, New York: American Management Association.

Owen, R. (1970 [1826]), 'Declaration of Mental Independence', in O.C. Johnson (ed.), *Robert Owen in the United States*, New York: Humanities Press.

Paastela, J. (1991), 'Sociobiology and Marxism: Some Preliminary Remarks', Paper presented at the XVth. World Congress of the International Political Science Association, Buenos Aires, July 21-25.

Parker, M. (2002), *Against Management: Organization in the Age of Managerialism*, Cambridge: Polity Press.

Perrow, C. (1986), *Complex Organizations: A Critical Essay*, 3rd ed., New York: Random House.

Perry, J. (1954), *Human Relations in Small Industry*, New York: McGraw-Hill.

Pessen, E. (1983), 'Builders of the Young Republic', in R.B. Morris (ed.), *A History of the American Worker*, Princeton, NJ: Princeton University Press.

Peters, T. (1992), *Liberation Management: Necessary Disorganization for the Nanosecond Nineties*, New York: Alfred A. Knopf.

Peters, T. (1994), *The Pursuit of Wow! Every Person's Guide to Topsy-Turvy Times*, New York: Vintage Books.

Peters, T. and Waterman, R.H. (1982), *In Search of Excellence: Lessons from America's Best-Run Companies*, New York: Warner Books.

Petit, F. (1979), *Introduction à la psychosociologie des organisations*, Toulouse: Privat.

Petty, R. and Guthrie, J. (2000), 'Intellectual Capital Literature Review: Measurement, Reporting and Management', *Journal of Intellectual Capital*, 1: 155-176.

Pfeffer, J. (1992), *Managing with Power: Politics and Influence in Organizations*, Boston, MA: Harvard Business School Press.

Pierce, B.D. and White, R. (1999), 'The Evolution of Social Structure: Why Biology Matters', *Academy of Management Review*, 24: 843-853.

Pinchot, G. (1985), *Intrapreneuring: Why You Don't Have to Leave the Corporation to Become an Entrepreneur*, New York: Harper & Row.

Pinchot, G. and Pinchot, E. (1993), *The End of Bureaucracy & The Rise of the Intelligent Organization*, San Francisco, CA: Berrett-Koehler.

Piore, M. (1992), 'Work, Labor and Action: Work Experience in a System of Flexible Production', in T. Kochan and M. Useem (eds.), *Transforming Organizations*, New York: Oxford University Press.

Piore, M. and Sabel C. (1984), *The Second Industrial Divide: Possibilities for Prosperity*, New York: Basic Books.

Plessis, A. (1988), *The Rise and Fall of the Second Empire, 1852–1871*, Cambridge: Cambridge University Press.

Pollard, S. (1965), *The Genesis of Modern Management: A Study of the Industrial Revolution in Great Britain*, Cambridge, MA: Harvard University Press.

Popitz, H., Bahrdt, H.P., Jueres, E.A, and Kesting, A. (1969 [1957]), 'The Worker's Image of Society', in T. Burns (ed.), *Industrial Man*, Harmondsworth: Penguin.

Popper, K.R. (1976), 'A Note on Verisimilitude', *The British Journal for the Philosophy of Science*, 27: 147-159, quoted in P. Diesing, *How Does Social Science Work? Reflections on Practice*, (1991), Pittsburgh, PA: University of Pittsburgh Press.

Porter, M.E. (1980), *Competitive Strategy: Techniques for Analyzing Industries and Competitors*, New York: Free Press.

Porter, M.E. (1985), *Competitive Advantage: Creating and Sustaining Superior Performance*, New York: Free Press.

Purvis, T. and Hunt, A. (1993), 'Discourse, Ideology, Discourse, Ideology, Discourse, Ideology...', *British Journal of Sociology*, 44: 473-499.

Ramsay, H. (1996), 'Managing Sceptically: A Critique of Organizational Fashion', in S. Clegg, and G. Palmer (eds.), *The Politics of Management Knowledge*, London: Sage.

Raucher, A. (1987), 'Employee Relations at General Motors: The 'My Job Contest', 1947', *Labor History*, 28: 221-232.

Ray, C.A. (1986), 'Corporate Culture: The Last Frontier of Control?', *Journal of Management* Studies, 23: 287-297.

Redman, D. (1991), *Economics and the Philosophy of Science*, New York: Oxford University Press.

Reich, R. (1991), *The Work of Nations: Preparing Ourselves for the 21st. Century Capitalism*, New York: Alfred A. Knopf.

Reid, D. (1995), 'Reading Fayol with 3D Glasses', *Journal of Management History*, 1(3): 63-71.

Revel, J.-F. (1969 [1966]), *Contracensuras*, Buenos Aires: Ed. Losada.

Rexroth, K. (1974), *Communalism: From Its Origins to the Twentieth Century*, New York: Seabury Press.

Reynaud, J. (1964 [1877]), 'La Propriété' in *Oeuvres de Saint-Simon & d'Enfantin*, vol. 43, Aalen: Otto Zeller.

Ribeill, G. (1994), 'Courcelle-Seneuil, fondateur du management moderne des entreprises au milieu du XIXè siècle', in J.-P. Bouilloud and B.-P. Lecuyer (eds.), *L'invention de la gestion. Histoire et pratiques:* París: Editions L'Harmattan.

Ricoeur, P. (1986), *Lectures on Ideology and Utopia*, New York: Columbia University Press.

Ridderstrale, J. and Nordstrom, K. (2000), *Funky Business: Talent Makes Capital Dance*, London: Financial Times / Prentice Hall.

Riesman, D. (1954), *Individualism Reconsidered, and Other Essays*, Glencoe, IL: The Free Press.

Rifkin, J. (1995), *The End of Work: The Decline of the Global Labor Force and the Dawn of the Post-Market Era*, New York: G. P. Putnam's Sons.

Robb, R. (1970 [1910]), 'Organizations as Affected by Purpose and Condition', in H.F. Merrill (ed.), *Classics in Management*, New York: American Management Association.

Robbins, S. (1996), *Organizational Behavior: Concepts, Controversies, Applications* 7th ed., Englewood Cliffs, NJ: Prentice Hall.

Roberts, H. and Sergesketter, B. (1993), *Quality Is Personal: A Foundation for Total Quality Management*, New York: The Free Press.

Rockart, J.F. and Short, J.E. (1991), 'The Networked Organization and the Management of Interdependence', in M.S. Scott Morton (ed.), *The Corporation of the 1990s: Information Technology and Organizational Transformation*, New York: Oxford University Press.

Roehling, M. (1997), 'The Origins and Early Development of the Psychological Contract Construct', *Journal of Management History*, 3 (2): 204-217.

Roome, N. (ed.) (1998), *Sustainability Strategies for Industry: The Future of Corporate Practice*, Washington, DC: Island Press.

Ruitenbeek, H.M. (1963), 'Introduction', in H.M. Ruitenbeek (ed.), *The Dilemma of Organizational Society*, New York: Dutton.

Runciman, W.G. (1993), 'Has British Capitalism Changed since the First World War?', *British Journal of Sociology*, 44: 53-67.

Ruse, M. (1998), *Taking Darwin Seriously: A Naturalistic Approach to Philosophy*, Amherst, NY: Prometheus Books.

Saint-Simon, H. de (1832 [1802]), 'Lettres d'un habitant de Genève a ses contemporaines' in *Oeuvres complétes de Saint-Simon*, Prèmiere livraison, París: Ad. Naquet Libraire-Editeur.

Saint-Simon, H. de (1832 [1818]), 'Vues sur le propriété et la législation' in *Oeuvres complétes de Saint-Simon*, Seconde livraison, París: Ad. Naquet Libraire-Editeur.

Saint-Simon, H. de (1832 [1824]), 'Catéchisme politique des industriels' in *Oeuvres complétes de Saint-Simon*, Seconde livraison, París: Ad. Naquet Libraire-Editeur.

Salaman, G. (1980), 'Organizations as Constructors of Social Reality II', in G. Salaman and K. Thompson (eds.), *Control and Ideology in Organizations*, Cambridge, MA: The MIT Press.

Salas, E., Rozell, D., Mullen, B. and Driskell, J. (1999), 'The Effect of Team Building on Performance', *Small Group Research*, 30: 309-329.

Sampson, A. (1995), *Company Man: The Rise and Fall of Corporate Life*, London: Harper Collins.

Scarbrough, H. and Burrell, G. (1996), 'The Axeman Cometh: The Changing Roles and Knowledges of Middle Managers', in S. Clegg, and G. Palmer (eds.), *The Politics of Management Knowledge*, London: Sage.

Schein, E. (1980), *Organizational Psychology*, Englewood Cliffs, NJ: Prentice-Hall.

Schein, E. (1989), 'Reassessing the "Divine Rights" of Managers', *Sloan Management Review*, 30 (2): 63-68.

Scitovsky, T. (1976), *The Joyless Economy*, Oxford: Oxford University Press.

Scott Morton, M.S. (1991), 'Introduction', in M.S. Scott Morton (ed.). *The Corporation of the 1990s: Information Technology and Organizational Transformation*, New York: Oxford University Press.

Scott, W.G. (1992), *Chester I. Barnard and the Guardians of the Managerial State*, Lawrence, KS: University Press of Kansas.

Scoville, J.G. (2001), 'The Taylorization of Vladimir Ilich Lenin', *Industrial Relations*, 40: 620-626.

Senge, P. (1990), *The Fifth Discipline: The Art and Practice of the Learning Organization*, New York: Doubleday.

Sennett, R. (1998), *The Corrosion of Character: The Personal Consequences of Work in the New Capitalism*, New York: Norton.

Sewell, G. (1998), 'The Discipline of Teams: The Control of Team-Based Industrial Work Through Electronic and Peer Surveillance', *Administrative Science Quarterly*, 43: 397-427.

Sewell, G. and Wilkinson, B. (1992), 'Someone to Watch Over Me: Surveillance, Discipline and the Just-in-Time Labour Process', *Sociology*, 26: 271-289.

Shenhav, Y. (1999), *Manufacturing Rationality: The Engineering Foundations of the Managerial Revolution*, Oxford: Oxford University Press.

Shenhav, Y. and Weitz, E. (2000), 'The Roots of Uncertainty in Organization Theory: A Historical Constructivist Analysis', *Organization*, 7: 373-401.

Sherman, S. (1993), 'A Brave New Darwinian Workplace', *Fortune*, January 25: 50-56.

Sherwin, D.S. (1975), 'Strategy for Winning Employee Commitment', in *Harvard Business Review, On Management*, New York: Harper & Row.

Shuey, E.L. (1900), *Factory People and Their Employers*, New York: Lentilhon.

Silver, J. (1987), 'The Ideology of Excellence: Management and Neo-Conservatism', Studies in Political Economy, no. 24: 105-129.

Simon, H.A. (1957), *Administrative Behavior: A Study of Decision-Making Processes in Administrative Organization*, 2nd ed., New York: Macmillan.

Simon, H.A. (1960), *The New Science of Management Decision*, New York: Harper & Row.

Simon, H.A. (1992), '[book review of] Oliver Williamson (ed.) *Organization Theory: From Chester Barnard to the Present and Beyond*', *Journal of Economic Literature*, 30: 1503-1504.

Sims, H. and Lorenzi, P. (1992), *The New Leadership Paradigm: Social Learning and Cognition in Organizations*, Newbury Park, CA: Sage.

Sinclair, A. (1992), 'The Tyranny of a Team Ideology', *Organization Studies*, 13: 611-626.

Sklair, L. (2001), *The Transnational Capitalist Class*, Oxford: Blackwell.

Slater, P. and Bennis, W. (1990 [1964]), 'Democracy is Inevitable', *Harvard Business Review*, 68 (5): 167-176.

Slichter, S.H. (1919a), *The Turnover of Factory Labor*, New York: D. Appleton.

Slichter, S.H. (1919b), 'The Management of Labor', *Journal of Political Economy*, 27: 813-839.

Smelser, N. (1968), 'The Sociology of Economic Life', in T. Parsons (ed.), *American Sociology: Perspectives, Problems, Methods*, New York: Basic Books.

Smiles, S. (1860), *Self-Help: With Illustrations of Character and Conduct*, New York: Harper & Brothers.

Smiles, S. (1872), *Character*, London: J. Murray.

Solomon, N. (1997), *The Trouble with Dilbert: How Corporate Culture Gets the Last Laugh*, Monroe, ME: Common Courage Press.

Somit, A. and Peterson, S. (1997), *Darwinism, Dominance and Democracy: The Biological Basis of Authoritarianism*, Westport, CT: Praeger.

Sousa-Poza, A. and Souza-Poza, A.A. (2000), 'Well-being at Work: A Cross-National Analysis of the Levels and Determinants of Job Satisfaction', *Journal of Socio-Economics*, 29: 517-538.

Spencer, H. (1873), *Essays: Moral, Political and Æsthetic*, New York: D. Appleton.

Spender, J.C. (1996), 'Villain, Victim or Visionary?: The Insights and Flaws in F.W. Taylor's Ideas', in J.C. Spender and H. Kijne (eds.), *Scientific Management: Frederick Winslow Taylor's Gift to the World?*, Boston, MA: Kluwer Academic Publishers.

Sproull, L. and Kiesler, S. (1991), *Connections: New Ways of Working in the Networked Organization*, Cambridge, MA: The MIT Press.

Staw, B.M, Bell, N.E. and Clausen, J.A. (1986), 'The Dispositional Approach to Job Attitudes: A Lifetime Longitudinal Test', *Administrative Science Quarterly*, 31: 56-77.

Staw, B.M. and Barsade, S.G. (1993), 'Affect and Managerial Performance: A Test of the Sadder-but-Wiser vs. Happier-and-Smarter Hypotheses', *Administrative Science Quarterly*, 38: 304-331.

Staw, B.M. and Epstein, L.D. (2000), 'What Bandwagons Bring: Effects of Popular Management Techniques on Corporate Performance, Reputation, and CEO Pay', *Administrative Science Quarterly*, 45: 523-556.

178   *Capitalism, Social Privilege and Managerial Ideologies*

Stearns, L.B. (1994), '[book review of] Michael Useem, *Executive Defense: Shareholder Power and Corporate Reorganization*', *Administrative Science Quarterly*, 39: 174-176.

Sternberg, R.J. (1996), *Successful Intelligence: How Practical and Creative Intelligence Determine Success in Life*, New York: Simon & Schuster.

Sternberg, R.J. and Powell, J.S. (1982), 'Theories of Intelligence', in R.J. Sternberg (ed.), *Handbook of Human Intelligence*, Cambridge: Cambridge University Press.

Sternberg, R.J. and Salter, W. (1982), 'Conceptions of Intelligence', in R.J. Sternberg (ed.), *Handbook of Human Intelligence*, Cambridge: Cambridge University Press.

Stewart, E.W. and Glynn, J.A. (1971), *Introduction to Sociology*, New York: McGraw-Hill.

Stewart, T. (1997), *Intellectual Capital: The New Wealth of Organizations*, New York: Currency Doubleday.

Storey, D. (1998), *The Ten Percenters: Fast Growing SMEs in Great Britain. Third Report*, London: Deloitte & Touche.

Stout, R. (1980), *Management or Control? The Organizational Challenge*, Bloomington, IN: Indiana University Press.

Strassman, P.A. (1985), *Information Payoff: The Transformation of Work in the Electronic Age*, New York: The Free Press.

Sumner, W.G. (1881), 'Sociology', *The Princeton Review*, yr. 57 vol. 2: 303-323.

Sumner, W.G. (1882), 'Wages', *The Princeton Review*, yr. 58 vol. 2: 241-262.

Sumner, W.G. (1883), *What Social Classes Owe to Each Other*, New York: Harper & Brothers.

Sumner, W.G. (1918), 'The Forgotten Man', in A.G. Keller (ed.), W.G. Sumner, *The Forgotten Man and Other Essays*, New Haven, CT: Yale University Press.

Sutcliffe, B. and Glyn, A. (1999), 'Still Underwhelmed: Indicators of Globalization and Their Misinterpretation', *Review of Radical Political Economics*, 31: 111-132.

Sutton, F.X, Harris, S., Kaysen, C. and Tobin, J. (1956), *The American Business Creed*, Cambridge, MA: Harvard University Press.

Sveiby, K.-E. (1997), *The New Organisational Wealth: Managing and Measuring Knowledge-Based Assets*, San Francisco, CA: Berrett-Koehler.

Swiss, J.E. (1992), 'Adapting Total Quality Management TQM, to Government', *Public Administration Review*, 52: 356-362.

Tarrant, J.J. (1976), *Drucker: The Man Who Invented the Corporate Society*, Boston, MA: Cahners Books.

Taylor, F.W. (1947 [1903]), *Shop Management*, in *Scientific Management*, New York: Harper and Brothers.

Taylor, F.W. (1947 [1911]), *Principles of Scientific Management*, in *Scientific Management*, New York: Harper and Brothers.

Taylor, F.W. (1947 [1912]), *Testimony before the Special House Committee*, in *Scientific Management*, New York: Harper and Brothers.

Taylor, F.W. (1995 [1907]), 'Report of a Lecture by and Questions Put to Mr. F.W. Taylor: A Transcript', *Journal of Management History* 1 (1): 8-32.

Tead, O. (1921), 'The Problem of Graduate Training in Personnel Administration', *Journal of Political Economy*, 29: 353-367.

Terman, L.M. (1904), 'A preliminary study of the psychology and pedagogy of leadership', *Pedagogic Seminary and Journal of Genetic Psychology*, 11: 413-451, quoted in C. Insko and J. Schopler, (1973), *Experimental Social Psychology*, New York: Academic Press.

Tezanos, J.F. (1992), 'Transformaciones en la estructura de clases en la sociedad tecnológica Avanzada', *El Socialismo del Futuro*, n° 6: 65-84.

Therborn, G. (1980), *The Ideology of Power and the Power of Ideology*, London: Verso.

Therborn, G. (1992), *Peripecias de la modernidad*, Buenos Aires: Ed. El Cielo por Asalto.

Thompson, K. (1980a), 'Organizations as Constructors of Social Reality I', in G. Salaman and K. Thompson (eds.), *Control and Ideology in Organizations*, Cambridge, MA: The MIT Press.

Thompson, K. (1980b), 'The Organizational Society', in G. Salaman and K. Thompson (eds.), *Control and Ideology in Organizations*, Cambridge, MA: The MIT Press.

Thompson, J. (1967), *Organizations in Action*, New York: McGraw-Hill.

Thompson, P. and O'Connell Davidson, J. (1995), 'The Continuity of Discontinuity: Managerial Rhetoric in Turbulent Times', *Personnel Review*, 24 (4): 17-33.

Tilly, C. (1998), *Durable Inequality*, Berkeley, CA: University of California Press.

Timms, H. (1966), *The Production Function in Business: Management Decision Systems*, Homewood, IL: R. D. Irwin.

Toninelli, P.A. (ed.) (2000), *The Rise and Fall of State-Owned Enterprise in the Western World*, Cambridge: Cambridge University Press.

Towle, G.M. (1872), 'Saltaire and Its Founder', *Harper's New Monthly Magazine*, 44: 827-835.

Trist, E. and Murray, H. (1990), 'Historical Overview: The Foundation and Development of the Tavistock Institute', in E. Trist and H. Murray (eds.), *The Social Engagement of Social Science: A Tavistock Anthology*, vol. 1, *The Socio-Psychological Perspective*, Philadelphia, PA: University of Pennsylvania Press.

Tsutsui, W.M. (1997), 'Rethinking the Paternalist Paradigm in Japanese Industrial Management', *Business and Economic History*, 26: 561-572.

Tsutsui, W.M. (1998), *Manufacturing Ideology: Scientific Management in Twentieth-Century Japan*, Princeton, NJ: Princeton University Press.

Tullock, G. and McKenzie, R. (1981), *The New World of Economics: Explorations into the Human Experience*, Homewood, IL: Irwin.

Tully, S. (1993), 'The Modular Corporation', *Fortune*, February 8: 106-115.

Ure, A. (1861 [1835]), *The Philosophy of Manufactures, or, an Exposition of the Scientific, Moral, and Commercial Economy of the Factory System of Great Britain*, 3rd ed., London: Bohn.

Urwick, L. and Brech, B.F.L. (1951), *The Making of Scientific Management*, vol. 1, *Thirteen Pioneers*, London: Sir Isaac Pitman and Sons.

Urwick, L. and Brech, B.F.L. (1953), *The Making of Scientific Management*, vol. 2, *Management in British Industry*, London: Sir Isaac Pitman and Sons.

Üsdiken, B. and Çetin, D. (2001), 'From *Betriebswirtschaftslehre* to Human Relations: Turkish Management Literature before and after the Second World War', *Business History*, 43: 90-121.

Useem, M. (1984), *The Inner Circle: Large Corporations and the Rise of Business Political Activity in the U.S. and U.K.*, Oxford: Oxford University Press.

Useem, M. (1992), 'Corporate Restructuring and Organizational Behavior', in T. Kochan and M. Useem (eds.), *Transforming Organizations*, New York: Oxford University Press.

Useem, M. (1993), *Executive Defense: Shareholder Power and Corporate Reorganization*, Cambridge, MA: Harvard University Press.

Useem, M. and Kochan, T. (1992), 'Conclusion: Creating the Learning Organization', in T. Kochan and M. Useem (eds.), *Transforming Organizations*, New York: Oxford University Press.

Veblen, T. (1921), *The Engineers and the Price System*, New York: B. W. Huebsch.

Veblen, T. (1923), *Absentee Ownership and Business Enterprise in Recent Times: The Case of America*, New York: B. W. Huebsch.

Vroom, V. (1964), *Work and Motivation*, New York: John Wiley.

Wagner, J.A. (1994), 'Participation's Effects on Performance and Satisfaction: A Reconsideration of Research Evidence', *Academy of Management Review*, 19: 312-330.

Wallerstein, I. (1984), 'Long Waves as Capitalist Process', *Review*, 7: 559-575.
Walton, R. (1985), 'From Control to Commitment in the Workplace', *Harvard Business Review*, 63 (2): 77-84.
Waring, S. (1991), *Taylorism Transformed: Scientific Management Theory since 1945*, Chapel Hill, University of North Carolina Press, NC: Chapel Hill.
Waterman, R.H. (1987), *The Renewal Factor: How the Best Get and Keep the Competitive Edge*, New York: Bantam Books.
Waterman, R.H. and Waterman, J.A. (1994), 'Toward a Career-Resilient Workforce', *Harvard Business Review*, 72 (4): 87-95.
Wayne, S.J., Liden, R., Kraimer, M. and Graf, I. (1999), 'The Role of Human Capital, Motivation and Supervisor Sponsorship in Predicting Career Success', *Journal of Organizational Behavior*, 20: 577-595.
Webb, S. and Webb, B. (1920), *Industrial Democracy*, London: Longmans, quoted in R. Russell, *Sharing Ownership at the Workplace*, (1985), Albany, NY: State University of New York Press.
Webber, A.M. (1993), 'What's So New about the New Economy?', *Harvard Business Review*, 71 (1): 24-42.
Wellins, R.S., Byham, W.C. and Wilson J.M. (1991), *Empowered Teams: Creating Self-Directed Groups that improve Quality, Productivity and Participation*, San Francisco, CA: Jossey Bass.
Wheatley, M. (1992), *Leadership and the New Science*, San Francisco, CA: Berrett-Koehler.
White, E. (ed.) (1981), *Sociobiology and Human Politics*, Lexington, MA: Heath.
Whitston, K. (1997), 'The Reception of Scientific Management by British Engineers, 1890-1914', *Business History Review*, 71: 207-229.
Whyte, W.H (1963), 'Individualism in Suburbia', in H.M. Ruitenbeek (ed.), *The dilemma of organizational society*, New York: Dutton.
Whyte, W.H. (1956), *The Organization Man*, Garden City, NY: Doubleday.
Willmott, H. (1993), 'Strength is Ignorance; Slavery is Freedom: Managing Culture in Modern Organizations', *Journal of Management Studies*, 30: 515-552.
Wilson, E. (1972 [1940]), *To the Finland Station: A Study in the Writing and Acting of History*, New York: Farrar, Straus & Giroux.
Wilson, E.O. (1978), *On Human Nature*, Cambridge, MA: Harvard University Press.
Wilson, F. (1999), 'Cultural Control within the Virtual Organization', *Sociological Review*, 47: 672-694.
Wirth, A.G. (1992), *Education and Work for the Year 2000: Choices We Face*, San Francisco, CA: Jossey Bass.
Witte, J. (1980), *Democracy, Authority, and Alienation in Work: Workers' Participation in an American Corporation*, Chicago, IL: The University of Chicago Press.
Wolf, W.B. (1995), 'The Barnard-Simon Connection', *Journal of Management History*, 1 (4): 88-99.
Wolff, E.N. (1995), *Top Heavy: A Study of the Increasing Inequality of Wealth in America*, New York: Twentieth Century Fund.
Wolff, J. (1991), *Robert Nozick: Property, Justice, and the Minimal State*, Stanford, CA: Stanford University Press.
Wood, S. and de Menezes, L. (1998), 'High Commitment Management in the UK: Evidence from the Workplace Industrial Relations Survey, and Employers' Manpower and Skills Practices Survey', *Human Relations*, 51: 485-515.
Woodward, J. (1969 [1958]), 'Management and Technology', in T. Burns (ed.), *Industrial Man*, Harmondsworth: Penguin.
Wrege, C.D. (1995), 'F.W. Taylor's Lecture on Management, 4 June 1907: An Introduction', *Journal of Management History*, 1 (1): 4-7.

Wrege, C.D. and Hodgetts, R.M. (2000), 'Frederick W. Taylor's 1899 Pig Iron Observations: Examining Fact, Fiction, and Lessons for the New Millennium', *Academy of Management Journal*, 43: 1283-1291.

Wrege, C.D. and Perroni, A.G. (1974), 'Taylor's Pig-Tale: A Historical Analysis of Frederick W. Taylor's Pig-Iron Experiments', *Academy of Management Journal*, 17: 6-27.

Wrege, C.D. and Stotka, A.M. (1978), 'Cooke Creates a Classic: The Story behind F.W. Taylor's Principles of Scientific Management', *Academy of Management Review*, 3: 736-749.

Wren, D. (1994), *The Evolution of Management Though*, 4th ed., New York: John Wiley.

Wright, C. (2000), 'From Shop Floor to Boardroom: The Historical Evolution of Australian Management Consulting, 1940s to 1980s', *Business History*, 42: 86-106.

Wriston, W.B. (1992), *The Twilight of Sovereignity: How the Information Revolution is Transforming our World*, New York: Charles Scribner's Sons.

Yago, A. (1982), 'Leadership: Perspectives in Theory and Research', *Management Science*, 28: 315-336.

Yates, C., Lewchuk, W. and Stewart, P. (2001), 'Empowerment as a Trojan Horse: New Systems of Work Organization in the North American Automobile Industry', *Economic & Industrial Democracy*, 22: 517-541.

Yukl, G.A. (1981), *Leadership in Organizations*, Englewood Cliffs, NJ: Prentice Hall.

Zuboff, S. (1988), *In the Age of the Smart Machine: The Future of Work and Power*, New York: Basic Books.

Index